PARTY SYSTEM IN MANIPUR

PARTY SYSTEM IN MANIPUR

AYANGBAM SHYAMKISHOR

AKANSHA PUBLISHING HOUSE
NEW DELHI · GUWAHATI · VISAKHAPATNAM

AKANSHA PUBLISHING HOUSE
4649-B/21, Ansari Road
Daryaganj, New Delhi-110002
Phones: 23268193, 09435116718
Email: ektabooks@yahoo.com
visit us: www.akanshapublishinghouse.com

Party System in Manipur

First Published 2012

ISBN 978-81-8370-313-0

PRINTED IN INDIA

Published by Akansha Publishing House, New Delhi-110002 and printed at Harmain Offset Printers, Delhi.

Contents

Preface

Party system is inseparable to the modern form of democracy. The successful working of democracy largely depends on the political parties and party system inside the State. Party system is the pattern of inter-party relationship among the various political parties inside a political system or as Maurice Duverger puts, 'the forms and modes of their co-existences'. The present study, "Party System in Manipur is a modest attempt to study the nature and dynamics of the party system in Manipur.

The study starts from 1985. The year 1985 was a landmark year in the history of evolution of the party system not only in Manipur but in India. It was an important year in the sense that the 52nd Constitution Amendment Act, 1985 came into force in this year. It was a major step towards curving the problem of defection which has plagued parliamentary democracy in India. In Manipur also, the period from 1985 to 2002, in Manipur witnessed as many as nine ministries (not counting the SPF ministry led by O. Ibobi Singh which was formed after the 2002 Assembly Elections). Moreover, there were three instances of President's Rule during this period with one of them lasting for about one year i.e. from December 31st, 1993 to December 12th, 1994 exactly 346 days.

On the basis of the objectives and the hypothesis formulated, the study has been divided into six chapters. The first one being introductory introduces the study discussing the theoretical concept of party system. It studies the meaning of political party, party system, types of party systems and importance of party system in democracy. It also includes a review of literatures apart from highlighting the problems of the study, scope of the study, aims and objectives of the study, hypothesis and methods of the study.

Chapter 2 deals historical background of the evolution of political parties, party system and party-politics in Manipur up to 1985. The main focus of the chapter is on the emergence of the political parties and party system inside the State from the historical perspective. It highlights the socio-religious and political reform movements during the 1930s and the middle of the 1940s which witnessed the emergence of a number of political parties like the Nikhil Manipuri Mahasabha (1938), Manipur Praja Samelloni (1940), Manipur Praja Mandal (1946), Krishak Sabha (1946), Manipur Praja Sangha (1946), Manipur State Congress (1946), etc. It covered the political movement for a responsible government in Manipur till the Central Government granted Statehood in 1972. It also studies the nature and dynamics of party system in Manipur up to 1985.

The third chapter deals with the nature of relationship among various parties forming coalition ministries. There were four State Assembly elections during the period from 1985 to 2002. However, none of the parties could secure a majority in the elections. The verdict of the people forced the political parties to form coalition ministries in order to run the affairs of the State. In fact, out of the ten ministries during this period nine were coalition ministries. This chapter tries to examine the motive behind the parties while joining hands to form coalition ministries. It also studies the nature of relationship which the parties in coalition share among them, their unity inside and outside the house, factors contributing to their breakdown, the inter-party and intra-party conflicts, the tendency of the larger parties in the coalition to absorb the smaller ones, its effect on the political system and the party system, etc.

The main focus of the fourth chapter is the nature of relationship that the opposition parties share among themselves as parties in opposition. Their success or failure in the due discharge of their functions as opposition parties inside the political system, the factors that bind them together or lead to their breakdown, pre and post election alliances among them, etc. are also being highlighted here. It also highlights the inherent weaknesses of the parties in opposition which contributed to their failure to sustain their unity and solidarity and evolve as a meaningful institution of parliamentary democracy.

The focus of the fifth chapter is on the relation between the ruling and the opposition parties in all its comprehensiveness. It tries to understand the nature and dynamics of the relationship between the two by examining the pre and post election alliances between the two, conflicts or cooperation between them on basic issues and their efforts to consolidate or destabilizes the existing ministry. This has been done in the context of the nine ministries which were there during the period from 1985 to 2002. It highlights the tussle for power between the two; the impact which the chronic problem of defection, split, merger and the intra-party and inter-party conflict become the nature of the relationship between the two.

Finally the concluding chapter is a systematic summarization of the findings of the previous chapters with a view to suggest the possible remedies in case of any defect in the existing party system, so that democratic functioning of the political system is better secured in Manipur.

—Ayangbam Shyamkishor

Acknowledgements

Thinking to write acknowledgement is like in the heaven. Writing it is one of the happiest and memorable moments of my life. It is like a dream come true. Therefore, first and foremost, I would like to salute and express the appreciation I owe to my Supervisor Prof. Senjam Mangi Singh, Department of Political Science, Manipur University, Imphal, Manipur for his valuable guidance and worthy suggestions. It would have been highly impossible to complete my humble work without his immense help and full co-operation.

I would like to acknowledge the support and cooperation extended towards me by all the teachers from the Manipur University (MU) and the Mizoram University (MZU) particlarly Dr. MC Arun, Associate Professor, Department of Anthropology (MU) and Prof. J. K Paitnaik, HoD, Dept. of Political Science, MZU during the course of my work. I thank to Mr. Erengbam Arun, Editor, *Ereibak* (A local Manipuri daily) and Mr. PB Sharma, AIR, Imphal, for their pain in taking appointment of the political leaders for interviews. I am also thankful to the ex-Librarian, Mr. Radheshyam Singh, MU, all the staff of the library, MU and the staff of the archive, Government of Manipur for helping at my disposal the books, journals, magazines and other relevant literatures I needed in connection with my studies. I also admire all the staffs of the Department of Political Science, MU and MZU. Their co-operations, advises, comments and suggestions really help me in the process of completing my work. Indeed, I am extremely grateful to them all.

I shall be failing in my duty if I do not express my gratitude to all my friends and well wishers whose cooperation and encouragement were great help to me all the while, particularly Dr. Nongthombam Jiten (Boby), Centre for Myanmar Studies, MU.

Last but not the least; I also would like to express my heart-felt gratitude to my family members especially my better-half Mrs. Rebecca Angom and lovely daughter Daphne Ayangbam (Sanathoi) and son Kumnganba Ayangbam, (Athoiba) my parents, all my brothers and sisters for understanding me and share the pain and sorrow and provides their moral and financial supports which I need the most, while writing the book. Thank you all. Let the Almighty be with you always.

—Ayangbam Shyamkishor

Abbreviations

AICC	-	All India Congress Committee
AIDMK	-	All India Anna Dravida Munnetra Kazhagam
AMNU	-	All Manipur National Union
AMSDC	-	All Manipur Statehood Demand Committee
AMSDCC	-	All Manipur Statehood Demand Co-ordinating Committee
BJD	-	Biju Janata Dal
BSP	-	Bahujan Samaj Party
CEC	-	Central Executive Council
CLP	-	Congress Legislature Party
CPI	-	Communist Party of India
DLP	-	Democratic Legislature Party
DMK	-	Dravida Munnetra Kazhagam
DOC	-	District Organizing Committee
DPA	-	Democratic People's Alliance
DPP	-	Democratic People's Party
DRPP	-	Democratic Revolutionary People's Party
FPM	-	Federal Party of Manipur
GOI	-	Government of India
ICS	-	Indian Congress Socialist
INC	-	Indian National Congress
JD	-	Janata Dal

JD(U) - Janata Dal (United)
JD(S) - Janata Dal (Secular)
JNP - Janata Party
KNA - Kuki National Assembly
LKP - Lok Dal Party
MDF - Manipur Democratic Front
MHPC - Manipur Hill People's Council
MHU - Manipur Hills Union
MKS - Manipur Krishak Sabha
MNC - Manipur National Conference
MNDP - Manipur National Democratic Party
MNO - Manipur National Organization
MPC - Manipur People's Conference
MPP - Manipur People's Party
MPS - Manipur Praja Sangha
MPSC - Manipur State Congress Committee
MRCP - Manipur Regional Congress Party
MSC - Manipur State Congress
MSCP - Manipur State Congress Party
NC - National Conference
NCP - National Congress Party
NDA - National Democratic Alliance
NHMM - Nikhil Hindu Manipuri Mahasabha
NMM - Nikhil Manipuri Mahashaba
NPP - National People's Party
NSCN - National Socialist Council of Nagaland
NSDP - National Socialist Democratic Party
PDA - Progressive Democratic Alliance

PDF	- Progressive Democratic Front
PEPSU	- Patiala and East Punjab
PFPM	- Progressive Federal Party of Manipur
PMSD	- President of the Manipur State Durbar
PSP	- Praja Socialist Party
RJD	- Rashtriya Janata Dal
RSP	- Revolutionary Socialist Party
SAD	- Shiromani Akali Dal
SAP	- Samata Party
SDA	- Secular Democratic Alliance
SDF	- Secular Democratic Front
SJP (R)	- Samajwadi Janata Party (Rashtriya)
SP	- Samajwadi Party
SSP	- Sanyukta Socialist Party
TC	- Trinamul Congress
TDP	- Telugu Desam Party
UDA	- United Democratic Alliance
UDF	- United Democratic Front
UF	- United Front
ULF	- United Legislature Front
ULP	- United Legislature Party
UNIC	- United Naga Integration Council
UPA	- United Progressive Alliance

1 Introduction

Party system is indispensable to democracy. It is impossible to visualize a healthy polity in modern societies without a vigorous party system. The party system acts as a catalyst for the growth and stability of a democratic polity. The successful working of a modern democracy largely depends on the political parties and party system because the nature and style of functioning of political parties decide to a great extent the true character of the political system. They are often described as the backbone of modern democracy. Without organised political parties smooth democratic change over of the government, effective representation of the people and also the stability of government will become impossible. Political parties and democracy live and work together which also means that they go hand in hand. They are the two faces of the same coin. There can be no such things as non-party government in modern representative democracies.

Moreover, "The absence or suppression of parties is regarded as a mark of political backwardness or of retrogression in political development."[1] There is hardly any polity in the modern world without political parties. In fact even in the military regimes or dictatorships and authoritarian or totalitarian states, political party plays an important role. La Palombara and Myron Weiner rightly wrote:

> "The political party is creature of modern and modernizing political systems. Whether one thinks of Anglo-American democracies or totalitarian systems such as the Soviet Union, Fascist Italy, and Nazi

political recruitment, and that is committed to the capture or maintenance of power either alone or in coalition with others."[12]

Amal Ray and Mohit Bhattacharya define a party as "a group consisting of cross sections of human beings, more or less stably organised with the objective, in accordance with the constitution, of securing or maintaining for its leaders the control of a government, and giving to members of the party, through such control ideal and material benefits and advantages."[13]

Though different writers and scholars gave different definitions of political party, all of them more or less agree on what constitutes the most essential attribute of a political party. A political party is an organization or association of likeminded people from different sections of the society, irrespective of caste, creed, religion, sex etc. who have decided to work together under an agreed leader, with the aim to capture political power through elections, and trying to gain control of the government. So, in a sense, a political party generates power, shapes it and applies it to government, which in turn, translates it into various programmes, policies, decisions and acts. In short, it has four main characteristics: (a) it is an organisation; (b) it is an organisation of like minded people; (c) it is goal oriented; and (d) it aims to capture and retain political power.

La Palombara and Weiner also give four characteristics of political parties:

"1) Continuity in organisation - that is, an organisation whose expected life span is not dependent on the life span of current leaders;

2) manifest and presumably permanent organization at the local level; with regularized communications and other relationships between local and national units;

3) self-conscious determination of leaders at both national and local levels to capture and to hold decision–making power alone or in coalition with others, not simply to influence the exercise of power; and

4) a concern on the part of the organization for sucking followers at the polls or in some manner striving for popular support."[14]

political parties their unique importance. Political parties are publicly identified minorities, the labelled groups, which compete for a right to govern. And the party system is the matrix of competitive relationships between these parties. The party system is the whole assortment of inter-party rivalries in a country at any given time. It is this web of competition which makes the whole number of parties in a country something more than they would be counted singly. That something more is democratic competition for the right to rule.[31] Party systems have different kinds of relationships between parties in terms of competition, coalitions and ideology which lead to patterned interactions. This is the importance of party system in a democratic state. A party system has certain properties - the number of parties, electoral disproportionality, fragmentation, centripetal (towards the centre) or centrifugal (towards the extremes) party competition.

Classification of Party System

Party system is classified by different scholars and writers according to their understanding of the term. But, the most common way of distinguishing between different types of party system is by reference to the number of parties competing for power. On this basis, Duverger (1954) distinguished between 'one party', 'two party' and 'multi-party' systems. Although such typology is commonly used, party system cannot simply be reduced to a 'number game'.[32] According to J.C. Johari, "the classification of Maurice Duverger is too simplistic and is now out-moded."[33] Moreover, the traditional typology cannot be sensibly taken to mean literally what it says, and it is difficult to use in a non-literal sense. For instance, strictly speaking there can be no such thing as one-party system. If party systems involve interactions among party units, than the idea of a one-party system is logically absurd, for one cannot have a competition or an interaction with only one actor. The same is true of two-party systems. The category is not logically absurd but two party systems in the literal sense are extremely rare, if indeed they have ever existed. Not even Great Britain, usually considered the paragon of bi-partism. Minor parties like the liberal democrats (of today), the early Labour Party, Irish Nationalist, Scottish Nationalist, Scottish National Party, etc. have always operated alongside major ones in Britain. The concept of a multi party system also poses a logical difficulty. If taken literally, it is a classification that does not classify for virtually all party systems comes under it. Therefore, the categories, one-party, two-party and multi-party system, if taken at face value they yield a classificatory scheme that simply does not classify. To construct an adequate set of concepts for characterizing and classifying party systems, it requires (a) technical precision about establishing the number of competing party units so that the numerical dimension can be precisely used and (b) proper attention to other dimensions of variability.[34]

The traditional method of categorizing party system according to the number of parties violates the basic concept of competitive interaction patterns. The empiricists are critical of the theoretical dilemmas caused by the 'numbers approach' to party systems. Frank. J Sorauf suggests that such an approach is one-dimensional and leaves out the ideological rivalries between major and minor parties that do not actually compete electorally; that the range of competition extends to political groups other than parties; that party differences in organization are ignored; and finally, that the expectations of systems analysis far exceed the product of competitive party electoral analysis per se. Gabriel Almond classified party system by applying the concept of the aggregative function into four categories, namely:

(a) authoritarian party systems with a sub-category called "totalitarian",
(b) dominant non-authoritarian party systems,
(c) competitive two-party systems, and
(d) competitive multiparty systems.[35]

Jean Blondel studies the political system of the world which existed between 1945 and 1966 and classified party system into 5 categories:

(i) one party system,

(ii) two-party system,

(iii) two-and-a half party system,

(iv) multi-party system with a dominant party, and

(v) multi-party without a dominant party.[36]

The classification of party system as elaborated by Giovanni Sartori is also used most frequently. He analyses the European party systems in the seventies and produced his own typology with several sub-types within the one-party system and multi-party system, and separate the two-party and multi-party system on the basis of 'pluralism' and 'atomism.' His classification is based on the pattern of interaction among and between parties which he termed as 'competition'. For him, single party system belongs to the non competitive categories whereas two parties and multi-party system belong to the competitive categories. His classification is given in the diagram illustrated below:-

SARTORI'S CLASSIFICATION OF PARTY SYSTEM[37]

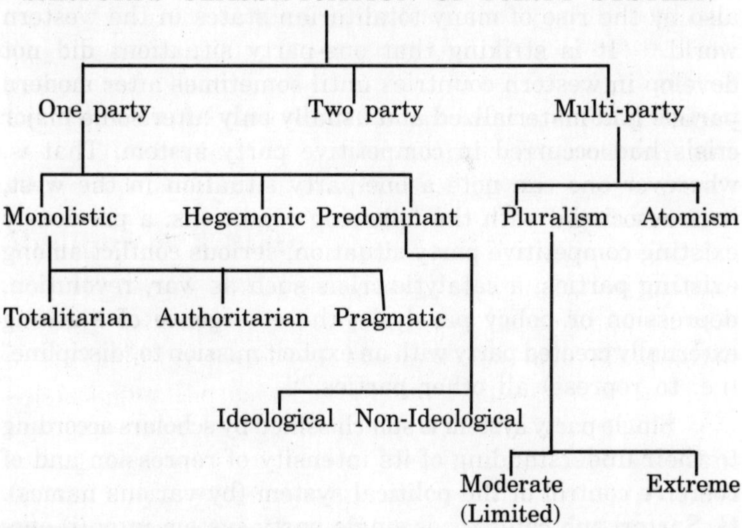

Though, different writers and scholars give their model of party systems, the party system as it exists today can be studied under the following heads:

(a) One Party system
(b) Two Party system
(c) Multi party system

One Party system

When there is only one party in the State, it is called one party system or mono-party system or single party system or unipartism. Literally, one party system means only one party exists and is allowed to exist. The single (one/uni) party system emerged only after the World War I. The first wave of single party states appeared from 1920-1940 period - the Soviet, Nazi and Fascist types of unipartism.[38] The wave spread very fast. "In the late 1960s slightly over a third of the world politics could be classified as single party systems."[39] The main reason for this was the decline of democracy. During the World War I, the allied powers claimed that an allied victory would make the world "safe for democracy". But such optimism was proven wrong as it was not only followed by the decline of democracy but also by the rise of many totalitarian states in the western world.[40] "It is striking that one-party situations did not develop in western countries until sometimes after modern parties had materialized and usually only after some major crisis had occurred in competitive party system. That is, wherever one can note a one-party situation in the west, it is associated with the following conditions: a previously existing competitive party situation; serious conflict among existing parties; a catalytic crisis such as war, revolution, depression or policy paralysis; the emergence of a strong externally created party with an explicit mission to "discipline" (i.e. to repress) all other parties."[41]

Single party system is sub-classified by scholars according to their understanding of its intensity of repression and of coercive control of the political system (by various names). G. Sartori sub-categorizes single party system into: (i) one-party totalitarian, (ii) one-party authoritarian and (iii) one-party pragmatic.[42] Joseph La Palombara and Myron Weiner also sub-divided it into three - one-party Authoritarian, one-party Pluralistic and one-party Totalitarian.[43] Single party system can also be studied under two heads: (a) one-party totalitarian and (b) one-party democratic, with many sub-categories.

In totalitarian state, the party in power allows no other party or group to live or act in opposition to its authority. This model of single party system is said to have two more sub-categories – (i) ideologically committed and (ii) ideologically neutral/non committed. It means the party in power may or may not be committed to a particular ideology. Moreover, such ideologically committed parties may be a rightist or a leftist party. The ideology of the right stands for the maintenance of the *status quo* while the ideology of the left aims at the liquidation of the present system and its substitution by a new one that is more equitable and just for the interests of the weaker, oppressed and exploited sections of the community. The Fascist and Nazi Party system are examples of totalitarian party system committed to an ideology of the right while the Communist political system which is single and totalitarian party system belongs to the committed and ideologically left category. Soviet Union, China, Yugoslavia, Czechoslovakia, etc. are in this category. Some of the countries like Indonesian National Party before 1965, Bangladesh under Awami League before 1975, Burma under the Lanzin Party, etc., come under the category of a totalitarian party system which is also ideologically non-committed party system.[44]

In democratic countries also the existence of single party system is sometimes witnessed. There, the ruling party tolerates the existence of other parties in opposition, or it may sometimes take the help of another party or parties for being in power. It may also so happen that there may be several parties which even when put together, may not be in position to wrest power from the dominant party. Further, it may also be a case where there is one party absorbing all other parties within its fold. The outstanding feature is that the party in power allows other parties and groups to exist and operate. The democratic single party system can be divided into three sub-types, - 'one-plus' party system, where the dominant party seldom takes the help of other party, e.g. Liberal Democratic Party of Japan; 'one dominant' party system where on party enjoys a position of far more influence than all other parties put together in a political system, e.g. Indian National Congress till 1967, and 'one absorbing' party system when one party absorbs all other major and minor political organizations within its fold, e.g. Institutional Revolutionary Party (PRI) of Mexico, Kenya African National Union (KANU) of Kenya and National Renovating Alliance of Brazil.[45]

Two-Party System

A two party system is a type of party system where only two political parties have a realistic chance of winning an election, and all or nearly all elected offices are held only by the candidates of the two parties. In this system, two major parties hold the scales of power, by winning a major portion of the votes despite the existence of minor parties, whose influence in politics and among voters, and in the legislature, is marginal and negligible. Political power really alternates between two parties - one becomes the ruling party and the other the opposition. "A two-party system, by definition, need not be free from third or fourth parties as long as the latter are too small to interfere constantly and substantially in the bipolar pattern of competition."[46] In two-party system "(i) two-parties are in a position to compete for the absolute majority of seats; (ii) one of the two parties actually succeeds in winning a sufficient parliamentary majority; (iii) this party is willing to govern alone; (iv) alternation or rotation in power remains a credible expectation."[47] According to Duverger, in two party system, "for practical purposes only two parties share the parliamentary seats: the one assumes the entire responsibility for government, the other limits itself to the free expression of criticism in opposition; a homogeneous and powerful cabinet has at its disposition a stable and coherent majority."[48] The most cited examples of two-party system are the U.K.

and the U.S.A. But, even they didn't appear to fulfil all the characteristic of a two party system.

The U.K., for instance, often portrayed as the model two party system, has conformed the criteria only for a particular (and some would argue, untypical) period of its history. Even the apparent Labour-Conservative, two partyism of the early post Second World War period (power alternating four times between 1945 and 1970) was punctuated by13 years of continuous Conservative rule (1951-64), a period during which time Labour's electability was called into question. Moreover, despite persistent major party domination of the House of Commons in the U.K., it is more doubtful that a two-party system has existed in the country since 1974. This is suggested by the decline of combined Labour-Conservative support (down from over 95 percent in the early 1950's to consistently below 75 percent since 1974), as well as by the dominance of one or major party since 1979. In the U.S.A. also, the Republicans and the Democrats holding between them all the seats in the House of Representatives and the Senate is questionable. In fact, there has been no instance of one party capturing the White House (the Presidency) and the other controlling Capitol Hill (Congress) in the U.S.A. since 1984 which means that it is not possible to identify a clear government-opposition divide. Besides 'third' party candidates are sometimes of significance. Ross Parots' 16 percent of the vote in the 1992 presidential election not only highlighted the decline of the Republican and Democratic parties, but also arguably proved decisive in securing victory for Clinton.[49]

The history of two party system in a country may also be interrupted, from time to time by a period when the system starts losing the nature of dualism. The two party system in England suffered this during the period between the two World Wars. Between 1918 and 1935, it was not possible to speak of the British two party system because British people were really divided amongst three major parties. A French Ministry of Information pamphlet published in 1945 declared that Great Britain (like France at that time) enjoyed a three-party system.[50] Sartori gave his hypothesis that not only Britain ceased to be the "perfect" two party system but also it would cease to be a two party system altogether. He wrote that "if a two party system is defined as one in which only candidates from two parties contest elections, then Britain has never had a two-party system." He further wrote that even if the four conditions of two party system are contrived, that also a lenient one and applied them in a political system as flexible as possible, even then, it turns out that two-party systems are rare.[51] Douglas Rae rightly described the party system in England as a "near two-party system" because only two parties have substantial shares, yet as many as a dozen parties often get some share of the vote.[52]

In the United States dualism has never been seriously threatened; the parties have changed profoundly since the rivalry between Jefferson and Hamilton which epitomized the conflict between the Republicans and Federalists with the former defending state rights while the latter argued for an increase in the powers of the Union. After the breakup of the Federalist Party and a period of confusion, the two-party system reappeared during the 1928 presidential elections with the rivalry between the Democrats grouped around Jackson and 'National-Republicans' led by Clay and Adams, who were also called 'Whig'. The Civil War naturally introduced considerable confusion into the rivalry of the parties and their organization. None the less it did not appreciably modify the two-party system, which reappeared after the war in the form of a renewed competition between Republicans and Democrats. Afterwards also frequent attempts have been made to create a 'third party' in the United States of America. However, so far, all have failed or have given birth only to minor parties, ephemeral and localized.[53]

Advantage and Disadvantage

Two-party politics was once portrayed as the surest way of reconciling responsiveness with order, representative government with effective government. Its key advantage is that it makes possible a system of party government characterized by stability, choice and accountability. The two major parties are able to offer the electorate a straightforward choice between rival programmes and alternative governments. Voters can support a party knowing that, if it wins the election, it will have the capacity to carry out promises it made in its manifesto without any negotiation or compromise with coalition partners. Two-party systems have also been praised for delivering strong but accountable government based on relentless competition between the governing and opposition parties. Although government can govern, it can never relax or become complacent because it is constantly confronted by an opposition that acts as a government in waiting.[54] It naturally follows that, under the bi-party system, discussion which is the soul of democracy may best be carried on when there are two main sides in a debate. When the conflicting arguments are two and only two, one can argue well and at the same time appreciate the arguments of the opponent. Moreover, balance in the political system which is éssential to political liberty is best secured under bi-party system. One party forms the government, another keeps a watchful eye in it; the two in fact form the scheme of government.[55]

It is sometimes argued that two-party system has to pay the price for its certainty and stability. It puts definite limits on the political expression of public opinion. The citizen has necessarily a narrow choice.[56] The restriction it imposes in terms of electoral and ideological choice is also a weakness of the two-party system. While a choice between just two programmes of government was perhaps sufficient in an era of partisan and class solidarity, it has become quite inadequate in a period of greater individualism and social diversity. In two-party system, two evenly matched parties are encouraged to compete for votes by outdoing each other's electorate which perhaps causes spiralling public spending and fuels inflation. This amounts to irresponsible party government, in that parties come to power on the basis of election manifestos which they have no capacity to fulfil.[57] It is also agreed that if the opposition party is weak, a dominant-party system may develop. Debate in the assembly of the country can often be adversarial and not constructive, sometimes revolving around narrowly perceived policy ideas rather than larger political issues. It leads sometimes the opposition disagreeing with everything the government proposes (and *vice versa*) for the sake of disagreeing. This may block important legislation especially reforms that may be beneficial for the country.

So, the two-party system has both advantages and disadvantages. The two partism "works" when spread of opinion is small and its distribution single peaked, opines Sartori. He further wrote that the smaller the spread of opinion, the smoother the functioning of two partism. Conversely, the greater the ideological distance the more a two party format is dysfunctional. Therefore, it is misleading to assert that two party systems always work. Rather, these systems represent an optimal solution only when they work, that is, whenever they presupposed and/or produced a highly consensual political society characterized by minimal ideological spread.[58] Duverger observed the correlation between the simple-majority single-ballot system and two party systems, and conclude that dualist countries use the simple-majority vote and simple majority vote countries are dualist.[59] This is popularly known as Duverger's law.

Multi-Party System

This is a system in which more than two parties compete for political power in a political system. Multi-partism is the characteristic of Western Europe with the exception of Great Britain.[60] The multiparty system lies in the logic of democracy. Since hospitality to a multi-plicity of opinion is the essence of democracy, every considerable volume of opinion must find expression through a particular political party. Multi-party system faithfully lives up to the democratic ideals and allows every opinion-group freely to organize itself. Under this system, groups can be freely organized, can unite and separate with every change of the situation. Opinion-groups, being liberated from a common organization, are able to formulate their doctrine without compromise. The modern society which is honey-combed with diverse interest-groups must necessarily possess a multi-plicity of political parties with a view to catering to their particular needs. The multiparty system offers many choices and options to the voters, and the voters can choose among many parties and candidates, according to their wishes.[61]

The principal criticisms of multiparty systems relate to the pitfalls and difficulties of coalition formulation. The post-election negotiations and horse-trading which take place when no single party is strong enough to govern alone can take weeks or sometimes months to complete. Another problem is that of the tendency towards moderation and compromise. This may further lead to the inability of the government to provide clear ideological alternative. Coalition politics which is characterized by negotiations and conciliation, and a search for common ground, rather than by conviction and the politics of principle, also follow. It is also criticized for encouraging the parties to abandon policies and principles in their quest of power.[62] The phenomenon of multiparty system is usually associated with three situations:

1) governments in multiparty parliaments must be minority cabinets, coalition cabinets or both;
2) by their very nature, minority cabinets and coalitions are quite transient;
3) multiparty systems are consequently undesirable since they produce transient governments.

Under the multiple-party system no party can normally expect to have an absolute majority of its own. This fact profoundly alters not only the tactics of parties but also the whole mechanism of government. The government of the day depends on a coalition of groups, and is the result of bargains and agreements between them. It is a bloc government rather than a party one. The bloc may be formed by groups from either wing or from the centre. There are several alternative governments which may take the place of a government which suffers defeat and it is often impossible to predict which shall be its successor.

Thus, the certainty of the two-party system and the clear-cut conflict for power disappears. Governments tend to be less stable and to be short-lived. If they offend a group of their supporters, the later do not feel obliged to continue with their loyalty to the coalition. It may even join with other groups outside the coalition to overthrow it. Governments are consequently more sensitive to changes in public opinion. There is less continuity of policy, especially if the executive depends on the support of parliament leaders and governments rise and fall with dramatic suddenness. They can seldom act with the assurance which the older system frequently bestows.[63]

In multi-party system, ordinarily coalitions are the only means of attaining a parliamentary majority and are by nature heterogeneous and unstable governments. But, stabilities and effectiveness vary greatly according to the discipline and organization of the parties involved. In the case of flexible parties that are undisciplined which also allow each legislator to vote on his own, the coalition will be weak and probably short-lived. The government tends to be most unstable and weak in such a situation. If, on the other hand, the parties in the coalition government are rigid and disciplined, it is possible to develop a (new) system which is similar to two-party system. This will be seen when two opposing alliances are formed, one on the left and one on the right, and when both are strong enough to endure through the legislative session. This type of coalition is referred as bipolarized, which introduces elements of the two party systems into a multiparty framework. Such a situation developed in Sweden in 1970. Moreover, it may also so happen that one party secure absolute majority of seats in the legislature so that no coalition is required. Such a situation is unusual (and rare) but did occur in West Germany, Italy and Belgium at various times after 1945.[64] Such a situation also emerged in India during the 1980s.

Formation of Multi-partism

Multi-party system may emerge as a result of two

different phenomena - internal divisions of opinion and their overlapping. In every party there are factions within it. It may be between extremists and moderates, or between left and right, or between radicals and liberals or between conservative and liberals etc. within party regarding their political ideas and outlook. Duverger wrote that:

> ".... inside all parties there are moderates and extremists, the conciliatory and the intransigent, the diplomatic and the doctrinaire; the pacific and the fire-eaters."[65]

These factions or groups may sometimes become exasperated and can no longer meet on common ground. If this happens, the basic tendency to unify is thwarted and it gives way to multi-partism. Multy-partism arises from the mutual independence of sets of anti-theses." These anti-theses overlay others when new anti thesis overlay old antithesis without destroying them, with the result that divisions of varying ages may coexist in the mind of the nation at the same point of time. In France, for example, the dispute between Monarchists and Republicans which was fundamental in 1875 no longer subsists today except amongst a very small minority of the population; on the other hand the division between 'clericals' and 'anti-clericals' which was dominant around 1905 still retains a large measure of influence in the provinces (and in the subconscious of Frenchmen) although for the most part events have made it obsolete; the Socialist-Liberal anti-thesis only really began to be important after 1940 and is only primordial so long as the economic situation is difficult (it has diminished somewhat since 1950-51); lastly, the East v. West antagonism, (Communists v. Non Communists), not born until 1947, is not always clear: many workers, farm labourers, and lower-middle-class people, who have no desire for a Soviet regime, vote Communist to show their discontent; moreover, the 'neutralists' are in an intermediate position.[67] It shows that, different opinions, beliefs, ideas, etc. in a society may ultimately bring multipartism in a state. The same is true for India also. A multi-faceted state like India which has many sets of anti-thesis is an obvious breeding ground for a multi-party system.

Classification of Multi-party System

Multi-party system is classified by scholars according to their observation and understanding of the parties in a political system. Scholars like Duverger classified according to the number of rival parties and others classified it according to the strength of the parties in a political system. Duverger classified it into three: tri-partism, quadri-partism and poly-partism. Tri-partism was found in 1900 in England, Belgium, Sweden, Australia, New Zealand etc., in the form of rivals among 'Conservatives-Liberals-Radicals', 'Conservatives or Liberals-Radicals-Socialists', and 'Liberals-Socialists-Communists'. Quadri-partism system is uncommon, but with the rise of agrarian party in 1900 in Europe, there were rivalry among 'Agrarian-Conservative-Liberal-Socialist' in Switzerland, Canada, Bulgaria, etc. Poly-partism or the tendency to extreme multiplication of parties has several types. One might distinguish a nationalist or ethnic poly-partism, peculiar to countries divided into several traditional or racial groups. Here racial antagonisms overlay the social and political, producing extreme complexity. Twenty-five parties were in Austro-Hungary on the eve of the 1914 war. This system was there in Czechoslovakia, France, Holland etc. between the inter war period.[68]

John H. Fenton divided multiparty system into three broad categories. The first is the classical variety, where many small parties that are highly competitive exist. These parties represent very particular points of view, and none of the parties is large enough to command a majority of the vote or a majority in the legislature. Therefore, government is always the result of coalitions of many parties. The classic example is France's Fourth Republic (1946-58). The second category of multiparty system exists where one party governs a sizeable proportion of the voters and the remainder of the electorate is divided among several small parties. This type of multiparty system resembles one-party system. Examples include India, where the Congress Party - until 1967 - ruled with about half the vote and the remaining vote was divided among various other parties. The third category of multiparty system prevails where coalitions of parties are successfully formed after or before elections, enabling one coalition to rule. Examples include the French Fifth Republic and the Netherlands. In France, the creation of a strong President and reformed or revised election laws in 1958 resulted in the formation of workable coalitions that provided reasonably stable and effective governments.[69]

Party System in India

The contemporary party system in India developed originally in the context of the struggle for freedom and since 1950 within the framework of parliamentary government; both these environments have exerted their influence on the present character and structure of the political parties.[70] The emergence of political party in India is different from those of western democracies. India had been a colony of the British. Most of the early political parties emerged out of the exploitative nature of the British rule. The exploitative nature of British rule provided a big fill up to the political activity in India in 1870s and the doctrine of Swadeshi was preached for the first time.[71] The centre of British India administration was in Calcutta and it became the hub of political activity. Many political associations came into being since 1830s in India. The first association of such type was the "Landholders Society" formed in Bengal in 1839. After that many associations emerged in India.

Name	*Year*	*Main Centre of Activity*
Landholders' Society	1839	Bengal
Bengal British India society	1843	Calcutta
British India Association	1851	Calcutta, Madras, Bombay
East India Association	1866	Main Indian Cities[72]
Poona Sarvajanik Sabha	1870	Poona
Indian Association	1876	Calcutta
Madras Mahajan Sabha	1884	Madras
Bombay Presidency Association	1885	Bombay
Indian National Congress	1885	Bombay

Dr. Sushil Kumar claimed that Asia's first political parties were founded in India and not in Japan as Horst Hartman has argued.[73] But, political parties emerged in India in the true sense of the term only after the emergence of the Indian National Congress in 1885. Indian National Congress gradually became an umbrella organization containing within its fold several splinter groups such as the Communist Party, the Socialist Party, Hindu Mahasabha, etc. at one time or the other. After independence, political parties like the Communist Party of India became a distinct political organization. And many political parties like Bhartiya Jan Sangh, grew and acquired prominence in the subsequent years. Yet majority of the Indian Political Parties had their roots in the Congress.[74]

Though the CPI, the Akali Dal and the DMK originated outside the Congress, parties like the Socialist Party, the Swatantra, the BLD, the BKD, the Janata Party[75], the NCP, the Trinamul Congress, etc. were formed by political leaders who were primarily important and erstwhile members of the Indian National Congress. At the regional level also, many parties like the Bangla Congress, the Jana Congress and Utkal Congress in Orissa[76] and Manipur Peoples' Party, Manipur State Congress Party, etc. in Manipur were the product of factional struggle within the Congress.

Some authors feel that the Indian party system is unique. It does not fit into generally prescribed types of one party, two parties, multiparty systems, etc.[77] According to Prof. Rashiduddin Khan, there are three vital factors in determining the pattern of the Indian party system. *Firstly*, "a major heritage of the national movement was the building of national consensus on certain essential issues of the three significant dimensions of national interest, namely, national unity and political integration, national socio-economic development and national defence and security. *Secondly*, the other heritage of the national movement was its broad ideological base, coalescing the many strands from the radical left to the conservative, traditional right. The co-existence of the left, centre and the right in the national movement during the freedom struggle not only gave it a wider support base and provided it with all Indian legitimacy but also laid down a tradition of toleration and accommodation of different points of view. *Lastly,* the Continental size of the country, comprising well defined and distinct socio-cultural regions, with their own languages and dialects, specific patterns of caste, community and tribal formations, provided the objective conditions for the rise of regional parties and groups.[78]

The party system in India has varied from time to time. In the beginning, it was a one-party dominant system. It was followed by a brief period of a two-party system and which subsequently led to a multi-party system, moving toward chaos with no semblance of a 'system'. The first phase was variously called as "Congress system" by Rajni Kothari, a "one-party dominant system" by W.H. Morris Jones, a "predominant party system" by Giovanni Sartori, the "ruling party system" by Maurice Duverger, which dated from 1952-1969. This was a phase of one-party dominance, as only the Congress was voted time and again with an overwhelming parliamentary majority on plurality (not majority) of voters in democratically contested elections. It coincided with the Nehru premiership, the Shastri premiership and the pre-1969 premiership of Indira Gandhi. The second party system was a brief spell of multi-partisan configuration following the 1969 Congress split between the Indira factions and the Syndicate faction when the Indira Gandhi government was reduced to a minority status and survived with the support extended (without formally joining the government) by leftist and regional parties. The third party system may be called the Indira Congress system of one-party dominance. It may be dated from 1971 to 1977. The fourth phase is the phase of bipartisan tendency. For the first time in India a two party system appeared and it was in existence from 1977 to 1979, when only two, the Janata and Congress, accounted for over 80 percent of both votes and seats. The fifth phase of the system may be called the Indira Gandhi and Rajiv Gandhi phase of Congress restoration. It may be dated from 1980-1989. The sixth is the phase of the multi-party system which followed the 1989 Lok Sabha elections.

Party System of India: The Present Scenario

A new party system has emerged in India since1989. It had a very bumptious and unstable start with a very precarious existence for about a year. Then, a mid-term election was held. But, the mid-term elections in 1991 brought a "hung Parliament." So, a coalition government led by Congress came into being. In the post-1989 scenario, no party secured majority in the general elections of Lok Sabha. Many parties specially the BJP rose and gained popularity and importance. Also, many regional and state-based parties like TDP, AIADMK, Shiv Sena, JD(U), TC, SAD, BJD, DMK, NCP, RJD, NC, BSP, SP, Left Front, etc. played an important role in National Politics during the period. At present, India has a large number of political parties in the system not only in numerical terms but also in terms of systemic relevance. Indian elections indeed have always been multi-party elections and since 1989, no single party could secure majority. As a result, coalition became the order of the day. There are pre and post poll alliances to get a workable majority in the legislature both at the national and state level politics. There are specially two alliances at present - one headed by the BJP which formed government in 1999 and known as National Democratic Alliance (NDA). The other is led by the Congress which is called United Progressive Alliance (UPA). It came into existence only after the 14th Lok Sabha election, 2004. So, the Indian party system is bipolar party system if not two party system.[79] In the 13th and 14th general elections of Lok Sabha (1999 & 2004), the two alliances got 433 (NDA, 299 + Congress allies, 134) out of 537 seats (six seats were deferred) in 1999,[80] which means both secured 80.63% of the total seats, and in 2004, they got 402 (NDA, 182 + Congress and Allies 217) out of 545 which means 73.76% of the total seats. In short, the competition in the Indian politics at present is between the two alliances.

The Indian party system is evolving over successive elections and the various trends and counter-trends are likely to play themselves out over the coming years. "It is too early to say whether the inexorable imperative to aggregate votes regardless of ideology will push the national party system to evolve towards loose bipolarity at the national level between two broad spatially compatible alliances, one broadly left and the other broadly right of the centre, or whether India's multiple social cleavages intertwined with geographical diversity will prevail to create so diversified an ideological space that bipolar consolidation is impossible at the national level."[81] Therefore, in general, the nature of party system in India remains a yet non-institutionalised, with ideological lines blurred and social support basis non-definitive.[82]

Review of the Literature

Review of literature is a major step in any social science research. It is necessary to understand the sequential development on both theoretical and empirical dimension of the problem under study. This helps researcher in delineating the problem area and provides a base for theoretical framework, insight and concept into the methods, procedure and also interpreting the findings.

A review of the existing literature of the party system in Manipur has clearly brought out the need for more historical, empirical and analytical studies in some specific settings. This study is a humble attempt in that direction. Thus, an attempt has been made to review some of the relevant existing literature on the topic. This review presents the importance of political party and party system in democracy, the problems and the prospect of political party and party system in modern political system and its effect on the stability of government, suggestion for successful working of the government and a summary of the review studies.

Maurice Duverger, 1964, 'Political Parties: Their Organization and activity in the Modern State' (translated by Barbara and Robert North) is a classic and authority on the subject (of political party and party system). Any study on political party and party system will have to begin from the studies and analysis of the M. Duverger. This is because the book tried to provide a general theory of party and party system for the first time in order to serve as a foundation for future studies. The main emphasis of the book is to theorize the party and party system. The book first discusses the origin of the political party, how political parties emerge side by side with democracy. Book one mainly examine the party organization, party membership and party leadership. In book two 'party system' is studied in detail. An attempt has been made to define the term party system and categories party systems according to the numbers of parties in the system. He also focused on the alliances of party, strength of the alliances and the relationship between the allies.

Giovanni Sartori, 1976, 'Parties and Party Systems: A Framework for Analysis' is one of the most celebrated books on the political party and party system. Any future study on the subject will have to start from and take into account, Professor Sartori's analysis, for it represents the first major attempt since Duveger's pioneering 'Political Parties', published in 1951, to provide a general theory of party - based politics, whether democratic, authoritarian or totalitarian. The primary emphasis of the book is on how different types of party systems perform very differently throughout the world. Part one consists mainly of a rationalisation of how and why parties came about, of what they are for, and of the perils involved in entrusting the one polity to its parts. Professor Sartori argues that despite the current dislikes for abstractions such as 'part' and 'whole', historically these have been the cornerstone of the debate about parties. The use of these terms, he feels, lends a sense of perspective to current analysis. In part two, 'party systems' are considered in detail and an attempt is made to sort them out on the basis of their mechanical tendencies or predispositions and explanatory and predictive power.

Richard Gunther, et al. edited 'Political Parties' (2003)

with the contributions from leading scholars in the field, present a critical overview of much of the recent literature on political parties. It systematically assesses the capacity of existing concepts, typologies, and methodological approaches to deal with contemporary parties. It critically analyses the 'decline of parties' literature both from a conceptual perspective and– with regard to anti-party attitudes among citizens - on the basis of empirical analyses of survey data.

'Political Parties and Party Systems' edited by Ajay K. Mehra, et al., (2003) is a collection of essays by eminent scholars drawn from diverse disciplines. It studies the evolution of political parties and party systems in India - the largest, the most complex and volatile democracy which reached a crucial stage at the turn of the century. The three general elections of India held in quick succession at the end of the nineties threw up three majors trends: the decline of the Congress Party as the dominant pan - national party; the emergence of a 'federalised' party structure and coalition politics; and the apparent demise of the Third Front as a force in national politics. They examine these wide - ranging changes in political parties - their leadership, ideological profile, support base and programmatic content- as well as in the texture of the party system in the country. In understanding these complex processes, this volume provides a comparative framework by bringing in the experiences of Germany and the European Union, which are also undergoing political transformation.

Sunil Kumar, (2004) in his book on *Parties and coalition Politics: A Comparative Study* examines the alliances and coalitions as they exist in the political system. It covers all important aspects of alliance politics in a comparative perspective, involving three federations - India, Canada and Australia. The book provides a comprehensive classification of alliance on the basis of an objective criterion. The nature and functioning of alliances is examined in detail with a special emphasis on the factors which cover their formation, durability and disintegration. Impact of coalition politics on various political institutions, particularly the behaviour of political parties is assessed critically. To attain all these objectives, the book explores the origin and nature of parties, party system and alliances of India, Canada and Australia.

In *India 50 Years of Independence: 1947-97, Status, Growth & Development of Political Parties*, Sadhna Chaturvedi (1999) discusses the gradual deterioration of the party system in India. In the initial years of its independence, the political scenarios were dominated by the Indian National Congress and call the Indian party system as 'Congress System'. The Congress at that time was an umbrella organisation; it embraced within it all shades of political opinions and factions which were based on different ideologies. Ultimately this gave way to parties based on personalities, castes, regions and communities. This resulted in a fractured polity as we find it today. It can be noted that there are parties which are only, in reality, one man party. Ideologies have been bid good-bye. Loyalty to the party means loyalty to the leader. Many times the word 'Supremo' is used for the party top leader. Policies, issues, and ideologies do not matter, what matters is the charismatic personality of the leader. Lastly, the book also asked that whether India can claim to have a genuine party system or not.

Peter Ronald de Souza and E. Sridharan (2004) edited a book, *India's Political Parties* which focused on political parties in India. The book covers an exceptionally wide terrain ranging from a discussion of individual parties, to their location in the context of nationalism and communalism, to more topical issues such as state funding of elections, party nominations, women's representation and defections. The book introduces the reader to the idea of a 'party less' democracy, which was a serious consideration in the early days of the Republic (India). It also examines the evolution of the party system in India at both the national and regional levels, explore the character of parties in terms of their ideology, social base and organisational forms, assess the issue of parties and political representation especially in the case of women, examine the policy options available for election, finance reforms and evaluate the significance of defections for a representative democracy.

Sven Groennings, *et al.*, edited the *The Study of Coalition Behaviour: Theoretical Perspectives and Cases from four Continents*, 1970 describes coalition activity at all levels of political involvement. The actors include individuals, interest groups, political parties, party factions and nation states. Political actors are frequently forming and dissolving coalitions for a variety of purposes. Coalitions influence the outcomes of elections, pass legislation, form governments and block legislation. Thus the analysis of coalition behaviour is a key to understand politics and the characteristics of political systems. This volume pursues two ends: (i) to demonstrate the variety of settings in which coalitions occur, and (ii) to present analytic studies leading to hypotheses and theories about behaviour in these settings.

In *Coalition Politics: The Indian experience*, N. Jose Chander (2004), provides an in-depth study of coalition government experiments in India, with particular reference to the coalition politics at the centre as well as in the states of Kerala and West Bengal. Focusing on the demands, stress and constraints of coalitions politics in the changed circumstances, it covers political developments upto the end of 2000. Also, it examines the impact of coalition politics on parliamentary institutions such as the executive, the legislature and the party system.

The book *Coalition Government and Politics in India* edited by Subhash C. Kashyap (1997) deals with the political development during the 1990s. The main focus is political developments following the fractured electoral verdicts from the 1990s, the emergence of a 'hung Parliament' which ultimately led to a coalition government at the Centre, etc. It studies not only the Coalition Politics in India but also in abroad.

D. Sundar Ram (1996) edited the *Indian Parliamentary Opposition*, Volume I & II with contributions from a group of distinguished scholars. These volumes examine important aspects of opposition parties' policy and strategy, particularly as they apply to the Indian Parliament, democracy and political system. Exploring the role of Parliamentary Opposition in legislative procedure in India, the contributors strongly urge the need of the responsible and viable alternative to the ruling party for the successful functioning of the Parliamentary democracy in the country. The book also provides an analytical description of the working of the Parliamentary Opposition in terms of its diverse political role as well as complex interaction.

In the book, *Opposition*, Ghita Ionescu and Isabel de Madariaga (1972), trace the development of parliamentary opposition in Western Europe and the United States and analyse its functions and the criticisms levelled against it. They then discuss states where there is no parliamentary opposition, such as Greece or the Soviet Union, demonstrating that political conflict nonetheless continues unabated and shows a recurrent tendency towards organization. At a time when the 'credibility gap' is widening and the parliamentary system is under attack from left and right, opposition offers a valuable perspective on an institution which is essential to democracy.

The book, *A Century of Government and Politics in North-East India* Volume IV: Manipur, V. Venkata Rao, T.S. Gangte and Ksh. Bimola Devi (1991) begin with a profile of Manipur and its geographical location, area and population. The book traces the beginning of Paramountcy which is to be found in the treaty of Yandaboo, 1826. The authors then delve into the tribal system and the powers of the chief. The Head of the state was the Maharaja of Manipur and later was subservient to the British Political Agent. The development of the legislature has been described in detail along with the formation of government. Insurgency in the state forms the next part of the book followed by the role of the women in the state, development of self government and administration of justice elections, etc.

In *Manipur: Culture and Politics*, Bimal J. Dev and Dilip K Lahiri (1987) describe the cultural heritage of the state of Manipur as unique with its potentiality as yet to be fully explored with imaginative planning and in full understanding of the socio-psychological factors governing the life and activities of the people. The authors have directed their single-minded attention in evaluating the cross currents of Manipur politics in different periods of time. Many of the ills of the Manipur today are in fact rooted in its wounds and this led the authors to analyse the cultural and political components of Manipur for facilitating a dispassionate assessment of the dimension of Manipur politics.

Prof. John Parrat (2005) *Wounded Land* assesses political developments in Manipur from the accession of Maharaja Churachand in 1907 until the present day. The first part deals with the growth in political awareness in the first half of the twentieth century and the popular reactions to feudalism and colonialism. After a detailed examination of the circumstances of the merger with India in 1949, the book then goes on to examine critically the crisis caused by insurgency, civil rights abuses and the failures of the government. The final chapter deals with the events of 2004 particularly the Manorama Case and the protest against the Arm Forces Special Power Act, 1958 and assesses prospects of the future of the state.

Th. Gokul Singh (1978), *Defection in Manipur* critically examines the politics of Manipur from 1963-1977. During the period of fourteen years or so there were ten ministries in Manipur though it should have been only three or four at the most. The book analyses in detail the political development during the period and shows clearly how MLAs change their loyalty both at the individual as well as at the party level and defect from one party to another. It highlights the political instability in the state.

B. Pakem (1999), *Coalition Politics in North-east India*, studies the theoretical considerations on coalition politics, coalition politics during the British period and coalition politics since India's independence. The coalition experiences in the region are not so much successful due to a number of problems. These problems cover a wide range of issues like insurgency activities, ethnic movements, student movements, community consideration rather than consideration of political ideology in coalitions and an entrenched regionalism leading to the regionalisation of Indian Government and politics.

N. Lokendra Singh (1998), *Unquiet Valley*, is an attempt to examine the dynamics of colonial penetration towards north east and the subsequent transformation of the traditional socio-political order of the erstwhile border state after the Anglo-Manipur War of 1891. The work not only explores the process of social restructuring but also examines the deeper socio-economic implications of the various anti-colonial and anti- feudal popular movements in Manipur Valley. While discussing the interplay of various social groups, emphasis is given on exploring the social roots and political ideas of the Manipuri middle class.

Naorem Joykumar Singh (2002), *Colonialism to Democracy: A History of Manipur, 1819-1972* is an analytical research work on the historical developments from the period of 'Seven Years Devastation' i.e. 1819- 1826 to the attainment of a full fledged state in the year 1972. During the period, the people witnessed a series of different historical developments which gave a new shape to the political history of Manipur. The occupation of Manipur by Burma in 1819 and its impact was a watershed in her history. It was followed by the reconstruction period of 1826-1834. The influence of the British started in 1835 and from the year 1891, Manipur got the experience of the colonial administrative system of the British that continued till 1947. During this long colonial period, Manipur passed through many stages like the outbreak of anti - British movements, growth of political consciousness and a series of political movements for the establishment of a democratic form of government. Then, after India's independence the people of Manipur again witnessed a series of political actions for the establishment of a responsible government under the Indian Constitution which continued till Manipur got a full fledged State in 1972.

Scope of the study

The period to be covered is from 1985 to 2002. Political parties have been there in Manipur right from 1938. Yet, their emergence as important structure inside a truly democratic and responsible framework of political system was from 1972 onwards when Manipur was granted statehood. Then, came the 52nd Constitutional Amendment Act in 1985. It was a landmark year in the history of evolution of party system in Manipur. It considerably solved the problem of defection inside the state thereby assuring the possibility for a more healthy, stable and meaningful party system to emerge Manipur. Besides, the period from 1972 to 1985 has already been the subject matter of a Ph.D research work of one of the scholars of the department. Therefore, the present study has been decided to start from 1985. About the year 2002, this was the year when the 8th State Legislative Assembly Elections were held, the last one before I did my registration in 2004.

Aim and Objective of the Research

The proposed research shall take different political parties inside the state as a set of elements standing in interaction, thereby constituting the party system in Manipur. As such inquiries shall be made to explore the possible pattern of actions and interactions among the parties. This will be done by keeping in view the most important concern of all parties i.e. having control over the decision making process. The main focus of the study shall be the following three areas:

(a) Relation between the ruling and opposition parties;
(b) Relationship among the various political parties forming a coalition ministry;
(c) The relationship among the parties in opposition.

The main objectives of the proposed research are:

(a) To study and explore the different stages in the evolution of party system in Manipur.
(b) To examine the relationship between the widespread

phenomena of merger and split of political parties during 1985 - 2002 and the nature of party system in Manipur during the period.

(c) To study the effect of the party system on stability of government.

(d) To examine the real motive behind the behaviour of political parties.

Statement of the Problem

Manipur was a princely state before joining the Indian dominion on 15th October 1949, and became a "Part 'C' State", when it merged with independent India. The first democratic election of Manipur was held on June 1948 under the then Constitution Act, 1947. The state which went to vote as early as 1948 is now riddled with confusion, instability and lack of direction. Perhaps, no other State in the country has witnessed such an unstable political climate as that of Manipur. Change of party loyalty, shifting alliances both in the individual and collective levels are so frequent and ruthless in the state. The people of Manipur faced as many as nine Assembly elections between the periods from 1972 to 2009. The State has also witnessed as many as 18 ministries during this period. Thus, the average life span of a government in Manipur is not even two years. And, the longest ministry that served in the State before the 97th Amendment Act, 2004, was a Congress ministry under the Chief Ministership of Shri. Rishang Keishing. It was from 19th June, 1984 to 4th July 1985, which was little more than 3½ years. Over and above, President's Rule was proclaimed on eight different occasions during the period.

The 52nd Constitutional Amendment Act, 1985 brought the 10th schedule of the Indian Constitution, which is also popularly known as "Anti-Defection Law." This Act was intended to control the phenomena of defection and instability of government. But, it has not brought much relieve to the people of Manipur. From 1985 till date, the state has witnessed as many as five Assembly elections and 10 ministries without counting the one formed in 2002. The normal life span of a government is five years, but in Manipur even after the enforcement of Anti-defection Law, the average life span of a government during 1985 to 2002 was just around 2 years. This clearly shows the kind of political instability the state has experienced over the years in spite of the Anti-defection Law. Splits and merger, intra-party faction, etc. have been responsible for this political instability in the state. The period also witnessed the emergence of Federal Party of Manipur (FPM), (1993), Manipur State Congress Party (MSCP) (1997), Manipur National Conference (MNC) (2001), etc. The proposed research work is an attempt to examine the nature and dynamics of the party system which was there during this period.

Hypotheses

The following hypotheses are formulated to give us a point of enquiry as well as specific direction in the study:

(a) Party system in Manipur is basically a game of power politics. In other words party system is a struggle for power in Manipur.

(b) Political defections, mushrooming of political parties, recurring phenomena of coalition ministries and the resultant instability of government etc. are all necessary fallouts of the nature of party system in Manipur.

Methods of the Study

No single method can be solely relied upon for making a meaningful enquiry to a topic like the present one. Therefore, a combination of traditional and modern method is being applied in the study. Historical and descriptive methods have been followed to explore the evolution of parties and party systems. The study is based on primary as well as secondary sources. Content analysis of various party documents, government publications, journals, newspapers etc. has been made in order to comprehend the changing ideological orientation of parties and the nature of their alliances. Besides, unstructured interviews with political actors and analysts helped largely in formulating and analyzing the principal hypotheses of this humble work.

NOTES

1. Robert, C. Bone, *Action and Organization: An introduction to contemporary Political Science*, New York, Harper & Row Publisher, 1972, p-72.
2. Palombara, Joseph La and Myron Weiner (Ed), *Political Parties and Political Development* , New Jersey, Princeton University Press, 1966, p. 3.
3. Das, Hari Hara and Choudhurry BC, *Political Theory, Traditional and Modern Theory* , National Publishing House, New Delhi, 1999, p. 378.
4. MacIver, R A. *The Modern State*, London, Oxford University Press, 1966, p-369.
5. Palombara, Joseph La *Politics within Nations*, New Jersey, Prentice Hall, 1974, p. 509.
6. Blondel, Jean *An Introduction to Comparative Government*, London, Weidenfeld and Nicolson, 1969, p-102
7. Gelb, Joyce and Marian Leif Palley (ed), *The Politics of Social Change: A Reader for the Seventies*, Holt, Rinehart and Winston Inc, 1971, p. 39.
8. *Lexicon Universal Encyclopedia*, Vol.15 (p), New York, Lexicon Publications Inc, 1983, p. 400.
9. *The New Encyclopaedia Britannica*, Vol.25, Micropadia, USA, Encyclopaedia Britannica Inc, 1998, p. 979.
10. Plano , Jack C. and Milton Greeberg (ed), *The American Political Dictionary*, Third edition, USA, the Dryden Press inc,1972 p-132
11. Sartori, Giovanni *Parties and Party System: A framework for Analysis*, Cambridge University Press, 1976, p. 64.
12. Palombara, Joseph La and Myron Weiner (ed), *op. cit.*, p. 29.
13. Amal Ray and Mohit Bhattacharya, *Political theory: Ideas and Institutions*, Twelfth revised edition, Calcutta, the World Press Private limited, 1966, pp. 438f.
14. Palombara, J. and Myron Weiner, *op. cit.*, p. 6.
15. Conn, Paul H. *Conflict & Decision Making: An Introduction to Political Science*, New York, Harper & Row Publishers, 1971, p.157.

16. Duverger, Maurice *Political Parties: Their Organization and Activity in the Modern State*, New York, John Wiley& Sons Inc.1954, p. xxiii.
17. *The New Encyclopaedia Britannica, op. cit.,* p. 979.
18. *Lexicon Universal Encyclopaedia, op. cit.,* p. 400.
19. Jennings, W. Ivor *The British Constitution*, Cambridge, Cambridge University Press,1971, p. 34.
20. Palombara, J. and Weinner, *op. cit.,* p. 7.
21. Duverger, M. *op. cit.,* pp. xxiiif.
22. *Ibid.,* pp.xxiv-xxxvii.
23. *Ibid.,* p-vii
24. *Ibid.,* p-xxiv
25. *Ibid.,* p-xxx
26. *Ibid.,* p-xxxviii
27. Lees, John D. and Richard Kimber (Ed), *Political Parties in Modern Britain: An Organizational and Functional Guide*, London, Routledge & Kegan Paul Ltd, 1972, p.1.
28. Harry Eckstein, Party System in David L. Shills (ed), International Encyclopaedia of Social Sciences (reprints, Vol. II, New York, Macmillan, 1972, p. 436.
29. Blondel, Jean *op. cit.,* p.128.
30. Sartori, G. *op. cit.,* pp. 43f.
31. Rae, Douglas W. *The Political Consequences of Electoral Laws*, (revised edition), New Haven, Yale University Press,1967, p.45.
32. Heywood, Andrew *Politics*, 2nd edition, New York, Palgrave, 2002, p. 258.
33 Johari, J.C., *Comparative Politics* (Revised & Enlarge edition) New Delhi, Sterling Publishers Private Limited,1998,p. 327.
34. *International Encyclopaedia of Social Sciences,* Volume II, *op. cit.,* pp. 439ff.
35. Rodee, Carlton Clymer Totton James Anderson, and Carl Quimby Christol, *Introduction to Political Science*, (third edition), New Delhi, Tata McGraw Hill Publishing Company Ltd, 1977,p-321
36. Jean Blondel, *op. cit.,* pp.143ff.
37. Johari, *op. cit.,* p. 336.
38. Sartori, *op. cit.,* p. 39.

39. Blondel, Jean *op. cit.,* p. 143.
40. Burns, Edward Mc Nall Philip Lee Ralph, Robert E.Lerner, and Standish Meacham, World Civilizations (seventh edition), Volume C, Delhi, Goyl Saab Publishers &Distributor 1980,pp-1251f.
41. Palombara, Joseph La and Myron Weiner, *op. cit.,* p.25.
42. Sartori, *op. cit.,* p. 222.
43. Palombara, Joseph La and Myron Weiner, *op. cit.,* pp. 37ff.
44. Johari, *op. cit.,* p-329
45. *Ibid.,* pp. 329f
46. Merki, Peter H. Modern Comparative Politics, Holt, Rinehart and Winston Ire, 1970, p. 285.
47. Sartori, *op. cit.,* p. 188.
48. Duverger, M. *op. cit.,* p-207.
49. Heywood, Andrew *op. cit.,* p-261
50. Duverger, M. *op. cit.,* p-208
51. Sartori, G. *op. cit.,* p-189f
52 Rae, Douglas D. *op. cit.,* p-55
53. M. Duverger, *op. cit.,* p-209.
54. Heywood, Andrew *op. cit.,* p-261.
55. Ray Amal and Mohit Bhattacharya, op cit, p-465.
56. *Ibid.*
57. Haywood, Andrew *op. cit.,* p. 262.
58. Sartori, G. *op. cit.,* p. 192.
59. Duverger, M. *op. cit.,* p. 217.
60. *Ibid.,* p. 229.
61. Ray, Amal and Mohit Bhattacharya, *op. cit.,* p-463.
62. Heywood, Andrew *op. cit.,* pp-264f
63. MacIver, *op. cit.,* pp- 417f.
64. *The New Encyclopedia Britannica, op. cit.,* p. 984.
65. Duverger, M. *op. cit.,* p. 230.
66. *Ibid.*
67. *Ibid.,* p- 234.
68. *Ibid.,* pp-234ff.

69. *Lexicon Universal Encyclopaedia*, Volume 15 (p). *op. cit.*, pp-402f.
70. Krishna, Gopal as cited in A.S. Narang, Indian Government and Politics, (Reprint) New Delhi, Gitanjali Publishing House, 1994-95, p-352.
71. Kumar, Sunil *Parting and Coalition Politics: A Comparative Study*, New Delhi, Uppal Publishing House, 2004, p-30.
72. It was originally formed by Dadabhai Naoroji in London. Later its branches were opened in all major cities in India.
73. Kumar, Sunil *op. cit.*
74. *Ibid.*, p. 31.
75. Puspa Asthana, *Party System in India: Development or Decay*, New Delhi, Criterion Publications, 1988, p.13.
76. *Ibid.*
77. Narang, A.S. *op. cit.*, p. 353.
78. *Ibid.*
79. Sridharan, E. "The Fragmentation of the Indian Party System, 1952-1989: Seven Computing Explanations" in Zoya Hasan (ed), *Parties and Party Politics in India*, New Delhi, Oxford University Press,2004, p. 492.
80. *Ibid.*, p. 490.
81. *Ibid.*, p. 503.
82. Narang, A.S. *op. cit.*, p. 360.

2

Emergence of Political Parties and Party System in Manipur

Introduction

Manipur lies in the North-Eastern corner of India. It is a land locked State having 352 km of international border with Myanmar on the east and south-east. In addition to it, she also has a 502 km long boundary with her neighbouring states, Nagaland on the north, Assam in the west and Mizoram on the south and south-west. The State has 22.327 sq km of area and populated by 22, 93,896 people according to the 2001 Census.[1] The State can be divided into two geographical regions, i.e. the hill and the valley. The hill region is the home of 33 different tribes. Prior to the Scheduled Castes and Scheduled Tribes Order (Amendment) Act, 2002, there were only 29 tribes namely[2]: 1) Aimol, 2) Anal, 3) Angami, 4) Chiru, 5) Chothe, 6) Hmar, 7) Gangte, 8) Kabui, 9) Kacha Naga, 10) Koirao (Thangal) ,11) Koireng, 12) Kom, 13) Lamkang, 14) Lushai, 15) Maring, 16) Maram, 17) Mao, 18) Monsang, 19) Moyon, 20) Paite, 21) Purum, 22) Ralte, 23) Sema, 24) Simte, 25) Sahte, 26) Tangkhul, 27) Thadou, 28) Vaiphei and 29) Zou. Later the Act,[3] added four more namely 1) Poumai Naga, 2) Tarao, 3) Kharam, and 4) Any Kuki tribes thereby increasing the total number of tribes in the State to 33. Each of these tribes has their own dialects, culture and tradition. The valley is overwhelmingly dominated by the Meitei, and other communities such as Meitei Pangal (Manipuri Muslim), Mayang (Bihari, Bengali, Assamese, Nepali, etc.) and tribals who had migrated from the hills are also found there. Overall, Manipur is a multi ethnic, multi-lingual and multi-cultural State.

Manipur was an independent State before it became a princely State in 1891 under the British Empire. When British left India, Manipur became a 'Constitutional Monarchy' for a short period from August 1947 till it joined the Indian Dominion on 15th October, 1949. Manipur up to the time of Maharaja Kula Chandra, April 27th, 1891, was an independent State. The existence of the State goes back to pre-historical and unrecorded times. The State was known by various names to different people in ancient times. The Shans called it *ka-se* (cassay); to the Burmese, it was *ka-the*; "the Ahoms called it *Mekhle*, the Kacharies, *Magli,* while the old Assamese name for it was *Moglau*."[4] The king was the head of the administration. But, the king did not have absolute power. He was assisted by 64 *Phamdous* (ministers). The sixty four *Phamdous* determined the laws and customs that should prevail in Manipur. They actually administered the land. They had the power of imprisoning the king in case he misbehaved. Similarly, if the nobles misbehaved, accepted bribes, or practiced nepotism, they were liable to imprisonment for a period of three months or could be removed from office or both. Thus, both the king and the nobles controlled each other.[5] There was a proper system of check and balance between the king and the *Phamdous* as evinced by the popular saying *Leipakna Nama,Ninghthouna Nama*[6] (The people on the one side and the king on the other side). Then there is also the saying, *Ningthouna wa ani ngangphade* which means that the King, by himself alone, should not change the decisions which he had taken along with his *Phamdous*.

The politics of ancient Manipur was the politics of the palace. The political power of the State was concentrated into the hands of the king and few noblemen. The power of the king of Manipur gradually and slowly went into the hands of the British after it came into contact with the British during the reign of Jai Singh in 1762. A treaty of alliance, offensive and defensive was negotiated on 14th September, 1762 with Hari Das Goswami on behalf of Manipur Raja Jai Singh and Mr. Verelst, Chief of Chittagong for the British.[7] Manipur was invaded and occupied by the Burmese from 1819 to 1826. This period in Manipur is popularly known as *Chahi Taret Khoontakpa* (Seven Years Devastation) in the history of Manipur. The King of Manipur was helped by the British in their efforts to expel the Burmese. Ultimately, the Burmese were driven out of Manipur by the Anglo-Burmese war of 1824. After the war, an Anglo-Burmese Treaty (Treaty of Yandaboo) was signed in 1826 which recognised Gambhir Singh as a Raja of Manipur. The war gave an opportunity for the British to interfere in the internal affairs of the State and they took full advantage of it. In 1833, the first Political Agent of Manipur (Lt. Gordon) was appointed.

Since then, the British interfered in every matters of Manipur. Because of their interference in the internal matters of the State, a war broke out between the British and Manipur in 1891. The British won the war and Manipur became a princely State under the British. Consequently, Manipur was granted Sanad in 1891 in favour of the Maharaja, making him subservient to the government of Assam. She continued to be under the British till they left the Indian Sub-Continent in 1947. The status of Manipur immediately before the attainment of independence was very low. Manipur was given only a very limited authority. The Governor of Assam exercised very important functions in the administration of Manipur.[8]

Political consciousness on democratic lines developed in Manipur during the British period especially in the 1930's. The introduction of modern education in Manipur resulted in the emergence of a new educated class whose involvement in the two World Wars directly or indirectly broadened their outlook, further. The new educated elite soon began to be imbued with the democratic values and the idea of nationalism. The Indian National Movement too had its own impact on the people and the people soon realized that the days of the British monarch were numbered and this realization further heightened the political consciousness of the people of this area.[9] As a consequence, many social and political organizations came into existence in the State.

Nikhil Manipuri Mahasabha (NMM)

A Socio-religious organization called 'Nikhil Hindu Manipuri Mahasabha' (NHMM) was established on May 30th, 1934, in Manipur under the Presidentship of His Highness Maharaja Churachand Singh.[10] The formation of NHMM was an important landmark in the growth of political consciousness among the Manipuris. Initially, the Mahasabha was designed to serve as a common forum for all the Manipuris who have settled in different parts of India, Myanmar and Manipur under the patronage of Churachand Singh, the king of Manipur. As such, every session of the Mahasabha was held at different places. The first session of the Mahashabha was held on 30th May, 1934 at Imphal, the second session was on 30th January, 1936 at Silchar; and the third session was held on 28th February 1937 at Mandalay, Myanmar. During this period, the main agenda of the NHMM was the integration of the Manipuris, in spite of inhabiting in different places.[11] In other words, the NHMM aimed to promote a sense of unity and oneness among the Manipuris who have settled in different parts of the neighbouring areas of Manipur.

This idea was promoted by some educated youths like Hijam Irabot Singh, Sorakhaibam Thambou Singh, Nongmaithem Thanin, Dwijamani Deva Sharma, Bankabihari, Nongmeikapam Gopal Singh, etc. They were greatly influenced by the idea of the Indian national movement. They were also concerned with the establishment of a new political system in Manipur based on democratic principles. However, they refrained from spelling out their plans and objectives clearly and openly, as the feudalistic rule of the Maharaja were in its zenith. The prevailing political situation compelled them to follow a moderate line. As a first step they strongly advocated for the removal of different forms of evil practices in the society.[12]

Some of the evil practices imposed by the State in the society were:

(i) *Chandan Senkhai* (tax for putting Chandan mark),

(ii) *Yairek Santri* (keeping vigil at night on the Government Officials),

(iii) *Peon Chakthak*, (serving food freely to the peon and other Government officials. It was a tax for the peon paid by the people by extending hospitality to the touring Government officials)

(iv) *Pothang* (helping the State government servants in carrying their belongingness when they went for tour in different places),

(v) *Dolaireng Puba* (carrying the king and government official in a palanquin by the people, while travelling in far away places), etc.

They even imposed taxes for growing 'simul tree' and cutting of it. During this period, there were also some sections of the society who were ex-communicated by the king. The volunteers of the Mahasabha made friends and intermixed with those people who were ex-communicated by the king in the name of *mangba-sengba*. (A social practice followed by the vaisnavaite Hindu Manipuri towards the non-Hindu community namely, the *Loi* and the tribal. The Hindu ex-communicated them, they didn't share food, didn't allow entering house, sacred places, etc. It was a social ostracize in the name of touchability or untouchability.) The dead bodies of the ex-communicated people were not cremated on the line of the Hindu rituals. The members of the Mahasabha cremated such bodies. The Mahasabha also took up many actions and programmes against other policies and activities of the King which discriminated the people.[13]

Soon the members of the Mahasabha led by Hijam

Irabot Singh realised that in the absence of political reforms the drive for socio-religious reforms alone won't produce the desire result. Therefore, they turned their attention more to political reforms. Such efforts ultimately led to the transformation of the NHMM into a political organisation with the new name 'Nikhil Manipuri Mahasabha' (NMM) after dropping the word 'Hindu' in the Chinga Session held on 29th and 30th December, 1938. This session was a landmark in the political history of modern Manipur in the sense that it culminated in the emergence of the first ever political party in Manipur. The newly formed party was headed by Hijam Irabot Singh as its President.[14]

Manipur Praja Sammelani

The 'Manipur Praja Sammelani' (MPS) was formed by a faction of Nikhil Manipuri Mahasabha, led by H. Irabot Singh. It emerged on 7th January, 1940 during the time of the Women Agitation of 1939 (2nd Nupi Lan). This political party was an immediate outcome of 2nd Nupi Lan. During the agitation, the members of the Working Committee of the Mahasabha had different views and opinions on the question of lending support to the agitation. Some of the members of the Mahasabha including the President H. Irabot Singh, and other leaders like Khogendrajit, Karam Bidur and Amuselung wanted to support the women agitation and launch a bigger agitation as a mark of protest against the police atrocities on the innocent women. Another faction of the Mahasabha led by Kh. Megho Singh, Lalitmadhop Sharma and Bangkabihari Sharma did not want to support the women agitation but wanted to extend cooperation in a peaceful and non-violent way. To find a solution on the differences among the leaders, an emergency meeting of the Working Committee was held on 7th January, 1940 (8 a.m.). In the meeting, members of the Mahasabha had a heated debate over the issue of the women's agitation and decided to settle the issue by vote. In the vote, H. Irabot Singh and his followers were reduced to a minority. Subsequently, they defected from the party and decided to launch a new political party. They organised a public meeting on the same day at Police Lane Ground at 2 pm. In the meeting, H. Irabot Singh delivered a highly explosive speech and proposed to form a new party called Manipur Praja Sammelani and seek the consent of the people who gathered there in the meeting. The people accepted the idea and the Praja Sammelani was formally established as a political party of Manipur. The meeting also constituted a Working Committee of 26 members. Hijam Irabot Singh was the President, Elangbam Tompok was the General Secretary and Longjam Bijoy was made the treasurer of the new party.[15]

Krishak Sabha

A new political party named 'Krishak Sabha' emerged in Manipur in the year 1946. Before it became a political party, it was a social organization which was known as 'Manipur Krishi Sammelani'. It worked for the cause of rural people particularly for the peasants. It was established in the year 1935 at Nambol in the Imphal - Churachandpur road, in the south of Imphal, under the Presidentship of S. Herananda Singh. The activities of the organization were mainly concerned with rural development. Emphasis was given on establishing Gram Panchayats in rural areas, schools in villages, introducing free education up to the primary level, providing medical and postal facilities, etc. On the 16th May 1946, the Krishi Sammelani held its second session at Nambol under the Presidentship of Khundrakpam Abungjao Singh. In this session Krishi Sammelani became a political organization and changed its name to 'Krishak Sabha'. H. Irabot Singh and Okram Ibomcha (Ibomcha Kabiraj) became the President and General Secretary of the party respectively. The Krishak Sabha emerged as a political party for the welfare of the peasant and became one of the most powerful left oriented political parties in Manipur.[16]

Manipur Praja Mandal

The Manipur Praja Mandal was formed on March,

1946. This political party is a product of the Second World War. During the war, the situation in Manipur, especially in the Imphal valley, was very tense. The socio-economic condition of Manipur became worse day by day. Essential commodities like salt, kerosene, sugar, cloths, etc. were scarce. Inflation rocketed sky high. Schools were closed down. The cycle tax which levied by the State also increased from Re 1 to Rs 5/- after the war.[17] People also suffered from tremendous psychological problems due to uncertainty of their life and property.[18]

It was in such an environment that Irabot returned from Cachar in the early part of 1946. He assessed the socio-economic and political realities of the State. He contacted political leaders like Laikhuram Khagendrajit Singh (Ibungohal), Karam Bidur Singh, etc. to discuss the situation of Manipur. A meeting was held on 7th March, 1946 at the residence of Karam Bidur Singh, Wangkhei Younglan Leirak. Some of the important political leaders who were present in the meeting were Shri Laikhuram Khagendrajit Singh, Shri Laishram Mera Singh, Khaidem Promodini Devi, etc. In the meeting they resolved to oppose the proposed plan for the formation of Purbanchal Pradesh (North East Frontier Provinces). They also resolved to demand the State government to provide the daily needs like cloth, kerosene etc. at a fairer price. The meeting unanimously decided to establish a political party called 'Manipur Praja Mandal' under the Presidentship of Hijam Irabot Singh. A working committee comprising 12 members was also constituted to look after the party affairs. Shri Laishram Mera Singh and Shri Laikhuram Ibobi Singh were elected as Vice-President and General Secretary of Committee respectively.[19]

Manipur Praja Sangha

The Manipur Praja Sangha emerged on 21st August 1946. After the World War II the political scenario of the Indian sub-continent experienced a sea change. It became obvious that the days of the British were numbered. Political future of the princely states became a major issue for discussion for one and all. Many political leaders of Manipur including Irabot wanted to have a responsible government in the State. So, he started efforts to form a strong political party which can demand a responsible government for the State.

Against this backdrop, a joint meeting of the Praja Sammeloni and the Manipur Praja Mandal was held at 5 pm on Wednesday, the 21st August 1946, at the temple of Gouramani Sharma, at Kwakiethel under the Presidentship of Raj Kumar Bhubansana Singh. These two parties were established earlier under the Presidentship of Hijam Irabot Singh. Most of their working committee members were common. The two parties also had more or less the same views regarding the conditions of British India and Indian native states, the political and economic conditions of Manipur, the common demand for a responsible government, the formation of a strong political organization by uniting of the Manipur Praja Sammelon and Manipur Praja Mandal, etc.[20]

In the joint meeting the two parties agreed that among the major political parties in Manipur, the two organisations reflect the people's aspirations, and that the two have the same aims and objectives. Therefore it was resolved that the two organizations be merged into one under the name of "Manipur Praja Sangha" in order to became a powerful political party in Manipur. A working committee of 25 members was also appointed. The President, Working President and General Secretary of the party were elected as Rajkumar Bhubonsana, Gouramani Sharma and H. Irabot Singh respectively.[21]

Manipur State Congress (MSC)

The Manipur State Congress was formed on 4th October, 1946 at the Aryan Theatre, Imphal. This was possible with the initiative of the young energetic educated youths of the State. The emergence of this party was another landmark in the political history of the State. It brought a new dimension and political outlook in the State. After the World War II, British government was ready to grant independence to the

Indian sub-continent. During the time, many educated youths felt the necessity to have a strong political party in Manipur to decide the future of State. They thought that there was a political vacuum in the State and it was inevitable to establish a powerful political party like the Indian National Congress. They wanted to invite the three major political parties in Manipur i.e. Nikhil Manipuri Mahasabha, Praja Sangha and Krishak Sabha. With a view to form such a party they contacted all the leaders of these parties and expressed their desire to form a common organisation and share a common platform. Their ideas and views were welcomed by the political leaders. They invited the leaders of the political parties for a meeting to discuss about the formation of a new political party.[22]

Subsequently, a meeting was held on 18th September, 1946, at the Aryan Theatre Hall. In the meeting, a 'Coordinating Committee' was formed and Yumnam Khoimacha Singh was made the Convenor. Sagolsem Indramani Singh, Sinam Krishnamohan Singh, Loitam Yaima Singh, Raj Kumar Maipaksana, and Sarungbam Ibohal Singh were the other members of the Committee. They resolved to invite three members from each party and convened a meeting on 4th October, 1946, at Aryan Theatre. In the said meeting, the three parties sent their representatives. They were:

1. Nikhil Manipuri Mahasabha- Sinam Krishna Mohan Singh, Laishram Yugeshwor Singh and Elengbam Tompok Singh.
2. Praja Sangha - H. Irabot Singh, Rajkumar Bhubon Sana Singh and Ayekbam Anggo Singh.
3. Krishak Sabha - M. Modhumangol Singh, Leiren Doctor and Kanhai Singh.
4. From the youths - Yumnam Khoimacha Singh, Sagolsem. Indramani Singh, and Rajkumar Maipaksana.[23]

At the very outset of the meeting all the members present unanimously agreed to form a strong political party and proposed to name it as 'Manipur State Congress'. This was followed by suggestions that once a person becomes a member of the newly formed party, he should resign his membership from any other political party in case he was a member of one. During this time, H. Irabot Singh was a member of the Communist Party of India. As a result some members strongly objected to the presence of H. Irabot Singh as he was a communist. Irabot took it as an insult to him. In the argument which subsequently followed, Irabot was asked to formally proclaim himself as a non-communist. At this, Irabot and his colleagues walked out of the hall as a mark of protest against the manner in which the coordinating committee conducted the meeting. Though Irabot and his colleagues left the meeting, the remaining members continued their business and ultimately formed the new party - 'Manipur State Congress' (MSC). The meeting constituted a Working Committee of 9 members with representatives from the Nikhil Manipuri Mahasabha, Praja Sangha and Coordinating Committee. Rajkumar Bhubonsana Singh was elected as the President and Yumnam Khoimacha Singh as the General Secretary of the party.[24]

Communist Party

The Communist Party emerged in Manipur on September, 1948. During the time, there were some political parties and political leaders who were left-oriented in their outlook and principles. But, there was no political party in Manipur who followed the principles and ideology of the Communists. The emergence of the Communist Party in Manipur was the handiwork of Hijam Irabot Singh. He became a member of Communist Party of India (CPI) in May 1943. He attended the historic Second Congress of the Communist Party of India held at Calcutta from February 28th to March 6th, 1948 as a special representative from Assam. In the year 1948, the political identity of Hijam Irabot Singh as a political leader who wants to use democratic revolution against the feudal and colonial administration became more distinct and clear. The new political developments in Manipur after the British's departure made him more disillusioned. Because, he felt that the transfer of power was merely from the hereditary feudal class to the educated bourgeoisies of Manipur. The mass especially the peasants were as exploited as before. So, he felt the need to establish a party on Communist lines in order to guard the mass (peasant) from the bourgeoisie.[25]

The Communist Party of Manipur was first established at the level of District Organizing Committee (DOC). It was formed in a meeting held at the residence of Takhellambam Ibotombi Singh at Hodam Leirak, Imphal, on 23rd August 1948. The meeting was attended by 22 members. The meeting also appointed Takhellambam Bokul Singh as the secretary of DOC and constituted a committee of 8 members. The members were

(1) Hijam Irabot Singh,
(2) Takhellambam Bokul
(3) Takhellambam Ibotombi
(4) Longjam Bijoy
(5) Laishram Kanhai
(6) Takhel Aamuselung
(7) Takhellambam Ongbi Juboti Devi and
(8) Thokchom Bira Singh.[26]

Praja Shanti Sabha

The Praja Shanti Sabha emerged as a political party of Manipur in 1948. During this time, 'demand for responsible government' was the slogan for every political party in the State. So, the Maharaja issued an order for an 'interim council' on 13th August 1948. The MSC made an attempt to participate in the interim government. In the process, the party split up into two. Some leaders tried to mediate the two rival parties but ended up by forming a new party called 'Praja Shanti Sabha'. It came into being by changing the nomenclature of a small party called 'Praja Party', which was led by Khongbantabam Ibotombi Singh, an ex-inspector of police. The Praja Shanti Sabha had no special and definite political objective and was regarded as the government party after forming the ministry along with other Hill members after the 1948 elections.[27]

Socialist Party

The Socialist Party emerged in Manipur in 1948. In the beginning, it was a branch of the Assam Socialist Party. Therefore, all the policies and programmes of the party were guided by the political objectives of the Assam Socialist Party. One of its objectives was to make Manipur a part of Assam Province. On this line, the Manipuri Socialist Party also launched a movement in Manipur in 1948. They believed that if Manipur became a part of Assam, then they would enjoy all the facilities which were available in Assam. The most important political slogan of the party was their demand for abolition of the Inner Line Permit System. In order to achieve it, Socialist leaders from other states made an attempt to enter into the State by violating the existing Inner Line System. The matter became very serious. However, the government was not in favour of their demand.[28]

Manipur People Party (MPP)

The Manipur People's Party (MPP) was established in 1968. Around 1967, the popularity of the Indian National Congress (INC) declined in some states. This brought a change in the political scenario of the country. As a result, non-Congress governments were formed in some states. The changing political trend also reached Manipur. A crisis had developed within the Manipur Territorial Congress Legislature Party on the issue of leadership and the policy of food. Ten Congress MLAs including the Speaker, S. Tombi Singh and Deputy Speaker, Kh. Chaoba Singh left the party. They formed the United Legislature Front (ULF) ministry, along with seven opposition members. The ULF ministry lasted only 12 days and the administration of Manipur was subsequently taken over by the President. This brought a political crisis in the State.

Moreover, the socio-economic position of the State was

in a very bad shape. In 1965, there was a famine in Manipur. There were wide spread unrest among the people in general and among the students in particular. As a result, students staged a demonstration in front of the residence of the Chief Commissioner, demanding supply of rice to the people. On that day, firing took place within the compound of the Chief Commissioner in which some students lost their life. These developments created a feeling of anti-congress in the minds of the younger generation, especially the students.

Under these circumstances, those ex-Congressmen who formed ULF ministry felt the necessity to have a local party in Manipur. Thus, leaders like Shri Chaoyaima Singh, Shri Nilachandra Singh, Y. Yaima Singh and S. Tombi Singh convened a meeting on 26th December, 1968 and formed the "Manipur People's Party' (MPP). The first conference of the party was held on 27th January, 1969 at the Aryan Hall, Imphal.[29] The party was formed with a view to safeguard the distinct identity of the people, protect Manipur's territorial integrity, check the worsening of the economy of the State and promote the interests of the people in general.[30]

Rise of Political Parties in the Hills

The political consciousness in the hills of Manipur developed more or less simultaneously with the valley. The introduction of modern education in Manipur produced educated elite in the State. With the introduction of modern education and arrival of Christianity in the early 20th century, the hill people became politically conscious and aware of their separate identity. This brought ethnic politics in the hill areas of Manipur.[31] Towards the end of British rule, community or ethnic based socio-political organisations emerged in the hills of Manipur. Among them, mention can be made of the Tangkhul Long (Tangkhul Naga Long) 1919, the Kabui Samiti of Rongmei (later known as Kabui Naga Association or Zeliangrong Naga Union) 1934, the Vaiphei National Organization, 1944, the Hmar Association, 1936 and Kuki National Assembly (KNA), 1947, etc. In the post-colonial period also, the trend continued with the emergence of similar community based organisations like the Hmar Congress (1954), the Paite National Council (1956), the Gangte Tribal Union (1958), the Hmar National Union (1959), the Baite National Union, (1962), etc.[32]

However, most of these organizations of the hills of Manipur did not last long. During the 1970's, except KNA, Hmar National Union and Zeliangrong Naga Union, all the others got merged into the Congress.[33] The 1970s also witnessed the emergence of two more political parties in the hills of the State. They are the United Naga Integration Council (1972) and Manipur Hills Union (1972). At present, The KNA is the oldest serving political party of Manipur.

Kuki National Assembly

The Kuki National Assembly (KNA) emerged in 1946. The historical background of the KNA can be traced back with the establishment of the Kuki Chiefs Association around the year 1935-36. During the British period, the chiefs were not happy with the practice of Pothang (helping the State government servants in carrying their belongingness when they went to a far away places without any tips) and also with the officials in the hills known as *Lambus* (hill peons). The *Lambus* were alleged to be corrupted. Therefore, the Chiefs Association demanded to abolish the post of *Lambus*. Moreover, three government employees filed a petition against the corrupt *Lambus* on behalf of the Association. Instead of looking into the matter, the government suspended them. The action of the government infuriated both the Chiefs and the public. As a consequence, the Chief convened a meeting in Imphal to discuss the situation and the prevailing practices like *Pothang*. In the meeting Kuki National Assembly (KNA) was formed on 24th October 1946, with Mr. Zavum Misao and Mr. Kipgen as the President and the Secretary of it respectively.[34]

The United Naga Integration Council (UNIC)

The United Naga Integration Council (UNIC) was formed

in 1972. This party was established under the leadership of Shri Rishang Keishing, a Naga leader who was expelled from the Congress party. After getting expelled from the party, he consulted some Naga leaders and formed the United Naga Integration Council (UNIC). This was on the eve of the first General Elections of Manipur in 1972.[35]

The Manipur Hill Union

The Manipur Hills Union (MHU) was formed as a local party, by seven MLA's from the hills of Manipur in December, 1972. This party was led by Shri Yangmaso Shaiza.[36] The life of the party was very short. The party was extinct by the end of 1974 due to a series of defections committed by its members.

Emergence of Party System in Manipur

The evolution of party system is related with the emergence of the political parties in Manipur. The first political party of Manipur emerged in 1938. In due course of time, many political parties also emerged in the State. This made Manipur a multi-party State. They were competing for power among themselves. But none of them succeeded in asserting dominance over the rest. In the 1930s and 1940s their main agenda were to educate democratic ideas and principles to the people, to promote and safeguard the interests of the farmers and downtrodden, to demand responsible government, etc. During the time, Manipur was a princely State under the British Government. The government inside the State was not democratic, society was feudal in nature and political consciousness among the people was very low. The policies and programmes of the political parties were mainly in the form of demands for democratic political reforms and organise people's support to these demands. As a result, the nature of the party system was not very competitive.

The first political party of Manipur, Nikhil Manipuri Mahasabha (NMM), played an important role for the growth of political consciousness among the people. It pioneered the cause for the uplift of the socio-religious life of the people. Its members gave strong emphasis on social unity among different ethnic groups of the State. Their main demand was the establishment of a responsible government in Manipur.[37] During the time, there was scarcity of rice in Manipur. As a consequence, the 2nd Nupi Lan (Women Agitation) broke out in 1939. It brought intra-party conflict within NMM, and divided the party into two groups – one group within the Mahasabha supported the agitation and the other opposed it. Subsequently, the party split into two. Those who want to support the agitation were led by H. Irabot Singh. They came out of the party and formed a new party called Praja Sammelani. The political agenda of the new party was more or less similar with that of the NMM. They were responsible for the abolition of colonial and feudal administrative system and establishment for a responsible government.[38]

During 1941-1945, there was hardly any political movement in Manipur as the State was engulfed by the Second World War. From 1945 onwards all the left oriented leaders of Manipur joined the political parties like Praja Sangha, Krishak Sabha, etc. As already stated, the Manipur State Congress (MSC) also emerged during this time. All these developments led to the intensification of the demand for responsible government inside the State. After the 2nd World War the Indians realised that the end to the colonial rule was now only a matter of time. The princely states were fully aware of this. Taking advantage of the new political development, the Maharaja of Manipur took an initiative to constitute an 'Elected Advisory Assembly'. But it seems that the Maharaja was not in favour for a responsible government in Manipur. This was not acceptable to the political parties of Manipur because they felt that it did not fulfil their demand for a responsible government under a separate constitution of the State. They urged the Maharaja to kindly make a royal declaration for the establishment of Legislative Assembly on democratic principles.

Understanding the people, the Maharaja formally

proposed to constitute a 'Constitution Making Committee' to draft a constitution on 12th December 1946. The Constitution Making Committee was to comprise of 15 members –

(i) Five nominee (three Durbar members including the President of the Manipur State Durbar, (PMSD), one member from judicial department, one nominee of the Maharaja),

(ii) one representative from each of the five tehsils in the valley, and

(iii) one representative from each of the five hill areas viz, Ukhrul, Mao, Tamenglong, Churachandpur and South-East area.

On 24th December 1946, the chairman of the Election Committee notified that the nominations should be filled on or before 5th January 1947. There was lot of misunderstanding and confusion among the people regarding the election for the representative of the five tehsils. The Krishak Sabha and Praja Sangha strongly protested the order of election. Because they felt that the time was very short and as such, it would not be possible for the people to decide within such a limited time the future Constitution of Manipur. Also, it was notified that any interested person from the valley could contest in any tehsils provided he had land in the tehsils.[39] It was alleged that the intention was to facilitate the candidature of the richer elites, many of whom were Congress supporters. The protests made by Manipur Praja Sangha (MPS) and Manipur Krishak Sabha (MKS) were ignored. Ultimately they decided to boycott the Constitution Making Committee and organized a series of protest meetings. On the contrary, the MSC was fully prepared for the election of the 5 tehsils in the valley. Since the other two parties boycotted the elections, the MSC got full advantage. And as expected, the MSC secured 4 seats out of 5 tehsils and they joined the Committee. The Committee submitted a proposed draft constitution on 27th July 1947 and it was enacted later.

During the time, the MKS and MPS organized a number of mass mobilization programmes. In one such programme of MPS (3rd Annual Conference) held in Khurai at 16 and 17th March, 1937, Irabot highlighted the undemocratic method in forming the Constitution Making Committee. He also called upon all sections of people and all the organizations in the State to unite in the ensuing struggle for socio-economic and constitutional changes. The Conference resolved to demand the scrapping of the recently formed Constitution Making Committee, reduction of land tax, and abolition of the 'passport system'.[40]

The popularity of the MKS and MPS was gaining its momentum and the members of the parties were increasing day by day. This was a great concern for the MSC because they could not tolerate the growing popularity of other parties. Therefore, the MSC started looking for opportunities to isolate the MKS and MPS from the masses. In the months of May and June, 1947, MSC tried to discredit MKS and MPS leaders particularly Irabot Singh by slanderous propaganda that the latter wanted to merge Manipur with Burma. In the Hindusthan Standard, 12th May, 1947, it was reported that Aung San, the then Deputy Chairman of Burmese Interim Government was invited by the people of Manipur and Manipuri wanted their State to merge into Burma. Again, on 14th May issue of the same paper, a news item under the title 'Claim of border State of Burma' came out, by quoting U Ba Choe, the then Information Minister of the Burmese Interim Government, which said that the Manipuri preferred to merge with Burma rather than with Muslim Bengal. The MSC which had been waiting for opportunities to embarrass Irabot and other fraternal organizations took full advantage of the new development. In a public meeting organized by MSC on 18th May, they charged the 'Communists' in Manipur to be responsible for the new developments. In another Congress meeting at Kakching on 15th May, Lalita Madhab Sharma accused Irabot by saying *Irabotna Manipur Burmada Yonthok khre* (Irabot has sold out Manipur to Burma). Such propaganda stirred the minds of the people. Irabot clarified that it was false propaganda and argued that the allegation was absolutely baseless. He further clarified that what the Praja Sangha and Krishak Sabha stood for was the integration of State by acquiring the Manipuri inhabited areas of Cachar and Kabow Valley to Manipur. He further argued that the activities of the State Congress was to destroy his credibility among the people and also to sabotage the people's struggles, as they had already done during the Nupi lan by collaborating with the Marwari traders and the authorities. All the organisations with which Irabot was associated with including CPI defended Irabot. The struggle for socio-economic and constitutional changes under the banner of MKS and MPS got intensified further. On 26th May, a meeting of the MKS was held at Pungdongbam. The meeting resolved to demand immediate payment of war compensation, and rationalization of government policy of encroaching upon the fishing and forest rights of the people. The MKS carried out mass mobilization programmes during the month of June. The MSC also protested against the non-payment of war compensation.[41]

On the eve of India's Independence, all the princely states were ready to take the administrative responsibility of their respective states from the British. The Maharaja of Manipur also prepared for the same. First of all, the Maharaja abolished the Manipur State Durbar on 1st July 1947 and established the 'Manipur State Council' in place of it. Secondly, he established an 'Interim Council' by dissolving the Manipur State Council on 15th August 1947. The formation of the 'Interim Council' was not accepted by political parties except few Congressmen. Even a large section of the Congress Party also severely criticized the designs of the Maharaja and the manner in which the members of the Council were appointed. They were particularly critical about the appointment of Krishnamohan and Dwijamani, both Congressmen, in the Council.[42] It was reported that some congress leaders met the Chief Minister and decided that the number of Minister in the Council will be 6 (two each from the Congress, officials and hills). They submitted the name of Krishnamohan and Dwijamani from the Congress without informing the Congress Working Committee. As a consequence, the MSC split into two groups, which were known to the people as Tomal Congress and Tompok Congress. The manoeuvrings of some of the congress leaders to capture the Interim Council were highly condemned by the Praja Shanti, another political party in Manipur. The later claimed that all the members of the Council should be elected by the people through proper election.

The Tompok Congress faction formed its Working Committee and started a political movement. They strongly urged that a 'Popular Interim Government' should be established at the earliest; otherwise the progress towards the formation of a responsible government would be obstructed and delayed. They also threatened the authority that if their demands were not fulfilled, they would take up their own course of action to achieve the goals. Later, as the Government did not give an appropriate response to their demands they decided to launch a political movement. They held a meeting of the Working Committee on 4th October 1947 and resolved to urge the government to declare the grant of 'Responsible Government' before 1st April 1948. They asked the government to respond before 31st October 1947 failing which they would immediately take up political agitation from 1st November 1947. Ultimately, as the government refused to fall in line with their demands they started a movement from 6th November 1947. The movement was supported by the Praja Sangha, the Krishak Sabha, the Mahila Sammelani, the Manipur Student Federation, etc. As the movement got more intensified, the government used force to stop the movement. There were some casualties. The government also issued a notice which mentioned that distribution of war compensation would be stopped from 10th November 1947, if the Tompok Congress did not suspend their agitation. Instead of suspending the movement the agitators further intensified their movement. Ultimately, having no choice the Chief Minister officially announced on 23rd November 1947 that a responsible government would be established in Manipur. As a result, the political movement launched by Tompok Congress was called off on 26th November 1947.[43]

Accordingly, steps towards the establishment of responsible government was taken up with elections to be conducted under the Manipur Constitution Act, 1947. A 'Franchise Sub-Committee' which was formed on 14th October 1947 was entrusted with the task for the election. In the meantime, the two Congress factions were reunited. As per plan of the Committee, the election was held on June and July1948.

Many political parties like Praja Shanti Sabha, the Krishak Sabha, the Socialist Party, the Manipur State Congress, etc. contested the election. In the election, no party could secure majority in the legislative Assembly. Out of the 53 seats in the Assembly, the Congress won 14 seats, the Praja Shanti 12, the Krishak Sabha 5 and the Socialist Party 3. The remaining 18 seats were filled by Hill members and election in one of the constituencies in the hills was not held. Though Congress became the single largest party, it failed to form the Government. Their dream of forming the government and controlling the State was shattered. The MLAs of the Hills and Krishak Sabha extended their support to the Praja Shanti. As a result, the Praja Shanti formed a coalition ministry headed by Maharaj Kumar Priyobrata Singh.[44]

The Merger with India

In the initial years of her independence, the Government of India adopted a policy of integration of all the princely states of British India. They wanted to integrate them including Manipur and initiated necessary steps for it. Meanwhile the MSC which was really frustrated because of its inability to form the Government started toying with the idea of merger of Manipur into the Indian Dominion. They saw merger as the only opportunity to get the patronage of Indian National Congress (INC) and also to control political power in Manipur.[45] With this purpose in view, the MSC tried to have a good relation with the INC. During the time, there was a proposal for the formation of a Purvanchal State from the Indian Government, by amalgamating the areas of Manipur, Tripura, Cachar and Lushai Hills. The MSC supported the proposal. Moreover they invited Prafulla Chandra Ghose, an eminent Congress Leader of West Bengal to Manipur. But, all other political parties of the State and government of Manipur were totally against the move, and so the proposed Purvanchal State did not materialize. However, Prof. N Joykumar Singh argued that it produced an indirect positive impact in favour of MSC as the MSC was able to establish a direct contact with the leaders of the All India Congress Committee. It also gave an opportunity to the Indian leaders to interfere in the domestic affairs of the State which, in turn, further open up the path that ultimately led to the merger of Manipur into India.[46]

Understanding the intrigue between MSC and the Indian Union, other political parties of the State began to oppose the merger movement. A strong reaction came from one of the ruling party - the Praja Shanti Sabha - of the State. It stressed that if integration was made without the consent of the people, then it might lead to a serious problem in the relationship between India and Manipur.[47] On the contrary, MSC demanded the King of Manipur to integrate with India. They gave three reasons for it. Firstly the Government of Manipur has failed to maintain law and order. Secondly, the danger of Burmese Communist entering into Manipur was there. Thirdly, the integration of Manipur into India would bring peace and development. They also believed that after merger, a responsible government would prevail in the State.[48] They also decided to send its members to meet Indian leaders to discuss the possible ways and means for the merger of Manipur. This clearly shows that the MSC were giving a very good and encouraging support to the Government of India (GoI). Meanwhile, a serious conflict also developed between the 'Dewan' and 'Maharaja' of Manipur, on the issue of the power and position of the two offices. So, in order to have a permanent solution, the Maharaja left Imphal for Shillong on 15th September 1949. But after reaching Shillong, the Governor of Assam, under strict instructions of the Home Ministry, pressurized the

Maharaja to sign the merger agreement. The Maharaja was not allowed to move out of his residence and all communications were cut off and soldiers were kept around his residence. In this situation, the Maharaja was in a helpless position and he had without any alternative. So, the Maharaja was under tremendous pressure from the Indian authority and compelled him to sign the Merger Agreement on 21st September 1949 and it became effective from 15th October 1949.[49]

The merger brought a drastic change in the political status of Manipur. The Manipur Constitution Act, 1947 was scrapped and the Council of Ministers, the Legislative Assembly and the Judicial System which were established under the Act were abolished. Manipur was declared as a province of the Chief Commissioner under the provision of the States Merger (Chief Commissioner's Province) Order. Under the new administrative set up, the entire administration went into the hands of the Chief Commissioner. Subsequently, Manipur was put under the category of the 'Part C State' of the Indian Union. This was highly unexpected and undesirable to the people of Manipur. Even the MSC which was very keen to join the Indian Dominion (with the hope that they will be treated equally and enjoy the same facility like other states) was shocked.

Manipur as a Part 'C' State

Manipur became a "Part 'C' State" with effect from 1952 till it was upgraded to the status of a Union Territory in 1957. Among the Part C States Manipur, Kutch and Tripura did not have a legislative assembly of their own. Instead of an Assembly, an Advisory Council for each of them was constituted. The Advisory Council consisted of not less than two members appointed by the President and they hold the office during the pleasure of the President. The primary duty of the Council was to assist the Chief Commissioner. The Advisors did not have any executive power or otherwise except giving advice to the Chief Commissioner in administrative matters. The first Advisory

Council of Manipur consisted of five members. They were N. Ibomcha Singh, S. Indramani Singh, A. Suisa, L. Jugeshwar Singh and Dwijamani Deva Sharma. It was inaugurated on 9th October, 1950.[50]

During the time, political leaders from West Bengal and Assam initiated a movement to include Manipur in their State. Leaders from both the states put their argument in favour of their demands. But, the Central Government was against it and the demand withered away within no time. At this juncture, the First General Election of India, 1952 was held throughout the country. The people of Manipur participated and elected two MPs (one each from the Inner and Outer Constituency). Five political parties of the State viz. Gandhi Sevak Sabha, Praja Shanti Sabha, All Manipur National Union (AMNU), Historical Research Committee of Manipur and Kuki National Assembly and three national parties viz. Indian National Congress, CPI and Socialist Party of India contested the election. The INC candidate won the Inner seat by defeating his nearest rival CPI candidate with a margin of 9718 votes. In the Outer Constituency, the Socialist Party candidate Rishang Keishing won with a margin of 5354 votes from his nearest rival A. Suisa, the AMNU candidate.[51]

In the middle of 1953, an Advisory Council was constituted. The Council consisted of four Congressmen and one independent. It means the Council was not represented by all the major political parties. Naturally, the parties which were not represented in the Council felt upset and frustrated. They went on demanding for a responsible government in Manipur. The establishment of the Council also failed to satisfy the people. The people wanted to establish a responsible government in Manipur. The Socialist Party began a movement from the middle of 1953 to fulfil the wishes of the people. They threatened the government to establish a responsible government on or before September 1953 and that they would launch a State wide strike otherwise. Their initiative was supported and later joined by many organisations like the Tangkhullong,

Paite Union, the Zeliangrong Union, Achumba Pamba Congress, Young Socialist League, Mizo Union, Gandhi Sevak Sabha and Manipur Revolutionary Nationalist Party. In the meantime, the President of India, Dr. Rajendra Prasad visited Imphal and discussed the problem of the State with all the leaders of different political parties. They submitted memorandum to the President whereby they expressed the wishes of the people to establish a responsible government in the State.[52]

In the early 1950s, the issue of Purvanchal State affected the politics of Manipur. The State Reorganisation Committee of India also planned to visit Manipur in the month of April, 1954. The Socialist Party took all the issues very seriously and decided to consolidate their demand. In order to intensify their demand for a responsible government in the State, a series of agitations began in the State. The law and order of the State became very bad. All the educational institutions were closed down. The students also joined the movement. As the situation intensified, the government took repressive measures to control the situation and bring peace and normalcy in the State. On 25th November 1954, the agitators and State police clashed at the gate of Advisory Council office where 25 persons got injured. Next day, another 50 persons were injured in the police action. The movement spread like a wildfire and reached Delhi. The opposition members in the Parliament put up the matter for discussion in the House. However, the then Union State Minister, Dr. Kailash Nath Katju contended that the Government shall have to wait for the recommendation of the State Reorganisation Committee to examine the feasibility or otherwise of the establishment of responsible government in Manipur.

The movement got intensified further with the adoption of new strategies. People gheraoed the houses of the members of the Advisory Council. They blocked all the major roads in Imphal. On 17th December, the police opened fire to the protestors injuring three persons. They also arrested as many as 150 persons. After five days, the then Socialist

Party MP from Manipur, Rishang Keishing was also arrested from his house. Till then, the movement was mainly spearheaded by the Socialist Party. But, from then onward, all the political parties in the State including the INC also joined the movement and demanded establishment of a responsible government in Manipur. The INC was the ruling party both in the Centre as well as in the Council. So, the movement became very strong.[53]

Manipur as a Union Territory

Manipur become a Union Territory from 1st November, 1956. The territorial council Act of 1956 (No. 103 of 1956) provided a provision for a territorial council, consisting of 32 members. Out of 32, two were to be nominated by the Central Government and the remaining 30 were to be elected by the people. The powers and functions of the Council were very limited. The primary duty of the Council was to look after the developmental works of the State like construction of roads, provide facilities for education, irrigation, agriculture, etc. No financial independence was given to the Council. At the most, they could prepare a State budget. But it was to be approved by the Centre. People were not satisfied with the new Act (the Union Territorial Act, 1956) and they remained discontented as what they wanted was a responsible government in the State. As Prof. N Joykumar Singh opined, in spite of their best efforts, "Manipur was not able to rise from the political status of a Union Territory."[54]

The election of the Territorial Council was held in January 1957 along with Parliamentary elections. In the Lok Sabha election, three political parties, viz. the INC, PSP and CPI contested the election with some independent candidates. The Inner parliamentary constituency was won by independent candidate Shri, Laishram Achow Singh and the Outer seat went to the INC candidate, Rungsung Suisa.[55] In the Election for Territorial Council, various political parties (Congress, SSP, CPI and PSP) were in the fray. In the election no party could secure an absolute majority. But the Congress party became the single largest party securing 12 seats out of 30 whereas the SSP, CPI and the Independents won 6, 4 and 8 seats respectively.[56]

The introduction of the territorial council once again failed to satisfy the people because; the Council had no political power. Their main duty was simply to follow the wishes and directives of the Central Government in every aspect of the State administration. Moreover, the State political leaders especially the Congressmen could not work collectively and independently from the All India Congress Committee (AICC) directives. The people had looked towards the Congress party to solve all the ills of the State as it was the party in power both at the Centre and in Manipur. The people were disillusioned. As a result, from the early part of 1960, a fresh movement for a responsible government was initiated by the Communist and Socialist party. They formed a Joint Committee on March 26th 1960 called the Assembly Demand Coordinating Committee with a view to demand responsible government in a more systematic and effective manner. Two more Assembly Demand Committees followed, viz., the Manipur Youth Assembly Demand Committee and Women Assembly Demand Committee. They submitted memorandums to the President of India demanding the establishment of a responsible government in Manipur.[57]

The Assembly Demand Co-ordinating Committee started its agitation from the second week of April 1960. They planned to paralyse the State administration. Subsequently, they didn't allow the employees to attend the office. They blocked the road and the markets were closed down. Students came out of their classrooms and joined the protests. As a consequence, all the institutions including the educational institutions were closed down. To control the situation and bring normalcy in the State, the government not only imposed Cr.P.C. section 144. It also proclaimed curfew in the Imphal area. The police arrested a large number of agitators including students for violating curfew. The movement reached every nook and corner of the State. Now, the movement suddenly turned into a mass movement as it got support from all sections of the society. The Congress Party which remained silent till then, also suddenly raised their hand demanding a responsible government in the State. It also submitted a number of memorandums to the Prime Minister, Home Minister and the President of the AICC in which they demanded the up gradation of the status of Manipur to the level of a State.[58] Demands for the preservation of the territorial integrity of Manipur and more developmental programmes for the State were also made in the memoranda submitted on 8th September, 1960.[59]

The Second Territorial Council election was held along with the Second Lok Sabha elections in February 1962. All the major political parties in the State i.e. INC, Socialist Party, Communist Party of India, and PSP participated in the elections. In the Territorial Council election, Congress once again emerged as the single largest party with 15 seats, Socialist Party won five seats and the remaining 10 seats went to the Independents. In the parliamentary election, the INC won the Inner Constituency whereas the Socialist got the Outer Constituency.[60] The Congress candidate Shri M. Koireng Singh was elected the Chairman of the Council.

In the meantime, the Government of India passed the Union Territories Act, 1963. It came into force in Manipur from July 1963. The Act converted the Territorial Council into a Territorial Assembly with the same number of members (30 elected and two nominated members). The Manipur Territorial Legislative Assembly started functioning from 22nd July, 1963 and Shri M. Koireng Singh was elected the Chief Minister of Manipur. This new arrangement was a step - forward towards transferring the entire responsibility of development of the State to the democratically elected representatives of the people. But, the people of Manipur were not satisfied with it. The people argued that Manipur was an independent State before the merger into India and she deserved to be a State under the Indian Constitution also. She had already experienced right to self government earlier under the Manipur Government Act, 1947. So, the political status of the State should not be degraded to the level of a Union Territory. At this crucial moment, Nagaland was granted statehood by the Indian Government in 1962. This development outraged the people of Manipur. Because, all the while, the Government of India said that the area and population of the State was very small and, hence Manipur cannot be a viable State. But the area and population of Nagaland was smaller than that of Manipur. All the political leaders of Manipur were deeply disappointed and they strongly pressurised the Government of India for the establishment of a responsible government in Manipur by granting statehood to Manipur. Various political parties including the CPI, National Socialist Democratic Party (NSDP), Socialist Party, Manipur Territorial Congress Committee, etc, strongly demanded statehood for Manipur. In 2nd September, 1966, the Manipur Territorial Assembly also passed a resolution for the establishment of a responsible government in the State.[61]

The first Territorial Assembly Election of Manipur was held along with the 4th Parliamentary election in the early part of 1967. Five political parties namely the CPI, INC, PSP, CPM and SSP contested the elections. In the parliamentary election, the CPI got the Inner-constituency and the Outer constituency went to an independent.[62] In the Assembly election, the Congress emerged as the single largest party but short of majority by one. It won 16 seats in the house of 32 members, followed by the SSP - 4, CPI - 1, and the rest 9 went to independents.[63] The Congress tried their best to persuade the independent MLAs to join them. Seven independent MLAs out of nine supported them and later joined the party and became Congress MLAs. The Congress Party also nominated two MLAs as per the Union Territories Act, 1963. So, the Congress secured majority with 25 MLAs in the House of 32 members. Subsequently, a Congress Ministry headed by M. Koireng Singh was sworn in on 20th March, 1967.[64]

Very soon Manipur was plagued by the problem of political defections. It badly affected party politics in the State. It also brought a new chapter in the political history of Manipur. Struggle for power, intra-party conflicts and inter-party conflicts became the order of the day. From the middle of 1967, a crisis emerged within the Congress Party which ultimately led to the expulsion of two MLAs from the party. Some Congress leaders were also not satisfied with the CM. Evidently the CM had promised them ministerial berths and contract works but did not keep his promise. Moreover, law and order in the hills of Manipur was deteriorating day by day and the life of the common people became very insecure. Economic health of the State was also in a very bad shape. So, taking advantage of the prevailing situation some Congress MLAs started efforts to overthrow the Koireng ministry. The CM tried his best to suppress the crisis, but could not solve the problem. Finally, he initiated a move to the Congress Legislative Party and adopted a resolution to remove the Speaker Shri S. Tombi Singh, and Deputy Speaker Shri Kh. Chaoba Singh, the rebels within the party. Later, they were expelled from the party.[65]

The expelled leaders had the support of eight other Congress MLAs. They joined hands with all the opposition MLAs and formed a 'United Legislative Front' (ULF). These 17 MLAs of the Front met the Chief Commissioner of Manipur and requested him to allow them form a new Government. As a consequence, a tussle for political power erupted in the State. The CM also contended that he still enjoyed majority support in the house. At the same time, he tried his utmost to get support of some more MLAs and consolidate his position. Both sides used all the possible means such as money, position, force, etc. to get MLAs from either side. Both groups opened up their concentration camps. It shows that Manipur was in a State of political crisis. To solve the crisis, the Congress High Command sent Mr. T. Manean to Manipur. But, he failed in his mission and advised the CM to resign. Koireng also did not see any other alternative, so he resigned on 4th October, 1967.[66]

Nine days after the resignation of Congress Ministry (13th October, 1967), a new ULF ministry headed by Shri L. Thambou Singh was sworn in. One day after the ULF ministry was sworn in Shri Koireng Singh moved for a no confidence motion against the ULF Government to the Speaker. Actually, Koireng somehow won one MLA Shri Demjalam Kipgen after his resignation. So, he thought that it is the right time to pull down the government. On 16th October, the House met but it got adjourned till 23rd October, 1967 after admitting the no-confidence motion. When the House assembled on 24th October, the Speaker resigned. This created a serious problem in the Assembly. The opposition and the ruling had the same number of MLAs and no MLA was ready to preside over the House. Since, there was no one to preside the Assembly Secretary announced that the case would referred to the Chief Commissioner. Then, on the same day the Chief Commissioner prorogued the House. On the next day, the Assembly was suspended and President Rule was imposed in Manipur.

Within a couple of months after the fall of ULF ministry, Shri Koireng succeeded in consolidating his position by bringing back most of the dissident Congress MLAs including the Ex. CM, Shri L. Thambou Singh to his fold. Once he regained the necessary support, he staked his claim to form the government. A new Congress Ministry headed by him was installed on 19th February, 1968. But, the new ministry also did not last for even one year. After two- three months some Congress MLAs revolted against him for not inducting them in the ministry. In order to control the problem within the party and save the ministry, the CM inducted some MLAs into the ministry. However, this in turn enraged those MLAs who didn't get a ministerial berth. They collaborated with the opposition and overthrow the Koireng Ministry on 24th September, 1969. The President of India dissolved the Assembly and the administration of the State was taken over by him on the 16th October, 1969.[67]

During the time, the movement for statehood was also gaining momentum in Manipur. The degree of the intensity of the demand for statehood increased from the beginning of the year 1968. Various political parties came together and formed a Joint Committee which was known as 'All

Manipur Statehood Demand Committee'. The Sanyukta Socialist Party (SSP), Communist Party of India (CPI), National Socialist Democratic Party (NSDP) and other independent MLAs were the members of the Committee. They organised a series of public meetings, demonstrations, strikes, bandhs, etc. to secure statehood for Manipur. They also demanded inclusion of Manipuri language in the 8th Schedule of the Indian Constitution and establishment of a University in Manipur. They organised a political conference on 30th and 31st March at the Aryan Theatre Hall, Imphal. They called a hartal at Imphal on 8th June and organised a public meeting on the same day where they strongly urged the central leaders to grant statehood to Manipur as early as possible. The youths and the students also actively participated in the movement. In the meantime, the Manipur Territorial Congress Committee also began reiterating its demand for statehood. It organised a series of conferences, dharnas, etc. It also submitted memoranda to the centre in pursuit of the said demand. On June 12th, 1968, they organised a political conference at Imphal, and submitted a memorandum to the PM on 23rd September, 1969. Again, they launched a dharna from 11th- 13th March, 1970. Around 1000 Congressmen organised a mass hunger strike on 19th March demanding statehood for Manipur. In short, each and every political party in Manipur came out demanding statehood for Manipur.[68]

As their efforts continued to be persistently thwarted by the Centre, the parties decided to come together to pressurise the Centre into granting statehood to Manipur. Subsequently, they held a meeting on 28th February, 1970. In the meeting, all agreed to send an all party delegation to Delhi and meet the central leaders. They also decided to form a common political platform where they all may come together. Accordingly, an 'All Parties Statehood Demand Co-ordinating Body' was formed on 26th April, 1970 in order to demand statehood for Manipur.

The formation of the All Parties Statehood Demand Co-ordinating Body was a turning point in the statehood movement. Every section of the society gave their support and joined hands with them. The support of the people gave the Co-ordinating Body more strength and cemented their position. During the time, a team of MPs from different parties visited Imphal on 9th May 1970. On that day, the Co-ordinating Body organised a mass rally and also submitted a memorandum in which they urged the central leaders to grant statehood to Manipur as early as possible. All the visiting MPs were in favour of the demand of Manipur. At this juncture, the Central Government granted statehood to Himachal Pradesh. The act of the Centre was like adding salt to the injury to the people of Manipur. The people were deeply dissatisfied, upset and angered with such an attitude of the Centre. So, they called a bandh on 3rd August, 1970. They boycotted the Independence Day function at Imphal and Civil Disobedience Movement began from 16th August. A series of mass rallies were also organised. As a result, law and order in the State was completely paralysed. The situation in Manipur became a serious concern for the central leaders in Delhi. Lots of pressures were mounting on the Congress at the Centre from the opposition parties and the mass-media. Ultimately, the Government of India passed the North-Eastern Areas (Reorganisation) Bill in December, 1971.[69] As a result Manipur was granted statehood on the 21st January 1972 with a legislative assembly with 60 elected members of the State.

Manipur as a State

The long cherished dream of the Manipuri to see Manipur as a full-fledged State was fulfilled in 1972. A new chapter in the political history of Manipur was opened. Manipur entered into the ocean of Indian Democracy as a State. People wanted to live in peace with prosperity and they looked forward to a better life. But, political stability, accountability, responsibility, etc. evaded the State. After attaining statehood, the politics of Manipur became a field of political defection and a battlefield for political power. Not even a single government could last its normal tenure of 5 years till 2002. As a result, President's Rule (PR) was imposed very frequently in the State.

Manipur was under the PR when it attained statehood. It was imposed on 16th October 1969 and it continued till the formation of a new government. During the PR some political developments took place in Manipur and also in Delhi. The Congress party expelled seven ex-Territorial Assembly members. They joined the MPP. The MPP was earlier formed by some ex-Congressman on December 1968. During the time, All India Congress split into two-Congress (O) and Congress (R) - in 1969. As a result, the Manipur State Congress Committee got split up into two groups, though majority of them remained with Congress (R). Around this time, the SSP also split and a section of them floated a new local party known as 'Manipur National Organisation' (MNO). Moreover, on the eve of the 1st Assembly Election of Manipur, 1972, a hill based political party - United Naga Integration Council (UNIC) - also emerged. This party was headed by Rishang Keishing, another ex-Congressman.[70] All these are important instances of the emergence of new political parties during the PR period.

The first General Election of Manipur Legislative Assembly was held in March, 1972 (11th March for the valley and 6th and 9th March for the hill). In the election, both national and local parties contested the elections. Political parties like Congress (R), Congress (O), MPP, CPI, SSP, UNIC etc. contested the elections. However, no party got majority in the election. The party wise strength immediately after the announcement of the election results was as follows:[71]

Congress (R)	17
MPP	15
CPI	5
SSP	3
UNIC	3
Congress (O)	3
Independent	16

Note: UNIC contested the elections as an unrecognised party.

Ministries during the period from 1972-85

The First Ministry

Since no party secured majority in the Assembly election, struggle for power began right after the election result was out. The tussle for power was headed by Congress (R) on the one side and the MPP on the other. Both the groups put their best efforts to win the Independent MLAs specially and other parties in general, so that they can form a coalition ministry. Fortunately or unfortunately, all the MLAs wanted an assurance for a ministerial berth for their support. This was a problem on both sides. Both the parties set up concentration camps and kept their supporters there. Ultimately, the game of power was won by the MPP. They managed to get the support of 17 other MLAs from different parties. It means the MPP and its allies were able to get 32 MLAs. Eventually a United Legislature Party (ULP) headed by Md. Alimmudin was formed as the first ministry of the State. It consisted of 15 MPP, three SSP, one Congress (O), three UNIC and ten independent MLAs.[72]

The Congress (R) did not give up its hope of forming a ministry. So, they further tried to woo some more MLAs in order to strengthen their position in the Assembly. In July, 1972 MLAs of the UNIC left the ULP and merged with Congress (R). They left the ULP as they failed to get ministerial berths in the ULP ministry. However, the ULP survived by engineering defection from the opposition camp. Two Congress MLAs and two independent MLAs defected from the opposition party and joined the ULP ministry. Thus, the ULP survived for the time being. Yet problems started very soon, and the ULP ministry collapsed in the month of March, 1972.

During the Budget session in 1973, there was turmoil in the Assembly. First, one ruling MLA, L. Chaoyaima Singh expired on 10 March. Then, on 15th March, 12 MLAs (9 independent, 2 ministers and Deputy Speaker) of the ULP defected and joined the opposition bench by forming a Progressive Independent Group. With this, the number of opposition MLAs reached 31. They formed an alliance called Progressive Democratic Alliance (PDA) under the leadership of Athiko Daiho, the leader of Congress Legislature Party and staked its claim to form a new government. They raised a motion of no-confidence against ULP ministry on 22nd March, 1973. The motion was discussed for 4 days. However, before the issue could be settled the ULP ministry resigned on 26th March 1973. The House was adjourned sine-die. So, on the recommendation of the Governor, PR was imposed in Manipur and subsequently the State Assembly was dissolved on 28th March 1973.[73]

The Second Ministry

After the proclamation of PR, Manipur went for a mid-term poll in early part of 1974. On the eve of election, one hill based political party - the Manipur Hill Union (MHU) - emerged. This party was formed by seven tribal Ex-MLAs which were led by Shri Yangmaso Shaiza. They put up 16 candidates for the second General Election for the Assembly. Other political parties who participated in the election were the Congress, MPP, CPI, KNA, CPM, SSP, etc.[74] In the election, the Congress made an alliance with the CPI while other went to the poll individually. The election was held on 19th and 23rd February in the hills and on 25th February in the valley. The result of the election is given below:[75]

MPP	20
Congress	13
MHU	11
SSP	2
CPI	6
Independent	8
Total	60

Once the result was declared, the MPP and the Congress tried to win the MLAs of different political parties and independent so that they can form the government. The MPP managed to get the support of 15 more MLAs from different parties and independents (6 - MHU, 2 - SSP and 7 - Independent). This meant that the MPP had the support of 35 MLAs. They formed a United Legislature Party (ULP) and formed a coalition government again headed by Md. Alimmuddin on 4th March 1974.[76] The Alimmuddin government failed to survive for long. There was serious problem right from the very beginning. As the ULP ministry was about to take swearing in ceremony, some MLAs of the MHU walked out of the ULP alliance. The MHU was not happy because their leader Yangmaso was not made the CM. However, the ULP ministry survived for some more months due to defections from the Congress party to its side. In the meantime, the parties in opposition i.e. the Congress, CPI, MHU and independent MLAs formed an alliance called Progressive Democratic Front (PDF). The PDF tried to lure as many MLAs as possible from the ruling side with promises of ministerial positions and other benefits. Finally it managed to secure as many as 31 MLAs to their side and pulled down the ULP ministry on 28th July 1974. The ULP ministry survived only 4 months and 4 days.[77]

The Third Ministry

After the fall of ULP ministry, the PDF met the Governor and staked its claim to form a new government. This was followed by the formation of a coalition government by the PDF under the leadership of Shri Yangmaso Shaiza on 10th July, 1974.[78] The fate of Yangmaso Shaiza was same with that of Alimmuddin. His government fell within five months due to internal conflicts within the PDF itself. Within one month after the formation of PDF ministry, a rift emerged between Yangmaso Shaiza and the Congress. The CM who was not from Congress wanted to select by himself those Congress MLAs who would be given ministerial berths. On the other hand, the Congress wanted to select these MLAs by itself for the CM to appoint them as ministers. As the problem become very serious, they set up their respective camps. In the tussle for power the Congress and the ULP won the battle by collecting 31 MLAs. The 31 MLAs met the Governor and requested to allow them to form a new government. They also claimed that 3 more MLAs were kept under duress in the Yangmaso camp. The Governor called upon the three concern MLAs and took their statement in which they expressed their support to the Congress-ULP collision. Then, the Governor advised Shaiza to step down and Shaiza resigned on 5th December, 1974.[79]

The Fourth Ministry

The Congress and ULP formed a Democratic Legislature Party (DLP) and another coalition ministry came into existence on 6th December 1974. The DLP ministry was headed by R. K. Dorendra Singh. After the formation of government, the Congress started the politics of absorption with a view to bring its coalition partners as well as other MLAs within its fold. It brought back its former General Secretary, Md. Habibur Rahman from the opposition party. Again, on 20th July 1975 three MHU MLAs and four MPP MLAs merged into the Congress. Moreover, the Congress encouraged all the other parties to do the same. The ULP was obviously not happy with such acts of the Congress. As a consequence, there were frictions between the ULP MLAs and Congress MLAs. The situation worsened as the Congress tried to form a pure Congress government. In the middle of 1975, the number of Congress MLAs reached to 34. So, some Congress leaders including the CM Shri R. K. Dorendra Singh met the Governor and requested him to allow them to form a Congress Ministry in place of the coalition ministry. But, the Governor advised them to incorporate the support of the CPI. Because, the Governor felt that the politics of Manipur was very fragile and political defection was the order of the day, and as such some more MLAs were desirable.

The Fifth Ministry

Accordingly, Shri R. K. Dorendra Singh resigned from his DLP ministry on the 23rd July, 1975. He was sworn in as CM of the Congress-CPI coalition on the same day.[80] Yet there was no end to the problem of political defection. In fact, a series of defection followed within no time. This time all the defections were more on the lines of a one way traffic in the sense it was a case of MLAs from opposition parties joining the Congress. For instance, on 17th September, 1975, five MPP and three MHU MLAs defected from ULP and joined the Congress. In the early part of 1976, two more MLAs from MPP joined the Congress party. So, the numbers of Congress MLAs become 42 in February, 1976 from an insignificant 13 MLAs in February, 1974. The party wise figures as on 26th February, 1976 were as follows:[81]

Name of Party	*Position in 1974*	*Position in 1976*
Congress	13	42
MPP	20	5
MHU	11	3
CPI	6	6
SSP	2	—
Independent	8	4

The trend continued till 1977 February. On 26th March, 1976, Shri Th. Chaoba Singh defected from MPP and joined the Congress. Again, on 2nd July N. Paoheu, Haokholal Thangjom and Jangamlung defected from MHU and joined Congress. So, all the MLAs of the MHU have defected to one party or another. On the same day, three Independent members also joined Congress. The defection continued further in the early part of 1977. On 17th February,'77, Shri M. Meghachandra Singh and M. Hera Singh defected from the CPI and joined Congress. As a result, the numbers of Congress MLAs got increased to 51in February 1977. The party strength as on February is shown below:[82]

Congress	51
MPP	4
MHU	Nil
CPI	4
SSP	Nil
Independent	1

In the meantime, the Sixth General Election for the Lok Sabha was held on 16th and 19th March, 1977. Various political parties contested the elections but Congress won the two seats in Manipur. However, Janata Party formed the government at the centre on 23rd March, 1977. It severely affected the party politics in Manipur. The political leaders of Manipur always looked toward Delhi and they love to dance according to the tune of the Delhi. Within two months most of the MLAs defected to the Janata Party. First, the lone independent MLA claimed himself to be the Janata MLA. Then, on 2nd May, 1977, 26 MLAs defected from the Congress and joined the Janata Party. By 6th May 1977, the Congress which had 51 MLAs in February got reduced to only 22 MLAs. As a result, the minority government of R. K. Dorendra Singh resigned on 13th May, 1977, and President Rule was proclaimed in Manipur on 16th May, 1977. The defectors did not form the government because the State Janata Party preferred dissolution of the Assembly and fresh elections to be held.[83]The defections continued during the President Rule as well. Shri. Yangmaso Shaiza, the Congress MP from Outer Manipur Parliamentary Constituency resigned from Congress and joined the Janata Party. On 24th June the Congress party which had 51 members immediately before the Lok Sabha elections was left without even a single MLA in the Assembly. Moreover, the MPP which played an important role in Manipur politics since its inception in 1968 declared their merger with the Janata Party. But, a section of the party didn't accept the merger and claimed to be true the MPP.[84]

The Sixth Ministry

The PR was revoked on 29th June, 1977 and Shri Yangmaso Shaiza was sworn in as the CM of Manipur. Actually, Shaiza was elected to the Lok Sabha and not to the Legislative assembly. So, he was required to seek election to the Assembly. This he did in December, 1977. Soon problems started in the ministry. Attempts were made to change the leader in the Janata Legislative Party. But central leadership did not accept the idea. Instead, they instructed him to expand the ministry and he immediately did it. However, it did not solve the problem. On 9th October 1978, nine Janata MLAs led by Ex-CM R. K. Dorendra Singh defected from the party and joined the Congress. It was also a time when the law and order situation in the State became deteriorated. Taking advantage of the situation, the opposition parties demanded imposition of President Rule in the State. Insurgent activities become increase in the State and slowly affected the entire State. The Governor reported the situation in Manipur to the centre and recommended President Rule. So, on 14th November, 1979 and President Rule was imposed in the State for the fifth time.[85]

The Seventh Ministry

Manipur went to the poll for the Legislative Assembly for the 3rd time in January 1980 since attaining statehood in 1972. This time also no party secured majority and coalition government became inevitable. The party wise position immediately after the declaration of the election results were as follows;[86]

Party	Seats
Congress (I)	13
Congress (U)	6
Janata	10
CPI	5
MPP	4
CPI (M)	1
KNA	2
Independent	19

Once again, the chronic problem of defections started soon after the election results were declared. Two independent MLAs joined the Congress (I). Another, two Janata MLAs also joined the Congress (I). So, the number of Congress (I) MLAs increased to 17. Even then, it was not possible to form a government. Therefore, Congress (I) negotiated with other parties to form a coalition government. As a result, Congress (I), Congress (U), MPP and KNA agreed on a 23 point - programme and to form a coalition government. They elected Shri R. K. Dorendra Singh as their leader and he was sworn in on 14th January, 1980.

The coalition ministry headed by R. K. Dorendra Singh did not last long. On 23rd October, the MPP President, L. Manoabi Singh announced the withdrawal of his party's support to the coalition ministry on the ground that it did not implement the 23 point agreement. Then, the MPP joined hands with Manipur National Democratic Party (MNDP). But, it did not affect the Dorendra ministry. Instead it affected the MPP itself as two of the four MPP ministers refused to resign and continued their support to the government for the time being. But, the two later on also decided to withdraw their support and ultimately in November, 1980 R. K. Dorendra Singh resigned from the CM.[87]

The Eight Ministry

On 27th November, 1980, Shri Rishang Keishing formed a new government with the support of the same parties in the previous government. But again this government lasted only three months. In February, 1981, a political crisis erupted in Manipur. Ten MLAs defected from the ruling party and joined the opposition in order to overthrow the Rishang ministry. Then the opposition party led by Kh. Chaoba Singh introduced a motion of no-confidence against the Rishang ministry on 27th February, 1981. By this time, 30 MLAs from the MPP, Congress (U), CPI and Janata came together and formed the People's Democratic Front (PDF) led by Kh. Chaoba Singh. They met the Governor and requested to allow them form a government. But, the

Governor refused it on the ground that the PDF would not able to form a stable government in Manipur. So, the Governor recommended for President Rule in the State and Manipur, once again, came under the President Rule for the 6th time on 28th February, 1981.

During the President Rule period, Rishang put his best effort to win back some of the defected MLAs. Ultimately, he won back 5 MLAs from the 10 defectors. They again joined the Congress (I). Subsequently, on 19th June 1981 the President Rule was revoked and Rishang Keishing again formed a new ministry. This was the 9th ministry since 1972. The ministry continued till the next general election which was held in December, 1984.[88]

Conclusion and Summary

The history of political parties in Manipur is not very old. The emergence of political parties in Manipur is of recent origin. The story of its origin lies in the British colonial period. The first political party of Manipur, Nikhil Manipuri Mahasabha (NMM) emerged in 1938. In the beginning, the NMM was a socio-religious organisation but slowly and gradually it turned into a political organisation. This organisation was established with a view to make it a common forum of all Manipuri who have settled in the neighbouring areas of Manipur. Soon it started working for socio-religious reforms. Later on, its members were convinced that without having a political organisation, it will be an impossible task to transform the society. So, they converted the socio- religious organisation into a political organisation.

Most of the political parties which emerged during the colonial period were related with the NMM in one way or the other. The Manipur Praja Sammelani, the Manipur Praja Sangha, the Krishak Sabha, Manipur Praja Mandal and CPI were formed with the initiative of Hijam Irabot Singh, who was the founder President of NMM. So, they were the brainchild of H. Irabot Singh. The Manipur State Congress (MSC) was established with the initiative taken up by the Manipuri youths. The NMM was also involved

Chief Ministers and Governments since 1963

Chief Ministers	*Governments*	*Period*	*Remarks*
M. Koireng Singh	Congress Ministry	22nd July 1963- 20th March 1967	Territorial Assembly
M. Koireng Singh	Congress Ministry	20th March 1967- 13th October 1967	First elected Territorial Assembly
L. Thambou Singh	ULP Ministry	13th October1967- 25th October 1967	
President Rule	————	25th October 1967 19th February1968	
M. Koireng Singh	Congress Ministry	19th February 1968 - 16th October 1969	
President Rule	————	16th October 1969 20th March 1972	
Md. Alimuddin	MPP-led ULP Ministry	20th March 1972— 28th March 1973	First Legislative Assembly
President's Rule	————	28th March 1973— 4th March 1974	
Md. Alimuddin	MPP-led ULP Ministry	4th March 1974—— 10th July 1974	Second Legislative Assembly
Yangmaso Shaiza	PDF Ministry	10th July 1974—— 6th December 1974	
R. K Dorendra Singh	DLP Ministry	6th December1974- 23rd July 1975	

R. K Dorendra Singh	Congress-CPI Ministry	23rd July 1975— 15th May 1977	
President's Rule	————	15th May 1977— 29th June 1977	
Yangmaso Shaiza	Janata Party Ministry	29th June 1977— 14th November, 1979	
President Rule	————	14th November 1979- 14th January 1980	
R. K. Dorendra Singh	Congress-MPP Ministry	14th January 1980- 27th November 1980	Third Legislative Assembly
Risfahang Keishing	Congress Ministry	27th November1980- 28th February 1981	
President Rule	————	28th February 1981- 19th June 1981	
Rishang Keishing	Congress Ministry	19th June 1981 — 4th January 1985	

in the formation of MSC. In fact, the NMM was merged into the MSC. Indeed, till its merger into the MSC, the root of the origin of all political parties of Manipur lied in the NMM.

Many political parties also emerged in the post-1947 era. But, they were mainly the product of the political defections. The Praja Shanti Sabha was formed by some defectors of MSC in 1948. The MPP was established by some expelled Congress MLAs in 1968. The Manipur National Organisation was formed in 1968 by splitting the SSP. The UNIC also emerged in 1972 because of Shri Rishang Kieshing an Ex-Congress MLA. Indeed, the changes of party loyalty both at the individual and party level were very frequent and no government was able to run the State without a problem even for a few months. It really affected the State. There was no political stability in Manipur.

The nature of party system in Manipur as emerged during the British period was not very competitive. The relations among the political parties were not very strained. The action and interaction among them were more friendly than conflicting because their aims and objectives were more or less the same. They all demanded a responsible form of government to be established in Manipur. They tried to educate the democratic ideas and principles to the people, so that political consciousness would grow among the masses. Another important agenda of the political parties during those times was that of the demand for socio-religious reforms.

In the post-British period, the nature of party system in Manipur did not change significantly in the beginning. In the 1940s and 1950s, the major agenda of the political parties was to demand for a responsible government. The people really wanted to establish a responsible government in Manipur. So, all the political parties took up the issue and fought for it. Though, there were differences among them, they coordinated and cooperated among themselves to fight the common cause. They joined together and formed the "All Manipur Statehood Demand Committee" in 1968 and "the All Parties Statehood Demand Coordinating Committee" in 1972 so that they could pursue their common goal together. This trend continued till the grant of statehood to Manipur. After that they parted ways in pursuit of their all-consuming desire to gain control over the State government.

Even then, slowly but surely, signs of conflicting rivalry emerged in the nature and character of party system in Manipur. The actions and interactions became increasingly competitive as they struggled for power. Defections followed at an alarming rate, both at the group level and individual level. As a result, the elements of cooperation and coalitional relationship among political parties evaporated from within the party system in Manipur to be replaced by a relationship characterised by lack of co-operation and co-ordination, conflicting rivalry, mutual distrust, etc. born out of reckless pursuit of power by the parties as well as its MLAs.

A sea change was witnessed in the nature of party system from the mid '60s. In 1963, the Territorial Council was converted into a Territorial Assembly. But, the Territorial Council members continued till the next election in 1967. The Territorial Assembly was headed by Shri M. Koireng Singh. The first election of the Territorial Assembly was held in 1967. No party secured majority. This has been the trend in all the State election in Manipur. All the time the people gave fractured mandates and no party could dominate the political scenario of the State alone. The governments which were formed in the State were coalition ministries. As a result, the politics of Manipur was coalitional in nature. No government could last its normal tenure of five year till 2002 as political defections and party-hopping became the order of the day. This indiscriminate party-hopping had no interest in pursuing policies with integrity; rather it represented short term individual opportunism.[89] Change of party loyalty and shifting of alliance both at the individual and party levels were very frequent that from 1963 till 1984. As a result, as many as thirteen ministries were formed and PR was imposed sixth times during this period. It means that at an average a ministry lasted less than 2 years. Moreover, on one occasion President Rule was imposed for more than two years (16th October 1969 to 20th March 1972). This clearly shows the kind of political instability the State had experienced during the time. According to Prof. John Parrat, the main factors for the political instability in Manipur are "the multiplicity of small parties, which ensures that none can have a majority without some form of coalition; the prevalence of defections and 'party-hopping'; and sacrificing of workable policies to self-interest and power-seeking."[90]

NOTES

1. *Statistical Abstract of Manipur*, 2004, Directorate of Economics and Statistics, Government of Manipur, p. 1.
2. Awasthi, Dr. S.K. *The Constitution of India* , Allahabad, Dwivedi Law Agency, 1999, p. 628.
3. *The Gazette of India*, Extra-ordinary, The Schedule Castes and Schedule Tribes Order (Amendment) Act, 2002.
4. Singh, N. Ibobi, *The Manipur Administration (1709-1907)*, Imphal, Friends & Co, 1976, p.18.
5. *Ibid.*, p. 48.
6. *Ibid.*, p. 60.
7. Dun, E.W. Gazetteer of Manipur, Delhi, Manas, 1886, First Print, Pr, 1992, p. 39.
8. Singh, R. K Jhalajit *A Short History of Manipur*, 2nd edition, Imphal, 1992, p. 335.
9. Dena, Lal Resistance, April 26th 1977.
10. Maipaksana, Rajkumar, *Manipurda Ihan Hanba Satyagraha Aandalon*, (A Manipuri book), 1996, Imphal, p-3.
11. Arun, M.C. *Meitie Socialization and Political Personality*, The Oriental Anthropologist, 2005(1), p. 1.
12. Singh, N. Joykumar *Colonialism to Democracy*, Guwahati, Spectrum Publication, 2002, p.147.
13. Rajkumar Maipaksana, *op. cit.*, p-4
14. *Ibid.*
15. Singh, Laikhuram Ibobi *Manipur Praja Sammelani AmasungAnisupa Nupi Lan*, (A Manipur book), Imphal, 1987, p-67ff
16. Singh, Soyam Chandradhari *Manipurgee Itihasta Irabot*, (A Manipuri book), Imphal, Soyam Publication, 1972, p. 70.

17. Karam Manimohan Singh, Hijam Irabot Singh and Political Movements in Manipur, Delhi, B R Publishing Corporation, 1989, pp-170f
18. Singh, N. Lokendra *Unquiet Valley*, New Delhi, Mittal Publications, 1998, p-167.
19. Singh, Soyam Chandradhari *op. cit.,* pp-67f.
20. Singh, Laikhuram Ibobi, *op. cit.,* pp-134ff.
21. *Ibid.*
22. Maipaksana, Rajkumar *op. cit.,* pp-8ff.
23. *Ibid.,* p-11, Also see Laikhuram Ibobi Singh, op cit, pp-136ff
24. *Ibid.*
25. Singh, Karam Manimohon *op cit,* pp-324f.
26. Joykumar, N. *op. cit.,* p.167.
27. *Ibid.,* p.168.
28. *Ibid.,* p.169.
29. Devi, Ksh. Bimola Manipur Peoples Party in Gassah, L.S (ed), *Regional Political Parties in North East India*, New Delhi, Omsons Publications, 1992, pp-170f.
30. Singh, Ng Kumarjit *'Emergence of regional political Parties'*, Volume I, North Eastern Region, Imphal, 1986, p.37.
31. Dena, Lal *op. cit.*
32. Chaube, S.K. *Hill Politics in Northeast India*, Orient Longman, Patna, 1999, p.210.
33. Dena, Lal *op. cit.*
34. Roy, Ashok Kumar *'the Kuki National Assembly*'s its Social Base and Working in Manipur' in Gassah, L.S : *Regional Political Parties in North-East India*, Omsons Publications, New Delhi,1992,pp-186ff.
35. Singh, Th. Gokul Defection in Manipur (1963-1977), Th. Achou Singh, Imphal, 1978, p. 35.
36. *Ibid.,* p-48.
37. Singh, N. Joykumar *Social Movements in Manipur (1917-1951),* Mittal Publications, New Delhi, 1992, p-96.
38. *Ibid.,* p.98.
39. Singh, N. *Lokendra Unquiet Valley*, New Delhi, Mittal Publications, 1998, p.198
40. It was necessary to take permission from the Government to enter Manipur and live in the State by outsider. It is like an Inner Line Permit.

41. Singh, N. Lokendra *op cit,* pp.200 ff.
42. Maipaksana, Rajkumar *op cit.,* p.15.
43. Singh, N. Joykumar *Social Movement in Manipur, op cit,* pp-105ff.
44. Shyamkanhai, Ksh. *Manipurgee Lungaklon Amasung Leingak Pathapki Itihas (1762 – 1949),* (A book in Manipuri), Author, Imphal, 1974, pp-79f.
45. Lokendra, i p. 226.
46. Singh, N. Joykumar *Social Movements in Manipur, op. cit.,* p.114.
47. *Ibid.,* cited by N. Joykumar from the Resolution of the meeting of the MLA belonging to the ruling Praja Shanti Sabha on 25.8.1949.
48. Shyamkanhai, Ksh. *op. cit.,* p.105.
49. Singh, N. Joykumar *Colonialism to Democracy*, *op. cit.,* p.193.
50. *Ibid.,* p. 202.
51. www.eci.gov.in, accessed on 24/5/07.
52. Shyamkanhai, Ksh. *Manipurgee Leingaklon Amasung Leingak Pathapki Itihas (1950-1972),* (A book in Manipuri) 1974, Author, Imphal, p-23.
53. N Joykumar Singh, Colonialism to Democracy, op cit, pp-200f
54. *Ibid.,* p. 213.
55. www.eci.gov.in, Accessed on 14/06/07.
56. Singh, P. Bhorot *Elections in Manipur*, Imphal, 1997, p. 9.
57. Singh, N. Joykumar *Colonialism and Democracy, op. cit.,* pp-214f.
58. *Ibid.,* pp. 217f.
59. *Ibid.,* p. 217.
60. www.eci.gov.in, Accessed on 14/6/07.
61 Singh, N. Joykumar *Colonialism to Democracy, op cit,* pp-219f.
62. www.eci.gov.in, Accessed on 14/6/07.
63. Singh, V.B. and Shankar Bose, State Election in India 1952-85 , *Data Handbook on Vidhan Sabha Elections, 1952-85*, Volume 3, The East and the North-East, 1987, pp-550f.
64. Singh, Th Gokul *op cit,* p.13.
65. *Ibid.*
66. *Ibid.,* pp-15f.

67. *Ibid.,* pp-18ff.
68. Singh, N. Joykumar Colonialism to Democracy, *op cit,* pp,221f
69. *Ibid.,* p-225.
70. Singh, Th Gokul *op. cit.,* pp-29ff.
71. *Ibid.,* p. 37.
72. *Ibid.,* pp.40ff.
73. Devi, K.Shusila *Origin and Growth of Legislature in Manipur upto 1972,* Unpublished Thesis pp. 256ff.
74. Singh, V.B. and Shankar Bose, *op. cit.,* pp-560ff
75. Th Gokul Singh, op cit, pp-48f
76. *Ibid.,* p. 52.
77. *Ibid.,* p. 55.
78. *Ibid.,* p. 56.
79. *Ibid.,* p. 58.
80. *Ibid.,* p. 62.
81. *Ibid.,* p. 64.
82. *Ibid.,* pp. 65f.
83. Devi, Ksh. Bimola, Gangte, T.S. and V. Venkata Rao, A Century of Government and Politics in North East India, New Delhi, S. Chand & Company Ltd., 1991, p.132.
84. Singh, Th. Gokul *op. cit.,* p.70.
85. Devi, Ksh. Bimola *op. cit.,* pp.133ff.
86. *Ibid.,* p.135.
87. *Ibid.,* pp.135f.
88. *Ibid.,* pp.137f.
89. John Parrat, Wounded Land: Politics and Identity in Modern Manipur, Delhi, Mittal Publication, 2005, p.195.
90. *Ibid.*

3

Relation among the Parties in the Coalition Ministries

Introduction

A coalition ministry is a ministry formed by an alliance or a union or a group of political parties. It implies sharing of political power at the governmental level, co-operation and co-ordination at the electoral and legislative level. In short, coalition ministry means two or more political parties working united and sharing the responsibility of a government. Coalition ministry occurs when political parties fail to secure majority in the legislature on their own capacity. This type of ministry is normally found in political systems where there is multi-party system like in India. In fact, coalition ministry has been formed both at the centre and the states in India on many occasions.

Coming to that of Manipur, the post-Independence history of government in Manipur has been, by and large, a history of coalition ministries. In fact, the first ever popular ministry established in Manipur in 1948 was a coalition ministry. It consisted of Praja Shanti, Krishak Sabha and Hill members. This was before the merger with India. The post-merger era in Manipur also saw a number of coalition ministries following one after another. In fact, there have been coalition ministry in 1967 before statehood. The tradition continued after statehood also. It is evident from the fact that there have been 15 coalition ministries[1] during the period from 1972 to 2002.

Coalition Ministry

The term "coalition" is derived from the Latin word '*coalito*' which is verbal substantive of coalescere. *Co* means together and *alescere* means to go or to go together.[2] According to the dictionary meaning, coalition means an act of coalescing, or uniting into one body, a union of persons, states or parts into one whole. The *Oxford Concise Dictionary of Politics* defines coalition as "any combination of separate players (such as political parties) to win a voting game. The commonest form of coalition arises where legislation required a majority to pass, but no one party controls as many as half of the seats in the Assembly."[3]

Politically, the concept emerged out of a multi-party government where a number of minority parties join hands with a view to run a government, which is otherwise not possible in a democracy. A coalition government is formed when many splinter groups agree to join hands on a common platform by sinking their broad differences and cobble a majority in the house. A coalition is also an alliance of parties formed for the purpose of contesting elections jointly and or forming a government and managing the governance by a process of sharing power. So, coalition implies co-operation between or among political parties and this co-operation may take place at one or more of the following different levels - electoral, parliamentary and governmental.[4] It is an astonishing chorus of discords. Though outwardly a coalition appears to be one solid mass inwardly it is riddled by party foibles and frantic party fervours and bickering and it is for this reason that coalitions prove to be transient.

An electoral coalition is formed by two or more parties to fight the election jointly against a common opponent. This may range from electoral alliance between parties at the national level to a mere understanding at the constituency level. Such alliances need not necessarily last beyond the elections after which the parties may consider themselves free to make new alliances to form the government. The existence and nature of such coalitions will depend upon the character of the electoral system.

Parliamentary coalitions on the other hand occur, according to Bogdanor, when no single-party gains a majority and the party asked to form the government prefers to rule as a minority government on an understanding with another for external support. The governmental coalition is a "power sharing". It occurs when parties unable to win a majority of its own combine to form a government. The parties comprising such coalitions might not have had a pre-poll alliance and they may compete elections with their own coalition partners later. This sort of power sharing is generally familiar to continental Europe, but comparatively unknown to British politics. In fact, power sharing is the end of all coalitions and therefore, it is the ultimate stage to be achieved in the election process. Any arrangement that stops short of this ultimate stage results in the lack of commitment to the coalition by the partners. Finally, there are what may be called 'integral' coalitions that link parties through the election process, parliamentary performance and governance. Continuous collaboration and cohesion of allies through the above stages of the potential process make them constitute stable coalitions while preserving separate identity of the parties.[5]

Coalition government is one of the features of the Parliamentary or Cabinet form of government where a government can remain in office with the support of other party or parties. Such coalition governments become necessary normally under the following two circumstances:

a) When no single party command even a working majority in the legislature;
b) In a situation of national emergency even if a party commands a majority in the Parliament, the government needs the support of all the parties.

The latter type of coalition governments were formed in Britain during the First and World Wars II. In India, we had this type of coalition government at the time of the transfer of power when the country was going through the trauma of partition and independence. Even though the Congress had a solid majority in the legislature, it had included in the Cabinet not only members of other parties like Dr. Ambedkar and Dr. Shyam Prasad Mukherjee but even persons not belonging to any political party like Mr. Ch Bhabha, Dr John Mathai and (after Dr Mathai resigned), Mr. C. D. Deshmukh.[6]

In normal times, coalitions of the first type are formed rather unwillingly and helplessly than out of volition because no single party is able to command even a working majority in the legislature. There are three types of contingencies necessitating the formation of such coalitions:

a) When there is a big party but falls short of absolute majority by a small margin and have to seek the help of some smaller parties or groups. Such coalitions are usually stable since the small groups supporting the coalition are not strong enough to dictate to the large party. For instance, the present UPA government at the centre. Another example is West Bengal. West Bengal has been continuing this type of coalition under the CPM for more than 30 years.

b) When there are two large parties of more or less equal strength but do not have an absolute majority. In such cases small groups can dictate terms to the main party as it happens in Israel where the two major party viz. the Linkud and the Socialists have almost equal strength but short of an absolute majority.

c) Where there is no single party with sufficient members to make a bid to form a government, parties form groups with like minded parties and stake their claim to form the government. Such coalitions consist of a large number of small parties or groups.[7] The NDA from 1999-2004 and UPA government from 2004 to 2009 at the centre is of this type.

As already stated, a coalition government comes into existence only when political parties fail to produce a majority in the legislature. It is a kind of solution to the problem faced by political party or parties to form a cabinet or ministry, when no party secures a majority in the legislature at the end of a general election. If politics is the art of the possible, then coalition politics is its highest expression. The art of forming a coalition involves passing through various bargaining, adjudging and sacrificing the ideologies and party or parties at times destroy the coalition formula or understanding at some opportune moment.[8] In a single-party system such a situation cannot arise. In two-party system in a strict sense also the contingency of a coalition does not arise. It is only when there are more than two political parties that a situation calling for a combination of two or more parties coming together to form a coalition may arise. Even in systems having a multiplicity of parties a coalition may not be necessary if there is a single dominant party which generally secures a clear majority. The Indian political experience during the first two decades following independence is an outstanding example of coalitions being not necessary in spite of multiplicity of parties (1947-67).[9]

Coalitions have become an inevitable and indispensable part of Indian polity in the present scenario both at the Centre and the States. India has been experimenting with various coalition ministries at the national level since the last two decades. With the decline of the one-party dominance system by the Congress Party and also with the emergence of various new political parties at various levels, the concept of the coalition government has gradually assumed a lot of significance in Indian political system. Coalitions have been constructed for the purpose of forming government and also to oppose and depose the existing governments. Coalitions have been formed before the elections and also after the elections depending on the demands of the circumstances.[10]

Coalition Governments in Manipur

The contemporary political history of Manipur is a history of coalition politics. Though it is basically a post-merger phenomenon, some sort of coalitional alliances were witnessed during the colonial period also. "The State Darbar was a very important institution where the seed of a coalition administration was carried on between the British component and the Manipur representation."[11] However, it was not a coalition form of government in the modern sense of the term. It was just a sort of an alliance made by the British with their subjects in order to administer the state. Coalitional politics in its real sense started in the post-colonial period. The government which formed under the Manipur Constitution Act, 1947 in 1948 was the first coalition ministry in Manipur. The government was formed by the Praja Shanti Sabha, the Socialist Party, the Communist Party and the hill members. After the merger with the Indian Dominion, Manipur did not have a Legislative Assembly till 1963. In 1963, the Manipur Territorial Council was upgraded to a Territorial Assembly. After that a government was installed in 1963 with Mairembam Koireng Singh of the Congress as the Chief Minister. "The principle of a coalition ministry did not figure out prominently at that time as the Congress had already secured half of the total seats. But, since the help of the Independents was very much there, it may still be called a Congress led coalition government."[12] Since then most of the governments which came into existence in Manipur have been coalitional in nature.

The coalition politics continued even after Manipur become a full-fledged state in 1972 as no political party secured majority in the Legislative Assembly. Though, the Congress Party was part of the government most of the time, it failed to secure majority in the legislature. The Congress party formed the government with the independent members or with small party or parties. People always gave a fractured mandate in the elections. This is due to the nature of the multi-party system prevailing in the state and no political party was able to dominate the political scene of the state. Manipur is a multi-ethnic and multi religious state. As a result, ethnic based political parties have also emerged in the state. Above all, many political parties emerged in the state by defecting from existing parties without having proper political agenda or ideology. These political parties did not last long. They either merged with one party or another or died a natural death. Because of the frequent mergers, splits and defections, ministries failed to last its normal tenure. Every now and then, changes of government took place in the state. From 1972 to 1985, there were nine ministries in Manipur. This clearly shows the kind of political instability which the state had experienced during the time. In order to control and check political defections in India, the Union Government amended the Indian Constitution in 1985 (the 52nd Amendment Act, 1985) and inserted the Tenth Schedule of the Indian Constitution. This is popularly known as Anti-Defection Law. Yet, coalition ministries continued to be the norm even after 1985. In fact, there were nine coalition ministries during the period from 1985 to 2002. Even the present Secular Progressive Front (SPF) ministry is a coalition ministry led by the Congress (I). Given this reality, the present chapter is an attempt to examine the relations between or among the various political parties among the coalition partners during the period from 1985 to 2002.

Coalition Ministries from 1985-90

The Congress Led Coalition Ministry (1985-88)

In the last part of 1984, the whole country was swept by a sympathy wave for the Congress (I) after PM Mrs Indira Gandhi was assassinated on 31st October 1984. Manipur was no exception. The 4th State Legislative Assembly Election was held on 24th and 25th December, 1984. In the election, 364 candidates were in the fray. Seven National Parties - the Congress (I), Janata Party (JNP), BJP, Lok Dal (LKD), Congress (S), CPI, CPI (M), and two state parties—the MPP and KNA, contested the election. The Congress (I) was the only party which contested in all the 60 seats. In the election, no party secured majority but Congress (I) won half of the seats. The election performances of the political parties immediately after the election results were out are given below:[13]

Falling one short of the require majority, the Congress invited other parties and specially the Independent MLAs to join and support the party in order to form a stable government in the state.

Performance of Political Parties

Party	*Seats*			*Votes Polled*		*Vote % in*
	Contested	*Won*	*FD*	*Votes*	*%*	*Seats Contested*
National Parties						
1. BJP	12	0	11	6163	0.71%	3.89%
2. CPI	17	1	10	35852	4.15%	15.63%
3. CPM	2	0	2	790	0.09%	3.35%
4. ICS	19	0	14	28156	3.26%	10.32%
5. INC	60	30	11	257809	29.82%	29.82%
6. JNP	21	4	9	52530	6.08%	18.06%
7. LKD	2	0	1	3653	0.42%	12.32%
	133	35	58	384953	44.53%	
State Parties						
8. KNA	4	1	0	13367	1.55%	19.93%
9. MPP	34	3	13	93421	10.81%	19.19%
	38	4	13	106788	12.35%	
Independents						
10 . IND	193	21	131	372766	43.12%	47.23%
Grand Total:	364	60	202	864507		

Eventually, it succeeded in admitting four independent MLAs to their side and a government led by Shri Rishang Keishing, the Ex-CM was sworn in on 4th January, 1985. The ministry was as good as a one party ministry. However, B. Pakem observed that as

> "the Independents had come to the rescue of the Congress I in the formation and continuation of the stability of the Government, it can safely be concluded that it is not entirely a single party government. The element of coalition politics persisted which had later on caused political instability."[14]

Because of the predominant position of the Congress (I), the people of Manipur expected that political stability will be there in the State. The previous Congress Ministry headed by Rishang Keishing also lasted about 4 years (19th June, 1981 - 4th January, 1985). So, the people who had experienced political instability a number of times before and after the attainment of statehood looked toward the Congress (I) to maintain political stability in the state. They look forward to the Congress (I) with new aspiration and hope for a progressive and stable government in Manipur. The CM himself declared that a new era of stability was being ushered with the coming of the ministry and he appealed to all to unite and strengthen the organization eschewing petty difference.[15] That the people will be disappointed within no time is altogether a different thing.

The Congress ministry which came into existence with lots of expectation and aspiration from the public could not sail smoothly for long. Yet the problem was not between the Congress and the Independents but within the Congress. Some Congress MLAs wanted to change their leaders. The pro-change group was led by the then Union Minister of State for Chemical and Petro-Chemical, Shri R. K. Jaichandra Singh, the Congress MP from Manipur. The crisis became more visible when the Union Minister of State visited Imphal and asked the pressmen that whether they have seen mini-stadia and swimming pools coming up in Imphal and other districts of the state. He also claimed that the centre has sanctioned Rs 5.51 lakhs for sports equipments and Rs 8.75 lakhs for construction of 100 rural sport centres both in the valley and the hill. The Chief Minister, however, informed the press that only Rs 87,000 have been sanctioned for rural sports. Referring to the construction of swimming pools at Thoubal, Imphal, Bishnupur and Churachandpur, the CM disclosed that the centre sanctioned Rs 50,000 only for each swimming pool and not Rs 1.5 lakhs as stated by Shri Jaichandra Singh.[16] The differences between the Union Minister of State and the CM regarding the development activities in the state created utter confusion not only among the people but also worsened the conflict between the two factions within the Congress.

Soon both sides opened up their concentration camps. This was followed by a series of resignations from the ministry. First, the Minister of State for power Shri L. Amujao Singh and the minister of state for Irrigation and Flood Control (IFC) Shri M. Babu Singh resigned from the Council of Minister. Then, the Deputy Chairman of State Planning Board, Shri S. L Paokhosei, Parliamentary Secretaries Shri Kh. Leirijao Singh and Shri Y. Kerani Singh and the Chairman of Khadi Board Shri O. Ibobi Singh also resigned. While submitting their resignation to the Governor, they mentioned that they have lost their faith in the leadership of Shri Keishing. They also demanded to elect a new leader.[17]

In the meantime, the minister of state for IFC Shri M. Babu Singh and Shri Jangamlung who withdrew their support from the leadership of Shri Rishang Keishing went back to the CM's camp. So, the pro-change group was left with only 20 members out of the total strength of 39. At this juncture, the then Union Home Minister Shri Buta Singh arrived in Imphal to look into the crisis. During his stay in Imphal, Shri Buta Singh met the State Congress leaders including the Speaker, W. Angou Singh.[18] Then, the struggle for power shifted to Delhi. Many Congress leaders of Manipur rushed to Delhi to meet the AICC leaders and bring a solution to the leadership crisis. A team of pro-change group led by the Speaker Shri W. Angou Singh left Imphal for New Delhi to press their demand to change the leader of the Congress Legislature Party (CLP). The other members of the team were Shri S. L. Paokhosei and O. Ibobi Singh. During the time, both the groups tried to win as many MLAs as possible to their side. The CM camp put up their best efforts to bring back some Congress MLAs at least if not all with promises of ministerial posts and large amounts of money.[19] On the other hand, the pro-change group tried their best to convince the Central leaders to change the CLP leader. They met the AICC members in

Delhi. At this moment, PM Rajiv Gandhi visited Dimapur and the pro-change group rushed to Dimapur and urged the PM to remove the CM Rishang Keishing.[20]

In the meantime, Union Minister of State for Chemicals and Petro-Chemicals, Shri R. K. Jaichandra Singh tendered his resignation to the PM. The move of the Union Minister Shri Jaichandra Singh convinced the people that change of ministry in Manipur was certain and that it might be only a matter of time. Jaichandra's supporters continued to camp in Delhi and pressurised the Congress High Command to remove Shri Rishang Keishing.[21] At last, the struggle for power was won by the pro-change group. The CM Shri Rishang Keishing tendered his resignation on 4th March 1988. This was followed by the election of Shri R. K. Jaichandra Singh as the leader of the Congress (I) Legislature Party. He was sworn in as the 11th CM of Manipur on 4th March 1988. With the change of leadership in the Congress party and also the installation of new government, the crisis within the ruling party was over. This is a Congress Government and not a coalition ministry. The new government continued till the next election in 1990.

It is evident from the above paragraphs that though there was a coalition ministry in Manipur comprising the Congress and some Independents, the ministry functioned more like a Congress ministry. This was mainly due to the fact that the Congress was only one short of the required majority and the Independents were not in a position to endanger the stability of the government. The stability or the otherwise of the ministry depended not so much on the relationship between the coalition partners but in the unity or otherwise of the Congress MLAs, and when the ministry failed it failed not because of fallout between the coalition partners but factions within the Congress.

Coalition Ministries from 1990-95

The MPP-led ULF Ministry (1990-92)

The years following the Fifth General Assembly Elections witnessed serious political instability inside the state. The elections were held on 12th February, 1990.[22] In the election, five national parties – the BJP, CPI, Indian Congress (S), INC and Janata Dal (JD), two state parties – the KNA and MPP, and two registered (Unrecognised) parties – the Manipur Hill Peoples Council (MHPC) and National People's Party (NPP) contested the elections.[23] The main issues of the election were the autonomy for the hills, the extension of Manipur Land Reforms Act, 1989 to the hills, inclusion of Manipuri language in the 8th Schedule of the Indian Constitution, insurgency, removal of Armed Forces Special Power Act, 1958, etc.[24] People went to the poll to elect new members for 58 seats because elections on two constituencies (9-Thangmeiband Assembly Constituency and 44-Ukhrul Assembly Constituency) were countermanded due to death of one contesting candidates each there. The countermanded elections were held on May, 1990. In the February 1990 elections, no party secured majority, but the ruling Congress (I) once again came out as the single largest party with 26 (two in the by-election) seats. A most significant thing about the election was that no independent was able to win. Otherwise, in the previous election held in December 1984, the independents won 21 out of the 60 seats. The detailed positions of the parties in the State Assembly after the elections were as follows: [25]

Performance of Political Parties

Party	*Seats*			*Votes Polled*		*Vote % in*
	Contested	*Won*	*FD*	*Votes*	*%*	*Seats Contested*
NATIONAL PARTIES						
1. BJP	11	0	8	18549	1.87%	10.11%
2. CPI	13	3	5	41012	4.14%	17.94%
3. ICS (SCS)	31	4	14	122829	12.41%	20.75%
4. INC	54	24	5	333765	33.71%	33.71%
5. JD	46	11	16	196207	19.82%	23.17%
	155	42	48	712362	71.96%	

(Contd.)

Performance of Political Parties *(Contd.)*

Party	*Seats*			*Votes Polled*		*Vote % in*
	Contested	*Won*	*FD*	*Votes*	*%*	*Seats Contested*
STATE PARTIES						
6. KNA	8	2	5	25867	2.61%	15.42%
7. MPP	41	9	7	192075	19.40%	25.46%
	49	11	12	217942	22.01%	
REGISTERED (Unrecognised) PARTIES						
8. MHPC	10	0	10	8820	0.89%	4.46%
9. NPP	5	1	3	7762	0.78%	9.38%
	15	1	13	16582	1.67%	
INDEPENDENTS						
10. IND	35	0	30	43101	4.35%	12.40%
Grand Total:	254	54	103	989987		

Immediately, after the election results were declared, party leaders put up their best efforts to win as many MLAs as they can. The Congress (I) being the single largest party tried very hard to get the support of other parties. At the same time, other parties led by MPP and JD also put up their best endeavours to win all the parties except the Congress (I) in order to form a government. The later somehow managed to win the CPI, Congress (S), CPM and KNA and formed a United Legislature Front (ULF). Even then, the Congress (I) did not give up their hope to form a new ministry. They paraded all their 24 MLAs with the lone NNP MLA to the Governor and staked its claim to form the government. Thus both the parties staked their claim to form the government. This was before the elections in the two Assembly Constituencies where elections were postponed. The Governor invited the ULF to form the government on 20th February, 1990. The ULF took three days to select their leader. Finally, it selected R. K. Ranbir

Singh of the MPP as the leader of the ULF and a coalition ministry was sworn in on 23rd February 1990 with R. K. Ranbir Singh as the Chief Minister of Manipur.

The partners of the ULF ministry worked with a 'Common Programme' which included the demand for the inclusion of the Manipuri Language in the Eight Schedule of the Indian Constitution. Moreover, the CM was an experienced veteran of the state politics. With a view to consolidate his position he went for a jumbo size ministry. In fact, his ministry had 27 ministers and the remaining 7 MLAs were also given the charge of Khadi Board, State Planning Board, etc. so that all the MLAs were satisfied and stability of the government secured. However, the ULF coalition could not provide a stable government due to internal bickering.[26]

The problem was actually one of intra-party conflict within the MPP leading the ministry. Earlier, the party had difficulties while selecting a consensus leader on the eve of the formation of the ULF ministry. The problem resurfaced within one year of the ministry. There were serious differences between the President of the MPP, Shri Houbam Bhuban Singh and R. K. Ranbir Singh, the CM who also belonged to the party. There was no issue to fight between the two, but their desire to control the party and the government.[27] The differences became so irreconcilable that Shri Houbam Bhuban Singh suspended the CM Shri R. K. Ranbir Singh from the party on 15th February 1991. In retaliation, a requisition committee meeting attended by MLAs and ministers of the party removed Shri H. Bhubon from the Presidentship of the party and suspended him along with Shri Kh. Chaoba Singh, an ex-minister, for six years from the party[28] and managed to survive.

Still, the ULP fell on 7th January 1992 before it could complete two years and the state was kept under the President's Rule with the assembly being kept in animated suspension. The main reason behind it was once again the internal bickering of the MPP.[29] The leadership crisis of the MPP divided the party into two groups and disturbed the stability of the ministry.

The fall of the ULP ministry marked the second consecutive instance when a coalition ministry failed not because of inter-party conflict among the coalition partners but because of the intra-party conflict within the leading party of the coalition. This also proves that inter party relations among the coalition are of less significance than that of intra party conflicts affecting the stability of the coalition ministries.

The Congress-MPP ministry (1992-93)

During the President Rule the political leaders of Manipur were very busy in bargaining among themselves to gain political power and form a new government. The battle for political power was won by the Congress (I) with the help of the MPP and a Congress (I) - MPP coalition ministry headed by R. K. Dorendra Singh of the Congress was sworn in on 8th April 1992. In politics, there are no permanent friends and enemies; the only permanent thing in it is the interest for power. This is quite true and prominent in Manipur politics. When the ULF headed by MPP was in power, Congress (I) was in the opposition. It was very critical of the ULF ministry and always trying to pull down the coalition ministry. Yet the two parties came together and formed a Congress led coalition government in Manipur.

The new Congress-MPP coalition ministry also faced the same fate with that of the previous government. It fell within a couple of years. Right from the beginning, the coalition Ministry had been functioning like a loose alliance where the parties do not have anything in common. There were no co-operation and co-ordination among the partners. A certain amount of cohesion and a partnership was expected between the partners of the ministry inside and outside the house. But both the parties were publicly criticizing each other which meant that the coalition partners were not serious about their coalition, the stability of the government, law and order and development of the state. The main problem between the parties was the Speaker, H. Borobabu Singh who belonged to the MPP. The Congress wanted to change the Speaker but the leaders of the MPP were totally against the idea. The Congress decided to move a no-confidence motion against the Speaker. The Congress leader M. Koireng Singh, a former CM, moved a no-confidence motion against the Speaker. However the motion was not admitted on technical grounds. This further worsened the crisis within the Coalition Ministry.[30] Shri Koireng Singh even asked the MPP to withdraw support.[31] Moreover, the Congress Legislature Party and the Congress party leaders had different opinions on the issue of going together with the MPP. While the party leaders insisted that the MPP should be dropped immediately from the coalition, many of the CLP leaders have a different story to tell. During the time, the Naga-Kuki clash took place in the hills of Manipur. Soon, the situation became very serious and alarming. This was followed by the imposition of President's Rule inside the state from 31st December, 1993 and the Governor took over the administration of the state.

The Congress led Coalition ministry (1994-95)

The President Rule continued till 12th December, 1994 which meant it continued for 346 days. On 13th December 1994, a new Congress (I) led coalition government was installed headed by Rishang Keishing. The government was supported by Congress (I) - 25, Congress (S) - 4, Janata Dal - 7, and Kuki National Assembly - 1.[32] The term of the Assembly was up to the end of February 1995. The restoration of a popular coalition ministry headed by Congress meant that the Central government headed by Congress (I) wanted to hold election in Manipur under a Congress ministry. Usually, the electorate of Manipur look towards Delhi at the time of assembly election. As a result, the ruling party in Delhi won more number of seats in most of the assembly elections of the State.

The new government also faced lots of problem coming from both within and outside the coalition. Just before, the installation of the popular ministry, there was leadership crisis within the Congress (I). Shri Radhabinod Koijam, R.

K. Dorendra Singh, M. Koireng Singh and Rishang Keishing wanted to become the leader of Congress Legislature Party (CLP) and formed a government. All of them tried to persuade the AICC leaders. In the struggle for power, Rishang Keishing won the battle. In the election held for the CLP leader, Rishang got the support of 20 MLAs out of 25 members. The election procedure was witnessed by the AICC observer Santosh Mohon Dev and P. M. Sayeed. As a result, Shri Rishang Keishing headed the Congress led coalition government. On the other hand, the Ex-CM, Shri R. K. Dorendra Singh tendered resignation from the membership of the State Legislative Assembly.[33]

Meanwhile, all the coalition partners wanted to get ministerial berths in the ministry. For instance, four MLAs viz. B. D Behring, Daisin Panmei and H. Bidur all from JD and one Congress (S), S. Brajagopal Sharma sent an ultimatum to the CM saying that they supported the government on the condition that they would be accommodated in the ministry before the trial of strength on 23rd December 1994. They also demanded concrete assurance from the Congress (I) party for giving party ticket in the coming election.[34] But the main problem was the controversial Speaker H. Borobabu Singh. The Speaker expelled 23 members by using the power given to the Speaker by the Anti-Defection Law in order to defeat the coalition ministry. But, the High Court passed an order staying the expulsion of the 23 members. Ultimately, the Speaker was removed and replaced by W. Angou Singh. So, the Keishing ministry survived and the Congress faced the Assembly Election in February 1995 as one of the parties in power on the eve of the elections.[35]

Coalition ministries from 1995- 2000

The Congress led JLP ministry (1995-97)

The 6th Manipur Legislative Assembly Elections were held in February 16th and 19th 1995. In the election, 14 political parties - seven national parties [BJP, CPI, CPM, INC, Janata Dal (JD), Janata Party (JP) and Samata Party (SAP)], three state parties [Indian Congress Socialist (ICS),

Kuki National Assembly (KNA) and MPP] and four registered (unrecognised) parties [Federal Party of Manipur (FPM), Manipur Hill People's Council (MHPC), National People's Party (NPP) and Samajwadi Janata Party (Rashtriya) (SJP (R)] were in the fray. Altogether there were 347 candidates including 67 independent candidates contesting the elections. The detailed of the election results of the Sixth State Legislative Assembly of Manipur were as given below:[36]

Performance of Political Parties

Party	*Seats*			*Votes Polled*		*Vote % in*
	Contested	*Won*	*FD*	*Votes*	*%*	*Seats Contested*
NATIONAL PARTIES						
1. BJP	20	1	14	38405	3.35%	10.82%
2. CPI	23	2	13	64026	5.59%	15.49%
3. CPM	2	0	2	2327	0.20%	6.44%
4. INC	60	22	7	328362	28.65%	28.65%
5. JD	40	7	21	136594	11.92%	18.19%
6. JP	4	0	4	1611	0.14%	1.73%
7. SAP	23	2	14	70887	6.19%	15.57%
	172	34	75	642212	56.04%	
STATE PARTIES						
8. ICS	13	1	10	44797	3.91%	16.06%
9. KNA	6	0	6	2832	0.25%	2.30%
10. MPP	55	18	13	271247	23.67%	26.59%
	74	19	29	318876	27.83%	
REGISTERED (Unrecognised) PARTIES						
11. FPM	22	2	15	56300	4.91%	13.62%
12. MHPC	1	0	1	2440	0.21%	10.61%
13. NPP	5	2	2	30417	2.65%	26.26%
14. SJP(R)	6	0	5	7194	0.63%	6.09%
	34	4	23	96351	8.41%	
INDEPENDENTS						
15. IND	67	3	54	88526	7.73%	12.45%
Grand Total:	347	60	181	1145965		

Like in the past, the verdict of the election did not favour any political party. No party secured majority in the house and a coalition form of government became the only solution again. The ruling Congress (I) emerged as the single largest party with 22 seats followed by MPP with 18 seats. As a result, a political battle for power between the Congress on the one side and MPP on the other started all over again. The group headed by MPP formed 'United Legislature Front (ULF)' comprising of six parties –MPP - 18, JD - 7, CPI - 2, SAP - 2, NPP - 2 and Congress (S) - 1 - and staked its claimed to form the government. The Congress (I) also did the same. But, the ruling Congress (I) ultimately won the political battle and formed a coalition government headed by Rishang Keishing on 24th February 1995. They formed a Joint Legislature Party (JLP) comprising of Congress (I), Progressive JD, NPP, SAP, JD (Sehpu Group) and Congress (S). The position of the ruling and opposition parties at the time of the formation of ministry are given below:-

Ruling (JLP)		*Opposition (ULP)*	
Congress (I)	22	MPP	18
Progressive JD	4	CPI	2
NPP	2	JD	2
SAP	2	BJP	1
JD (Sehpu Group)	1		
Congress (S)	1		
Independents	3		
FPM	2		
Total	37	Total =	23

The new coalition ministry was not free from problem among the coalition partners and also within the Congress party. Within a very short time a serious crisis developed among the coalition partners. Ten MLAs walked out of the JLP and formed a United Democratic Front (UDF). The

Front was constituted by Progressive Janata Dal (PJD), NPP, SAP, FPM, JD (Sehpu Group), Congress (S) and one Independent MLA. Subsequently, a no-confidence motion was brought against the Keishing coalition ministry on July 31st 1995. However, the speaker, W. Nipamacha Singh disqualified five opposition members and the lone BJP MLA abstained from voting and saved the coalition ministry. This clearly proves the lack of unity and solidarity within the JLP ministry led by Keishing. Its coalition partners failed to co-exist together for long.

The real challenge for the coalition ministry, however, was when 15 CLP members including nine ministers adopted a resolution demanding change in CLP leadership. The resolution was sent to the party high command of the Congress in Delhi. They also threatened that more MLAs would join the anti-Rishang Camp.[37] So, a problem cropped up within the Congress party. The pro-change group was led by the Speaker W. Nipamacha Singh. Both opened up their 'concentration camp' to keep their MLAs in it. They tried their best to get maximum support from other MLAs. In the meantime, AICC (I) observer Pawan Singh Ghatowar reached Imphal on 25th November 1997 to look into the matter and mediate the two groups so that an amicable solution can be brought in. But he failed in his mission. Then, the CLP battle shifted to Delhi. The leaders of both the groups went to Delhi to persuade and convince the AICC (I) leaders about their respective contentions.[38]

The crisis of the CLP leadership took a new turn when the CM dropped five of the rebel MLAs from the Council of Ministers after returning from Delhi. He also asked the MPCC (I) President Phungzathang Tonsing to take necessary action for the expulsion of Nipamacha from the party membership. This was followed by 16 dissident ministers and the Chairman of the IDA, Md. Hessamuddin and the Vice Chairman of the State Planning Board, Sochinkhup submitted their resignation letter to the CM. This clearly showed that the majority of the CLP had shifted their allegiance to W. Nipamacha Singh, the leader of the dissident faction. Even then, the Congress high command failed to dislodge Keishing who kept inventing mechanisms for remaining in power.[39] Ultimately, the rebel group led by the Nipamacha Singh left the Congress (I) and formed a new party entitled as "Manipur State Congress Party (MPSC)" on 7th December 1997.[40]

Subsequently, the House was summoned on 15th December 1997 for a vote of no-confidence. The motion against the Rishang Keishing ministry was won by a large margin of 22 votes. There were only 16 votes against the motion while the entire opposition having 38 members voted for it. The strength of the house at that time was 55 members as four have been disqualified and one was killed by extremists in November 1997. The break up of the party positions at this point was as given below:[41]

Party Position

Total Strength 60

Effective Strength 55

Nipamacha's Camp		*Rishang's Camp (Congress I)*		*Opposition*	
MSCP (including Dy Speaker)	24	Congress (I)	14	MPP	11
Independent	01	Independent	02	FPM	02
				CPI	01
Total	25	Total	16	Total	14

The entire episode as discussed above was yet another example of the coalition partners being driven by their own pursuit for power and the resultant failure to work as a team for long.

The MSCP-led UF ministry (1997-2000)

After Rishang Keishing was voted out, a new four party coalition government under the name 'United Front' was sworn in on 16th December 1997. The government was headed by Shri Wahengbam Nipamacha Singh. The parties in the Front were MSCP, FPM, MPP and CPI. The Nipamacha ministry created sort of a history for heading the biggest ever council of ministry in the state till then with 31 ministers. Out of these 27 were in the cabinet rank.[42]

This United Front ministry continued till the next election held in February 2000. This meant that the coalition partners were successful in working together for a considerable period of time. Yet, this had more to do with the fact that it was a jumbo size ministry in which almost everyone's desire to hold a position of power was assured, and not so much because they were bound together by a common ideology or policy and program and were successful in realising them.

The tenure of UF ministry was known for scandal and financial crisis. The state was rocked with scandals like that of a lottery scam which involved 1.77 crore[43] and fake appointments in Education Department.[44] The Government faced a deep financial crisis. The government also failed to pay even the salaries of its employee. The financial position of the state was very bad. Commenting on the financial situation, the 'Jokes Apart', a column in the Imphal Free Press (local English daily), remarked: "The government is bankrupt so it has decided to pay salaries in kind!!"[45] The Banks in Imphal refused to honour the government bills.[46] The government employees also went on strike for many months demanding implementation of the 5th Pay Commission recommendations. As a result, government offices were paralysed.[47] The situation remained unchanged when the state went to poll for the next assembly elections in February 2000.

Coalition Ministries from 2000-02

The MSCP-led UF Ministry 2000-01

The 7th State Assembly Elections were held in two phases, on 12th and 22nd February 2000. There were 15 different political parties - seven national parties [BJP, CPI, CPM, INC, Janata Dal Secular {JD (S)}, Janata Dal United {JD (U)}, National Congress Party (NCP)], six state parties [FPM, MPP, MSCP, Rashtriya Janata Dal (RJD), Revolutionary Socialist Party (RSP) and SAP)] and two registered (unrecognised) parties (KNA and NPP) - contesting the 60 seats. Altogether, these parties accounted for 353 candidates. In addition to it, there were 48 Independent candidates also. In all 401 candidates were in the fray.

Coming to that of the four coalition partners in the previous ministry, they failed to continue their partnership in the elections. For instance, three fronts were formed prior to the elections. The MPP and CPI joined hands with the Congress (I) and JD (S) to form the Secular Democratic Front (SDF) led by Congress (I). The MSCP decided to continue with the previous United Front of Manipur (UF) along with the FPM. The third front was the Manipur Democratic Alliance (MDA) led by the BJP which also had the SAP, JD (U) and KNA.[48] It also meant that some of the ruling UF partners have left and entered into alliances with the opposition parties.

The details of the party positions immediately after the elections results were as follows:[49]

Performance of Political Parties

Party		*Seats*			*Votes Polled*		*Vote % in*
		Contested	*Won*	*FD*	*Votes*	*%*	*Seats Contested*
NATIONAL PARTIES							
1.	BJP	39	6	22	142174	11.28%	18.32%
2.	CPI	15	0	7	45309	3.60%	14.33%
3.	CPM	4	0	4	3783	0.30%	5.44%
4.	INC	47	11	16	230748	18.31%	22.94%
5.	JD (S)	8	1	6	19945	1.58%	12.88%
6.	JD (U)	18	1	16	22576	1.79%	5.98%
7.	NCP	41	5	34	99128	7.87%	11.51%
		172	24	105	563663	44.73%	
STATE PARTIES							
8.	FPM	39	6	23	118916	9.44%	13.76%
9.	MPP	29	4	13	99487	7.90%	16.45%

(Contd.)

Party	*Seats*			*Votes Polled*		*Vote % in*
	Contested	*Won*	*FD*	*Votes*	*%*	*Seats Contested*
10. MSCP	57	23	15	331141	26.28%	27.36%
11. RJD	15	1	14	23037	1.83%	7.54%
12. RSP	3	0	3	1050	0.08%	1.08%
13. SAP	36	1	26	84215	6.68%	10.58%
	179	35	94	657846	52.21%	
REGISTERED (Unrecognised) PARTIES						
14. KNA	1	0	1	690	0.05%	2.17%
15. NPP	1	0	1	17	0.00%	0.05%
	2	0	2	707	0.06%	
INDEPENDENTS						
16. IND	48	1	45	37875	3.01%	7.44%
Grand Total:	401	60	246	1260091		

The results showed all the attributes that have characterised electoral politics in the state since it attained statehood in 1972: high turn out, political fragmentation and hung assemblies. Since 1972, no party has secured an absolute majority in the state. In the Seventh Assembly Election 2000, the parties took this into consideration and formed three alliances and fought the election in a triangular way. But, no party or alliances secured a clear majority. The UF came much closed with 29 seats (MSCP - 23, FPM - 6) but was short by two seats. Having failed to secure an absolute majority, the UF soon started looking towards the small parties to get the required strength.

W. Nipamacha Singh, the CM and leader of both the UF and the MSCP submitted a list of 36 MLAs to Governor Ved Marwah on 27th February staking his claim to form a government. Moreover, the Front leader claimed that three MLAs each had broken away from NCP and MPP in order to support the UF.[50] Subsequently, a mammoth 34 members, three tiers MSCP led UF ministry was sworn in on 2nd March, 2000 headed by W. Nipamacha Singh which marked his second innings as the CM of the state.

The new ministry was the largest ever in the history of Manipur after attaining statehood. The large size of the ministry was mainly because of the political leaders' belief that a large size ministry will bring political stability in the state. They thought that in order to sustain their unity and bring political stability, all the MLAs in the ruling party or parties were to be made happy and satisfied.[51] The number of the MLAs who were supporting the UF ministry was 38. Out of these, 34 were made the ministers - there were 22 of cabinet rank; five were ministers of state with independent charges, while the remaining six including a woman were ministers of state, and the remaining four were also given other assignments which were equal with the ministers in terms of status and ranking.

The belief that a jumbo size ministry would bring unity and solidarity among the coalition partners thereby bringing stability to the government was, however, proven wrong very soon. A tussle for power erupted specially between the Speaker Dr. Sapam Dhanonjoy Singh and the CM. Both were elected on the MSCP tickets. The Speaker blamed the government for its failure to control the law and order situation of the state. He also criticised the government for its failure to promote welfare of the people. He joined hands with the opposition to topple the UF ministry. The Speaker openly declared his firm resolve to bring down the Wahengbam Nipamacha government with the help of the Opposition parties. On the other hand, the front also decided to initiate impeachment process against the Assembly Speaker, Dr S. Dhananjoy Singh during the winter session. The official Spokesman of the then Front M. Kunjo Singh countered the Speaker by saying that the Speaker's threat was no threat as 37 of the 38 MLAs of the ruling front are solidly united and behind the CM W. Nipamacha Singh.[52] The two sides also opened up their respective camps.

Before one proceeds further, some observations about the role of the Speaker may be made here. The Speaker belonged to the MSCP, the party leading the coalition. Yet, because of his political ambitions, he failed to be impartial though his office was supposed to be above party politics, and joining hands with the opposition he tried to overthrow the ministry. Once again this was a case of history repeating itself too often. Most of the time coalition ministries failed to last not so much because of inter-party differences among the coalition partners but because of intra-party conflicts within the major party in the coalition. This, in turn, also underlies the failure of parties in coalition ministries to evolve a meaningful and effective relationship among them.

In the meantime, the Congress (I) which was in the opposition and had 11 MLAs in the Assembly got reduced to one, with all its MLAs except former CM Rishang Keishing splitting from the party and forming a new regional party called as the 'Manipur Regional Congress Party (MRCP)'. The break away group of 10 MLAs was headed by Radhabinod Koijam and he subsequently formed a new political alliance called as the Manipur Democratic Front (MDF) with six other opposition parties - BJP, NCP, Progressive FPM, MPP, SAP and Janata Dal (S) - with the objective of toppling the W. Nipamacha ministry. After the split, the breaks up of the political parties in the Assembly were as follows:[53]

Ruling (UF)		*Opposition*			
		Manipur Democratic Front (MDF)			
MSCP	30	MRCP	10	Congress (I)	1
FPM	4	BJP	6		
Independent	1	NCP	2		
		Progressive FPM	2		
		MPP	1		
		SAP	1		
		Janata Dal (S)	1		
Total	35		23		1

The opposition alliance 'MDF' stood united and ready to throw out the UF ministry by convincing some MLAs from the coalition ministry. They tried very hard using all the possible means to break the ruling coalition ministry. At this juncture, the UF coalition government began to crumble. Eight MLAs including three cabinet ministers, one minister of state (independent charge), two (MoS), one MLA and the Deputy Chairman Planning escaped from the ruling camp and walked into the opposition MDF camp held at the Speaker Dr S. Dhananjoy Singh's bungalow[54] and they later withdrew their support from the Nipamacha-led UF ministry. At this moment, another crisis rocked the MSCP, the main ruling party. The CM and the MSCP working president, the then Union Minister of State for Food Processing, Th. Chaoba openly criticised each other and expelled each other. The CM declared that the MSCP's Central Executive Council (CEC) resolved to expel the MSCP working president, vice-president (administration) and general secretary (administration) from the party for six years for their anti-party activities on 10th February 2001. Moreover, they sent a fax message to the central leaders of the NDA requesting them the removal of the Union Minister of State for Food Processing, Th. Chaoba Singh who was the Working President of the party.[55]

The Working President of the MSCP, Th. Chaoba also retaliated to the CM on the same day. He announced the expulsion of the CM W. Nipamacha Singh and Dy. CM Dr L. Chandramani along with six other ministers from the primary membership of the ruling MSCP for six years by the party Central Executive Council (CEC). They charged the CM and Dy. CM of failing to bring up the issue of the three month political crisis in the MSCP legislature party and failure of the government in maintains law and order. They also charged them for financial indiscipline. Both the groups claimed that they were the genuine MSCP. When the crisis reached its peak, Th. Chaoba and his group joined hands with the opposition to topple the Nipamacha ministry. Th. Chaoba also claimed that he enjoyed the support of 22

MLAs of the MSCP but 14 of them were being held as 'captive' at the Nipamacha side.[56] In the meantime, the MRCP and the PFPM merged into the SAP thereby increase the number of SAP to 13 from 1. The MSCP faction of Th. Chaoba withdraws its support to the government. Finally, the CM stepped down in favour of Shri Radhabinod Koijam of the SAP, following which a new ministry called the United Democratic Alliance (UDA) or Peoples' Front ministry was sworn in on 15th February 2001. It clearly shows that intra-party relationship of a party adversely affected the stability of a ministry.

The Samata Party-led Peoples' Front ministry 2001

Of all the coalition ministries, coalition partners of no other ministry was more disunited and fragmented than the Peoples' Front ministry. In fact, seeds of conflict were there from the very beginning. The MSCP in spite of having almost double the number of MLA than that of the SAP, and having led the previous ministry, failed to lead the coalition ministry. When the UDA was formed, it was supported by 39 members. The break up of the alliance was MSCP (Nipamacha group) - 22, SAP - 12, FPM - 4 and Independent - 1. The UDA invited all the parties including the BJP to join the government. Later on the six MLAs of the BJP also joined the UDA. With this, the ministry was like an all party government. Unfortunately, though the SAP and BJP were partners at the centre, the joining of the UDA by the BJP worsened the interparty relationship within the coalition ministry.

The real problem was that at the centre the BJP was leading the government whereas in the state the SAP was leading the ministry. Six BJP MLAs were elected in the 7th assembly elections whereas there was only one SAP MLA elected in the elections. Obviously, the BJP was not willing to play second fiddle to the SAP in the state. In fact, this was the reason for which the BJP was reluctant to join the ministry initially. Though both share power in Delhi, their relation in Manipur was not cordial as in the Centre.

Actually, the state BJP unit did not want to support the Front but the BJP central leaders asked them to join hands with the Peoples' Front alliance which was led the SAP. This was the result of the talk between Radhabinod and George Fernandes on one side and L. K. Advani and P. B. Acharya on the other. The CM also met L. K. Advani in Delhi.[57] It means that BJP joined the ministry after the intervention of the central leaders. Within no time, the two parties indulged in a cold war right after the formation of the UDA ministry. In the first week of May it turned out as a major crisis in the UDA coalition ministry. When the crisis became deeper, both the group set up different camps. If any political crisis erupted in Manipur, political leaders open up camps and kept their supporters camping together. This became a culture in the state politics. The two groups put up their best efforts to strengthen the number of MLAs by wooing maximum number of members from different parties in the state. The BJP group were camping at the Speaker Dr S. Dhananjoy Singh's Bungalow. The BJP group claimed that they were 32 in number including 7 - BJP, 19 - MSCP, 2 - FPM, 2 - NCP and 1 - JD(S). They said that they don't have any intention of abandoning the People's Front government but wanted to change the leader.[58]

In the second week of May, the crisis becomes more complex. The 18 MSCP members who were camping with the BJP defected from their party and formed 'Progressive Manipur State Congress (PMSCP)' and merged to BJP on 13th May, 2001. As a result, the BJP became the single largest party with 26 members in the house of 60. The BJP had originally only six MLAs but it increase first to eight with two FPM joining it, then with the addition of 18 MLAs, the BJP's strength now reached 26.[59] The SAP thought that this is a direct threat and challenge to the Radhabinod ministry from the BJP camp.

The UDA leader Chief Minister Radhabinod Koijam, on his part, tried his best to hold his post by giving ministerial berths to his allies as much as possible. This was proven by the fact that his ministry had 39 ministers, the biggest ever the state has witnessed so far. However as the conflict between his party and the BJP dragged on, he made a crucial move to challenge the power of the BJP and also to control his ministers tightly and properly. He dropped six ministers from the UDA ministry. Of these six, two were from the FPM and four from the BJP. The BJP strongly objected the action of the CM and term it as "dictatorial, deceptive and dubious." Party leaders of the BJP M. Bhorot and R. K. Dorendra accused Radhabinod of having failed to consult the BJP on administrative and political affairs of the People's Front and destroyed the ethics of a coalition ministry. So, the two leaders sought permission from the BJP President, K. Jana Krishnamurthi to withdraw from the People's Front government.[60] Moreover, two constituents of the People's Front government namely the FPM and NCP had withdrawn their support to the ruling front. The reason for their withdrawal was that of dropping the six ministers without proper explanation. They also demanded the resignation of Radhabinod Koijam from the post of CM. In addition to it, seven ministers - Kh. Loken Singh, MoS finance, K. Ranjit Singh MoS health, Danny Shaiza MoS tribal development, H. Borobabu Singh minister IFCD, Md. Alladin, minister CADA, Ngursanglur MoS works, Kh. Chandra Singh MoS agriculture - also tendered their resignation from the ministry.[61]

To add more woes to the Chief Minister, the militant groups in the state were causing serious law and order problems inside the state. Militants forced the closure of two prestigious girls' Catholic School in Imphal for an indefinite period following their failure to pay the money demanded by them. This followed the unilateral declaration of a ceasefire with 18 militant groups by the state government without consulting the Centre. But the Centre refused to endorse the state government's decision to extend the ceasefire period on the ground that there had been no change in the nature and extent of militant activity inside the state.[62] This meant that decision of the State government headed by the SAP was not endorsed by the Central government headed by the BJP though both were coalition partners both at the centre and the state. All these show the serious differences between the SAP and the BJP inside the coalition ministry in Manipur.[63]

Finally, the Governor summoned a special session of the 7th Manipur Legislative Assembly on 21st May, 2001 to prove the majority of the People's Front ministry headed by Radhabinod. At this crucial juncture, the Speaker recognised the split of the JD (S) by its lone MLA, Dr. Kh. Loken and formation of the JD (L) by the latter.[64] On 21st May, as per the plan of the Assembly, the vote of confidence on the council of minister was moved. The Radhabinod Koijam ministry lost the vote of confidence in the assembly. Only 17 MLAs - SAP - 13, MPP - 1, BJP - 1, MSCP – 1 and one independent voted in favour of the ministry and 39 MLAs from different parties (BJP - 24, FPM - 2, NCP - 2, MSCP - 10, JD(S) - 1) voted against the government. Two MLAs namely RK Dorendra Singh state BJP leader, who aspired for the CM's post and the lone Congress (I) MLA Rishang Keishing abstained from voting. One MLA Thangminlen Kipgen was not allowed to cast his vote because he was disqualified by the Speaker under 10th Schedule of the Indian Constitution.

The above discussion clearly evinces that the breakdown of the ministry was mainly because of the internal crisis within the coalition partners. Moreover, many MLAs did not follow the whip issued by their party leaders. For instance, the BJP's central leaders issued a whip to its MLAs to support the Radhabinod ministry. Yet 24 MLAs out of 26 voted against the government and one abstained from voting. This means that the decision of the Central leaders of the BJP was not respected by its MLAs in the state. This led to a serious crisis in the relationship between the BJP state unit and its national body. Equally significant was the fact that the developments embittered the relationship between the BJP and the SAP inside the state to a point of no return. Indeed, the relationship between the two parties became strained even in Delhi. The downfall of Radhabinod

Koijam's government, one of the shortest lived in the state, sent shock tremors all the way to Delhi, where for several days, the future of the NDA seemed to be in jeopardy.[65] The SAP was really shocked at the behaviour of the BJP MLAs. The opposition of the state BJP unit to the ministry was described as an "act of betrayal" by the Samata Party's central leaders who said that despite their party being the "most loyal" ally of the BJP in the National Democratic Alliance (NDA) and the BJP's top leaders having repeatedly assured support to the government, the BJP MLAs voted against the government.[66] In the same manner, the ten MSCP MLAs also betrayed the SAP by voting against their own party's whip. The fall of the Koijam ministry was followed by the proclamation of President's Rule inside the state on 3rd June 2001 with the State legislative assembly kept under animated suspension.

It is evident from the above discussions that there was failure on the part of the coalition partners to maintain even a semblance of unity among themselves which led to the fall of the ministry. The entire episode proves that the sole consideration around which parties in coalition tried to sustain their togetherness or part ways was that of sharing governmental power and not that of sharing any other common objectives, ideologies or policies and programs.

Meanwhile, the 39 MLAs who voted against the government formed a new alliance called the Progressive Democratic Alliance (PDA) under the leadership of R. K. Dorendra Singh with the intention of forming an alternative government. So, the struggle for power again continued after the collapse of the ministry. Then, the battlefield was shifted from Imphal to Delhi. Immediately, after the fall of the ministry, Dorendra and some other BJP legislators rushed to Delhi to convince the central leaders that the state BJP was capable to form an alternative government with the help of some regional parties. The Samata party did not approve the move. Its central leaders particularly George Fernandes who was the Convenor of the NDA and the then Union Minister Nitish Kumar threatened to pull out of the NDA if the BJP central leaders succumbed to the pressure from Manipur. So, a peculiar situation emerged out from the political crisis of Manipur within the partners of the NDA in Delhi. To ease the tension between the BJP and SAP and bring an amicable solution in Manipur, a meeting was held between the Samata party leaders and BJP leaders in the presence of A.B. Vajpayee and L.K Advani on 28th May 2001. It was decided that neither the BJP nor the Samata would be in the race for power in Manipur. Samata leaders urged the then BJP President, Jana Krishnamurthy to restrain the BJP legislators and respect the decision taken in the meeting. In the meantime, a number of political formations surfaced in the state, each claiming to be in a position to form the government. The BJP leader R. K. Dorendra Singh and Assembly Speaker Sapam Dhananjoy Singh tried to garner support from different political parties and prove to the Governor that they enjoyed majority. Actually, it was an attempt to thwart the move for President's Rule. But, the Governor recommended for PR because he felt that the entire claim made by the political leaders about their ability to form a stable government were all based on "hypothetical support."[67] So, Presidents' Rule was placed in Manipur on 3rd June, 2001 and the Manipur Assembly was kept under suspended animation. As destiny would have it, the Assembly was not to be revived again.

By June the entire state was in serious turmoil following the signing of a Cease-Fire Agreement between the GOI and the NSCN (IM).[68] The ceasefire between the NSCN and the Government of India extended without territorial limit on 14th June, 2001. This meant that it was applicable to all the Naga inhabited areas of NE India including Manipur as well. The people of the state got furious and protested against the ceasefire extension. Thousands of people took to the streets and targeted the politicians. The agitators destroyed the offices of the BJP and Samata Party while those of the Congress, the Manipur People's Party and the MSCP were set on fire. The State Assembly was also burnt down. Speaker Sapam Dhanonjoy Singh was roughed up as he tried to escape from the building and BJP MLAs N. Bihari Singh and K. Tomba Singh were trapped inside the Assembly Hall. They sustained 50 per cent burns. To control the situation, police opened fire and killed 14 protesters and more than 50 protesters were injured. The situation became critical. Curfew was imposed in the valley of Manipur. The protesters asked the MPs and MLAs of the state to resign and boycotted them socially. They were even asked to leave the state. With the opposition from various sections of the society mounting up, political leaders in Manipur were under pressure to oppose the cease-fire extension. A delegation of MLAs and MPs from all parties, including the BJP, met top functionaries of the NDA government and demanded the revocation of the agreement.[69] Ultimately, the clause 'without territorial limit' was dropped. The situation in Manipur become slowly and gradually normalizes around October 2001. Once the law and order prevailed in the state, the Election Commission of India announced in the month of December, 2001 that the election of the 8th Manipur Legislative Assembly will be held in the month of February, 2002.

In the elections which were held on 12th February and 21st, 2002, the Congress once again emerged as the single largest party winning 20 seats. This paved the way for yet another coalition ministry inside the State, the 15th one since 1972. It was known as Secular Progressive Front (SPF) ministry and led by the Congress (I) and the other partners were the MSCP, NCP and CPI. Later, all the parties except the CPI were to merge one by one into the Congress thereby leaving only the Congress and the CPI in the Ministry.

Conclusion and Summary

A coalition form of government is a government formed by two or more parties by entering into an alliance. The parties in the alliance work united by maintaining cooperation and coordination among themselves and they share all the responsibilities of the government. This type of alliance is formed by parties when none of them secured the required majority individually. A coalition government may also come into existence in times of emergency. Usually, such situations do not occur frequently. It happens only at the time of war or other extraordinary situations.

The Indian political system is a multi-party system having many political parties at different levels such as national, regional, state or local. The country is also experiencing the politics of coalition at all the levels of government i.e. national, state and local level. At the national level, the coalition politics have become the norm from the '90s onwards. At the state level, however, coalition ministries emerged as early as the 1950s as it happened in Patiala and East Punjab (PEPSU) in 1952. This was followed in Andhra Pradesh in 1953.[70]

Coming to that of Manipur, the state has also a long history of coalition governments. It was there right from the beginning when a coalition ministry was sworn in Manipur immediately after the 1948 elections held under the provisions of the Manipur State Constitution Act. After her merger into India, she did not have a legislative body of her own. Coalition ministries again followed during her period as a Union Territory. Social, cultural, linguistic, religious, ethnic and geographical diversities have provided a healthy background for the emergence of numerous political parties and multi party system inside the state. The legacy of coalitional governments got further entrenched after her becoming a full-fledged State. In fact, as many as 17 coalition ministries have been formed in Manipur so far since her statehood in 1972. Therefore, it may not be an exaggeration to say that the history of ministries in Manipur is one of coalition ministries.

So far as the relationship among the parties forming coalition ministries during the period from 1985 to 2002 is concerned, Coalitions were formed usually not on the basis of shared ideologies, principles or policies and programs but with sole intention of having a share of the governmental power. Pre-poll alliances also hardly mattered while forging a coalition with a view to form a ministry. Once the election results are out and a coalition ministry became the only alternative, anyone and any party became a prospective partner in the effort to garner the magic number. In the bargain, even parties who belonged to different pre-poll alliances became close partners. All the while, the main concern of the parties in a coalition ministry has been to garner maximum number of ministerial posts. The individual MLAs also remained more or less solely concerned with securing their own ministerial berths. These meant that the coalition partners do not have much of a common platform to stand together and secure unity and solidarity among them. The relationship they shared was often characterised by lack of coordination and cooperation and most of the time, the relationship they shared was not one of mutual trust and cooperation but one of conflict and distrust. Indeed, parties who have been partners of coalition ministries usually went separate ways once a new election is announced.

Inter-party conflicts among the coalition partners were one of the factors which led to the fall of coalition ministries. However, more significantly, intra-party conflict within the leading parties inside the coalition was the major factor which often led to the fall of ministries. Both these conditions, further underlies the failure of the parties to achieve unity and solidarity both individually and as a group. Small parties also often tended to change their political affiliation. Within the coalition they will support different leaders from time to time with a view to garner their own position of power. They don't even hesitate at all to cross over to the opposition side thereby leaving the ministry high and try and seriously endangering the stability of the ministry. This further proves the feeble and fragile nature of the relationship which the coalition partners share among them. All these also meant that the coalition partners failed to transcend their own ambition to grab power by any means. Prospects of sustaining their own position of power or gaining a position of power were the main concerns which kept the coalition partners together. They will also part ways for the same reason. As a result, all the time they failed to achieve unity and solidarity among themselves. This in turn led to the failure of the emergence of a healthy coalitional relationship among political parties forming a coalition ministry.

NOTES

1. MPP-led ULP in 1972 and 1974, MHU led-PDF Ministry in 1974, Congress led-DLP Ministry 1974, Congress-CPI Ministry in 1975, Congress-MPP Ministry in 1980, Congress-Independent Ministry in 1985, MPP led ULP in 1990, Congress-MPP Ministry in 1992, Congress led Coalition Ministry in 1994, Congress led JLP in 1995, MSCP led UF Ministry in 1997 and 2000, Samata led MDF Ministry in 2001 and Congress led SPF in 2002
2. Tiwana, S.S. Coalition Politics in India: Problems and Prospects in D. Sundar Ram (ed), Coalition Politics in India: Search for Political Stability, Jaipur & New Delhi, National Publishing House, 2000, pp-131
3. McLean, Iain and Alister McMillan (ed), Oxford Concise Dictionary of Politics, Indian edition, Oxford University Press, New Delhi, 2005, p-86
4. Jose, N. Chander, *Coalition Politics: The Indian Experience*, New Delhi, Concept Publishing Company, 2004 p-5
5. *Ibid.*, pp.5ff
6. Gadkari, S.S. United Front Coalition Government in India: Experiences and Prospects, in D. Sundar Ram (ed) *Coalition Politics in India: Search for Political Stability,* Jaipur & New Delhi, National Publishing House, 2000, p-78.
7. *Ibid.*, p. 79.
8. Pillai, K. Raman, Coalition Politics in India—A Review in D. Sundar Ram (ed) *Coalition Politics in India: Search for Political Stability*, Jaipur & New Delhi, National Publishing House, 2000, p. 201.
9. Singh, S.D. Coalition Governments: An Exercise in Political Futility in D. Sundar Ram (ed) *Coalition Politics in India: Search for Political Stability*, Jaipur & New Delhi, National Publishing House, 2000, p.182.

10. Sudhakar, E. *Third Concept,* April-May, 1998, p. 45.
11. Pakem, B. *Coalition Politics in North-East India,* Regency Publications, New Delhi,1999, p. 83
12. *Ibid.,* p. 87.
13. http://www.eci.gov.in/StatisticalReports/SE_1984/Statistical%20Report%201984%20Manipur.pdf
14. Pakem, B. *op cit,* p. 92.
15. 'Rishang Kieshing sworn-in as Chief Minister', The Manipur Mail (A Local English Daily), Imphal, January 5, 1985.
16. 'State vs Centre', Editorial column, *The Manipur Mail,* Imphal, November 1, 1986.
17 '2 State Minister Resign', *The Manipur Mail,* Imphal, September 11, 1987.
18. 'Babu, Jangamlung, back to CM's camp' *The Manipur Mail,* Imphal, September 13, 1987.
19. 'Angou, Paokhosie, Ibobi leave for Delhi', *The Manipur Mail,* Imphal, September 15, 1987.
20. 'Rishang's days are numbered', *The Manipur Mail,* Imphal, October 8, 1987.
21. 'R.K Jaichandra resigns', The Manipur Mail, Imphal, February 18, 1988.
22. B. Pakem, *op.cit,* p. 92.
23. http://www.eci.gov.in/StatisticalReports/SE_1990/Statistical%20Report%20Manipur%201990.pdf
24. Singh, Ksh. Kenedy , Parties and Politics in Manipur, Dissertation submitted to JNU for the M. Phil, *Centre for Political Studies,* 2000, pp-54f
25. http://www.eci.gov.in/StatisticalReports/SE_1990/Statistical%20Report%20Manipur%201990.pdf
26. Poknapham Kunmathoishuba Chahi (*Special issue of Poknapham, a Local Manipuri Daily*) Akhannapa Chephong, 1st February 1996, p. 4.
27. 'Ranbir cease to be MPP leader says Bhubon', *The Manipuri Mail,* Imphal, February 18, 1991
28. 'MPP in deep crisis', *The Manipur Mail,* Imphal, February 17, 1991.

29. B. Pakem, *op cit,* p. 93
30. 'It is time for Borobabu's resignation?', *The Manipur Mail*, Imphal, March 24, 1993
31. 'Congress (I) MPP relations badly strained', *The Manipur Mail*, Imphal, April 13, 1993.
32. 'Rishang led Ministry sworn in' *The Manipur Mail*, Imphal, December14,1994.
33. 'Rishang group commands absolute majority', *The Manipur Mail*, Imphal, December14, 1994.
34. 'Minister berth: Price of support ultimatum: A real bomb shell from 4 MLAs,' *The Manipur Mail*, Imphal, December19, 1994.
35. B. Pakem, *op cit.,* p. 93.
36. http://www.eci.in/StatisticalReports/SE_1995/StatisticalReport-MR95.pdf
37. '15 CLP members demand change in leadership', *The Imphal Free Press*, the Anniversary Special Supplement 2003, Imphal, p. 9.
38. *Ibid.,* 'CLP battle to shift to Delhi, CM and Speaker to air dash to capital' p.11.
39. 'Manipur coming apart', *Economic and Political Weekly*, December 13, 1997, p. 3169.
40. 'Five rebels axed, 18 resign in defiance'. *The Imphal Free Press*, the Anniversary Special Supplement , op cit, p-12
41. *Ibid.,* 'Congress split rebels forms new party', p.13.
42. 'Nipamacha inducts six new ministers', *The Imphal Free Press*' Imphal, May 5, 1998.
43. 'Manipur's minister for scandal's Rs 1.77 crore scam', *The Imphal Free Press*, May 18, 1998.
44. 'Fake appointment inquiry commission reduced to a big farce', *The Imphal Free Press*, December 2, 1998.
45. 'Jokes Apart', *The Imphal Free Press*, October 1, 1999.
46. 'Banks refuse to honour government bills', *The Imphal Free Press*, May 7, 1998.
47. 'Strike puts administration in the limbo', *The Imphal Free Press*, August 19, 1998.
48. 'Manipur assembly election', *The Economic and Political Weekly*, March 11, 2000, p. 883.

49. http://www.eci.in/StatisticalReports/SE_2000/STAT_REPORT_MR_LA_2000.pdf
50. 'Fuzzy verdict in Manipur', *Frontline,* Volume 17- Issue 05, March, 04-17, 2000.
51. 'Mara chetba sarkar amasung People's Frontgee maraipak', *Poknapham* (A local Manipuri daily), February 23 2001
52. 'Speaker Dhananjoy draws first blood', *The Imphal Free Press*, Imphal, November 17, 2000.
53. 'Congress splits in opposition power gambit', *The Imphal Free Press*, Imphal, December 9, 2000.
54. 'UF Government on a tailspin', *The Imphal Free Press*, Imphal, February 11, 2001.
55. 'Nipamacha, Chaoba expel each other from MSCP', *The Imphal Free Press*, Imphal, February 12, 2001.
56. 'Seven of eight who left CM's camp tender resignation', *The Imphal Free Press*, Imphal, February 13, 2001
57. 'Radhabinod ministry expansion proposal still under cloud', *The Imphal free Press*, Imphal, February 19, 2001.
58. 'Samata Party-BJP cold war breaks into open', *The Imphal Free Press*, Imphal, May 9, 2001.
59. 'Merger okayed, BJP set to be largest party in Assembly', *The Imphal Free Press*, Imphal, May 14, 2001
60. 'BJP seeks central permission to withdraw from ruling front', *The Imphal Free Press*, Imphal, May 17, 2001.
61. The Imphal Free Press, 7th Anniversary Special Supplement, *op cit.*, p. 54.
62. 'Continuing instability', *Economic and Political Weekly*, June 9, 2001, p. 2012.
63. '4 MSCP MLAs request separate seats, Thangminglien debarred', *The Imphal Free Press*, Imphal, May 21, 2001.
64. *Ibid.*
65. 'Manipur continuing instability', *Economic and Political Weekly*, June 9, 2001, p. 2012.
66. 'A spell of President's Rule', Kalyan Chaudhuri, *Frontline*, Volume 18 - Issue 12, June 09-22, 2001.
67. *Ibid.*

68. A Cease-fire agreement was signed between Government of India and National Socialist Council of Nagalim (NSCN), IM faction on 25 July, 1997. Then, renew every after six months or one year. But, from 31stJuly2007, the Cease-fire extended indefinitely without territorial limit. See www.angelfire.com and http://www.satp.org/satporgtp/countries/india/states/nagaland/data_sheets/Chronologynscnim.htm Dated 11 /9/07

69. 'Truce and violence', Kalyan Chaudhuri, *Frontline*, Volume 18- Issue 14, July, 07-20, 2001.

70. D. Sundar Ram, *op cit.*, p. 61.

4

Relationship among Parties in Opposition

Introduction

The present era is the era of democracy. Democracy has surpassed all forms of government and it has been the best. In a democratic setup, one party or group of parties form a government and the rest become the opposition in the assembly. The ruling and the opposition have equal responsibility for the proper functioning of the government and leading the State on the path of progress and prosperity. The opposition is indispensable in a democracy. It is an inseparable part of every party system. The nature and character of opposition however, vary from one party system to another.[1] For instance, in one-party system, opposition is not allowed to exist. In two-party system, the opposition is very strong and it is the real shadow cabinet. In a multi-party system like India, the oppositions have been weak, heterogeneous and divided among them. The opposition in Manipur is also more or less similar with the one at the centre.

The opposition in Manipur are normally weak and divided on the party lines. Most of the times, the opposition are busy either trying to dislodge the party in power or trying to defect from the opposition and join the ruling party. They are more concerned with the struggle for power than anything else. They hardly play the role of an opposition in the true sense of the term and do not act or work as a watchdog of the interests of the public. They come together only when they want to pull down the government. In fact, the role of the opposition is played by the interest groups or pressure groups inside the society rather than by the opposition parties in Manipur. The pressure groups or interest groups tries to check the moves of the government whenever they posed a serious danger to the interests of the people and the opposition followed them most of the time. For instance, when the Indian Government extended the cease-fire with the National Socialist Council of Nagaland (NSCN) without territorial limits on 14th June, 2001, the civil societies reacted first and the political parties followed them.

Opposition

The success of democracy depends on many factors. One of the most important factors is the role of the opposition party. It plays a vital role in the democratic set up. As Benjamin Disraeli rightly said in 1844, "no government can be long secure without formidable opposition."[2] The absence of opposition party virtually means one-party system. One party system is usually associated with authoritarian or totalitarian form of government and not with democracy. In democracy two or more political parties are allowed to function in the system. One or more party runs the affairs of the State. The remaining party sits in the opposition bench and checks the actions of the government. The opposition is an inseparable part of the democratic political set up. There can be no democratic government without opposition and a responsible opposition is as important as the party in power in the parliamentary system. Actually, the opposition makes the functioning of a government truly democratic since it keeps a close vigil on the working of the government closely.

The opposition comprises all those political parties which as a result of the last general election did not become part of the government. The largest opposition party becomes the official opposition. The word 'opposition' has many meanings. In the first place, opposition may mean total resistance to the form and basis of the State, and a determination to overthrow it by whatever means. Secondly, it may denote resistance to the power of the State when the later is viewed as an oppressive institution. Thirdly, the term 'opposition' refers to resistance to the group, faction, or dynasty in command of the State, and to the denial of its legitimacy. Fourthly, it may be used to denote a loyal opposition which opposes the commanding group without either contesting its legitimacy or threatening or rejecting the basis of the State or the Constitution. Fifthly, opposition may also be used to mean the system of checks and balances whereby the Constitution guards against and corrects its own excesses, or to identify a belief in a composite or divided sovereignty. Finally, the term has been used to describe the methods whereby the citizen or group, without condemning government as inherently oppressive, modifies its action, mellows its harshness, and prevents its tyrannies.[3]

The opposition functions as a watch-dog of the rights of the people. The parties in opposition make a national debate possible on important issues facing the country. It is said that the chief function of the opposition is to propose, oppose, expose and depose. They must propose several measures with a view to furthering the cause of their ideology which may or may not find favour with the majority party. Another function of the opposition is to oppose those policies and programs of the government which they may consider as being unjust, unreasonable and not in the interest of the people. The opposition never miss a chance to expose the misdeeds and lapses of the government. Corruption, favouritism, nepotism, unaccountability, inefficiency in government offices, misuse of authority, induction of tainted ministers, etc. are the main targets of the opposition. The opposition is always on the lookout for skeletons in government's cupboard. The ultimate objective of the opposition is to depose the government and provide an alternative of its own.[4]

The role of the opposition in democracy is very broad and comprehensive. It virtually includes everything under the sky. It is very difficult, if not impossible, to contain the subject in specific boundaries and to jump on certain conclusions.[5] They are expected to offer positive counter proposals and initiatives of their own. They need to present themselves as a credible and responsible alternative government by performing a very responsible and effective role. They examine and scrutinise each and every policy, programme and departments of the government of the day. If they find faults in any of these, they criticize the government and make the flaws public. The opposition not only highlights the mistake or defect or weakness of the government but also offer alternative policies for better ensuring the good of the people. Moreover, they also cooperate with the government in times of emergency, national calamity and natural disaster. The opposition should be loyal to the interests of the State and of the nation. It is also necessary that they use constitutional methods in the pursuit of their goals. Otherwise they cannot be considered as a healthy structure of a system of constitutional democracy.

The cooperation between the governing and opposition party is an essential element for constructive and efficient governance. The government need to recognize the effective and responsible role of the opposition. The effective and responsible role of the opposition and the recognition from the government is an essential element for the success of parliamentary democracy.[6] The effective and responsible role of the opposition party however depends on the type of party system. In one party system the institution of opposition is not allowed to exist. Therefore, it takes the form of a dissident group with minority tendency and criticise the government at party meetings with varying degrees. In Myanmar, for instance, the opposition party is not allowed to function by the military junta. In China also the Communist Party of China does not allow and other party to exist. In two-party system, the opposition party is very strong and have the potential to rule the country. The two parties have a very clear policy and programme for the people. The people choose between the two parties. The competition is very tight and strong. This type of competition exists in

U.K. and U.S.A. In multi-party system, opposition consists of heterogeneous groups and they often fight against each other. They are weak and do not talk and act as an alternative to the government. The role of opposition in such circumstances is different.[7] Because in multi-party systems opposition is likely to be dispersed among several parties and strict competition is actually impossible, unless one party formed the government. Moreover, parties may not be strictly competitive even during elections, for they may enter into electoral alliances that limit competition in various ways.[8] The numerous groups composing the opposition work in a State of frustration. Such situation is frequently witnessed in India both at the centre and the states.

History of Parliamentary Opposition

The word opposition is derived from the Latin word '*oppositio*' which means to oppose.[9] The origin and emergence of opposition can be traced from the ancient Greece and Rome. A limited form of democracy prevailed in ancient Greece and Rome and from there discovered many indications for having a separate organization of the opposition. According to Ghita Ionescu and Isabel de Madariaga, in the Roman world "one institution came near to the modern idea of an institutionalized opposition. . . . The Roman tribunes (first two and then ten) had the right (intercessio) on behalf of the Council of the Plebs to veto measures approved of or initiated by the Senate, and to prosecute magistrates who attempted to carry out such measures. Therefore the tribunes were organs through which the people could oppose decisions taken by the government."[10] This role was later on played by the church towards the feudal monarchs of the Middle Ages.[11]

The modern idea of parliamentary opposition however, emerged in British parliament. With the emergence of Tory and Whig party groups in the latter part of 18th century, the term 'opposition' has been applied to the party or parties whose elected members do not support the ministry of the day and offered themselves to the voters as an organised and disciplined alternative government which came to be known as 'Shadow government'. The opposition became formally known as "His Majesty's Opposition." The term "His Majesty's Opposition" was coined during a debate in the House of Common in 1826.[12] It was used for the first time by Sir John Cam Hobhouse to deride the members opposite. The opposition was financially recognised however first in Canada (1905), then in Australia (1920) and Tasmania (1927) and reached the 'mother of parliaments' in 1937.[13] The concept of opposition ultimately reached to all the democratic countries of the world.

Parliamentary Opposition in India

The Indian democracy started with the advantage of being the offspring of a mature democracy, which has been described as the 'mother of democracy'. The Indian experienced democracy during the British period though in a limited way. They however adopted parliamentary democracy after independence. In parliamentary democracy, the role of the opposition is very crucial and important. But in India, the opposition were very weak and ineffective for about two decades after independence. It was because of the evolution of one-party dominant system in India. The Congress party dominated the political scene both at the centre and in the states. As a result, the Congress enjoyed an unchallenged hegemony so much so that the opposition became comparatively weak and ineffective.[14]

A strong and healthy opposition was not able to grow in India for many years after independence. It was, indeed, very unfortunate for the Indian democracy. Until the Congress split in 1969, no party or group other than the Congress could succeed in securing 50 seats in Lok Sabha. A party requires to secure at least 1/10 seats of the legislature in order to recognise for the official opposition status and avail the facilities as an opposition.[15] In 1969 the Lok Sabha recognised the Congress (O) as the opposition party and its leader Dr Ram Subhag Singh as the leaders of the opposition. The recognition did not improve the status of the opposition.

The absence of a viable opposition in the Lok Sabha encouraged the Congress Party and its leader (Mrs. Indira Gandhi) to become more and more authoritarian during the 1970s. It virtually outlawed the Opposition and reduced the Parliament to a status of a captive body.[16] Still, the opposition slowly and gradually improved their strength and status in India. The opposition came to power at the centre in 1977 and formed the first non-Congress government in Delhi. It was formed by Janata Party headed by Morarji Desai. From there onwards, the role of opposition in the Indian democracy became more visible even though most of the time they were weak and not united.

Relationships among parties in Opposition in Manipur

Emergence of democratic form of government on the lines of parliamentary democracy started in Manipur in the year 1948. This was the year when Manipur had her first ever assembly elections based on the principle of universal adult franchise for constituting a popular legislative assembly having 53 representatives. The assembly was inaugurated on October 18, 1948.[17] The government was formed by the Praja Shanti, Krishak Sabha and the Hills members and the Congress was in the opposition.[18] The tradition of parliamentary system of governance, however, came to an abrupt end with the merger of Manipur into India on 15th October 1949 because this resulted in the abolition of both the democratically constituted assembly as well as the then existing council of ministers. Later she became a Part C State within the Indian Union. All these also meant that the institutions like the ruling and opposition parties ceased to exist in Manipur as there was no popular legislative assembly inside the State and a government responsible to it. Instead, the State was under the rule of a Commissioner. A significant step towards the evolution of ruling and opposition side inside the political system of Manipur could be seen with the coming of the territorial assembly in the year 1963. The Congress was in the ruling side whereas the

SSP was the lone opposition party. Manipur was upgraded into a full-fledged State on January 21, 1972. It led to the emergence of the ruling and opposition parties in a democratic and parliamentary system of governance inside the State. When the first ministry after statehood was sworn in on, the MPP, SSP, Congress (O) and UNIC[19] were in the ruling parties and the Congress (R) was in the opposition. The present chapter is an attempt to discuss and examine the relationship that the opposition parties in Manipur share among themselves as parties in opposition, their success or failure in the due discharge of their function as opposition parties inside the political system, the factors that bind them together or otherwise, the pre and post election alliances among them, etc. from 1985 to 2002.

Relationship among parties in Opposition from 1985-90 in Manipur

Relationship among parties in Opposition during the Congress ministry (1985-88)

The composition of the parties in opposition was very fragmented and divided during this time. In the last part of 1984 the Fourth State General Assembly Election was held and Congress (I) formed the government with the support of the Independent MLAs. The opposition parties comprised the CPI (1 MLA) Janata Party (4 MLAs), Kuki National Assembly (1 MLA), and Manipur People's Party (3 MLAs).[20] This meant that there were four parties in the opposition but only nine MLAs. This further meant that none of them were individually qualified to become an official opposition in the House, because to become an official opposition party, parties have to secure 10% of the strength of the House.[21] The strength of the Manipur Legislative assembly is 60 which meant that to become an official opposition, a party has to secure at least six MLAs in the election. They did not fight the election as a unit by forming an alliance. Moreover they failed to unite as a team after the election also. As a result they were very weak and became mere observers.

It was not as if they did not make an effort to achieve unity among them. But their efforts were only half-hearted. There was clear schism between the two national parties, viz., CPI and Janata Party, on the one hand and the two State parties, viz., the MPP and KNA.[22] Between the State parties also, the KNA was a party based on a particular community of the hills whereas the mass basis of the MPP was confined mainly to the valley. Thus, they represented different people having different interests and aspirations. Moreover the ruling party also tried to divide and absorb the smaller parties into their fold so that their own strength got increased. Indeed, when it succeeded in absorbing four MLAs of the Janata Party, it came as a serious blow to the latter party.[23]

Relationship Among Parties in Opposition during the Congress ministry (1988-90)

The opposition parties got an opportunity to put up a combined fight against the ruling Congress when the by-elections to the Sagolband Assembly Constituency was held in July 1988. They decided Shri Moirangthem Kumar Singh of the MPP as their common candidate. However, Shri R. K. Jaichandra of the Congress won the elections. It may be noted here that Shri R. K. Jaichandra was sent to the State as the CM by the Congress which was the party in power at the center. The defeat of the combined opposition during the election was a huge moral boost for the ruling Congress whereas the same was a great blow to the strength of the opposition.

The division among the parties in opposition was again exposed during the 9th Lok Sabha elections in 1989. The opposition in Manipur headed by the CPI decided to put up a common candidate inside the State in order to fight the common enemy, i.e. the Congress (I). They also decided to isolate the BJP from the public as they believed that the party was based on religion by joining hands with all the other secular parties.[24] The decision of the opposition, however, did not materialize. As the day of election came closer, the opposition parties decided to go their own separate ways and contest the elections individually in both the Inner and Outer Parliamentary Constituencies. It once again showed the failure of the parties in opposition to transcend their different ambitions and aspirations. [25] This significantly helped the Congress in winning both the seats in the elections.

The 5th State Assembly Elections scheduled for February 1990 gave the parties in opposition another opportunity to come together. As the elections approached, there were some efforts among them to fight the elections collectively. Yet, once again it was not to happen. The MPP decided to go alone in the assembly election. Other opposition parties also put up their respective candidates to contest the election. However, they could reach some understanding about seat adjustments, and wherever they failed to arrive at it, they decided to go for what they conveniently termed as "friendly contests".[26] The reality in election, however, is that there is no such thing as 'friendly contest' in the true sense of the term. Every candidate wants to win the election. All the candidates try their best to win the election. So the understanding of the seat adjustment of the opposition parties was more or less meaningless.

Relationship among parties in Opposition from 1990-95 in Manipur

Relationship among the parties in opposition during the MPP led ULF ministry (1990-92)

When the results of the 5th State Legislative Assembly came out, none of the parties won a majority of the seats. The Congress was the single largest party winning 26 seats. However, the parties who failed to form a well united opposition succeeded in coming together to form a coalition ministry called the United Legislature Front (ULF) Ministry. It consisted of the MPP, JD, Congress (S), CPI (M) and the KNA. This once again shows the ultimate reality of State politics in Manipur where parties come together or part ways just to gain or sustain or strengthen their own position of power. The ULF ministry was led by R. K. Ranbir Singh of the MPP. During this period, the Congress which was the single largest party after the elections remained as the only party in opposition.

Though left alone in the opposition, the Congress (I) continued with its own tirade against the government with a view to bring it down. Time and again it declared that it won't last even one year. It pressurised the Governor to sack the ULF Government on the ground of the worsening law and order situation in the State.[27] The opposition also alleged that the Governor misused power and destroyed the sanctity of the 'Governor's Office' by involving in State politics. It questioned the style of functioning of the Governor[28] and boycotted the Governor's address on the beginning of the budget session.[29]

Yet, when the coalition ministry fell apart, it was not so much because of the efforts of the Congress, the party in opposition, but because of the internal conflicts inside the MPP, the leading coalition partners of the ULP. An internal erupted within the MPP due to differences between the H. Bhubon, the President of the party, and R. K. Ranbir, the CM. The President suspended the CM from the party on 15th February, 1991. The CM also retaliated on the same day. He convened a requisition meeting of the party which was attended by the party's MLAs and ministers. The meeting suspended H. Bhubon, the party President and Kh. Chaoba Singh, an ex-minister from the party membership for six years.[30] With the crisis inside the MPP, it was only matter of time before the ministry fell apart. Ultimately, Manipur was imposed Presidents' Rule (PR) on 7th January, 1992 by keeping the assembly under animated suspension.

Relationship among the parties in opposition during the Congress-MPP ministry (1992-93)

The political parties did not remain idle during the PR. There were hectic negotiations among the political parties. Once again, two parties which were perched opposite to one another in the previous ministry, i.e. the MPP and the Congress came together to form a coalition ministry led by R. K. Dorendro of the Congress. It was sworn in on April 8th 1992 after lifting PR the same day. The opposition comprised the KNA (2 MLAs), CPI (3 MLAs), JD (11 MLAs), and Congress (S) (6 MLAs).[31]

The compositions of the ruling and opposition sides during this period were as follows:

Ruling Parties		*Opposition parties*	
Congress (I)	26	KNA	2
MPP	11	CPI	3
		JD	11
		Congress (S)	6
		NPP	1
Total	27	Total	23

It is obvious from the number of parties in opposition that, as compared to the opposition during the previous ministry where only Congress was there, this time it was a very heterogeneous opposition. This, inevitably also meant that it was very weak. They were not united and did not function as one unit. They could not pose a challenge to the ruling side at all. There was no proper coordination among the different constituent units of the opposition. Apart from condemning the Congress led coalition ministry as responsible for the outbreak of the ethnic clashes in the hills and their failure to control them, and also for the overall failure of law and order inside the State, they remained most of the time silent spectators of the rumblings going on between the two partners in the coalition ministry. They neither had the political will nor the numerical strength to make use of the situation to their advantage. Thus, once again, when the Congress led Congress-MPP ministry fell apart in December 1993 and PR was imposed on 31 December 1993, it was not because of the manoeuvrings from the opposition but because of internal crisis within the coalition ministry itself.

Relationship among the Parties in Opposition during the Congress-led Coalition Ministry (1994-95)

Once again, all the parties indulged in political horse-trading among themselves during the PR. The Congress which was the single largest party after the 5th Assembly Elections continued to be embroiled in deep internal crisis. It concerned the leadership of the Congress Legislative Party (CLP). The crisis reached Delhi and many national leaders of the Congress (I) visited Imphal to solve the crisis and restore a new Congress government in Manipur. The internal problem of the Congress (I) ended after the Congress MLAs choose their CLP leader through secret voting. In the voting Shri Rishang Keishing, the former CM won and he became the leader of the CLP.[32]

The election of the CLP leader solved the tension within the party. Subsequently, the Congress (I) staked its claim to form a popular ministry to end the Presidents' Rule in the State. Eventually, the Governor invited the Congress (I) to form the government and a new Congress led Coalition under the leadership of Shri Rishang Keishing was sworn in on 13th December, 1994.[33] The composition of the ruling and the opposition side as claimed by both sides on the day of swearing in of the new ministry was as follows:

Ruling Parties		*Opposition Parties*	
Congress (I)	25	MPP	9
Congress (S)	4	CPI	3
Janata Dal	7	Congress (S)	3
KNA -	1	KNA	1
		JD	4
		NPP	4
Total -	37	Total	24

From the above table it is very clear that there were overlapping in the number of MLAs as each side claimed to be within their respective folds. As a result, there were confusions about the parties in the ruling and opposition side.[34]

Further confusions were to follow soon. A one day Special session of the Assembly was called on 23 December 1994. However, one day ahead of it, the Speaker, Dr. H. Borobabu, had disqualified 23 MLAs from the ruling side. In protest to this action of the Speaker, the Treasury side boycotted the session. The assembly session started without a Governor's address, and the opposition moved a no-confidence motion against the government and passed it.[35]

The same day, Shri O. N Srivastav also sworn in as the new Governor of Manipur. The decision taken by the opposition was rejected by the new Governor. He summoned a one day session on January 9, 1995 so that Rishang may prove his majority in the House. In the meantime, the Gauhati High Court stayed the expulsion of the 23 MLAs by the Speaker. This gave an advantage to the ruling parties. Rishang not only succeeded in proving his majority but also replaced the Speaker by W. Angou Singh of the Congress (I).[36] All the while, the opposition parties remained weak and helpless, unable to assert themselves in the deep crisis in the assembly and within the ruling side.

Overall, the duration of this ministry was too short. It lasted only for about three months. Therefore, this period was not so viable a period for examining the relationship among the different parties in opposition. Besides, the debates over the disqualification of not less than 23 MLAs after issuing notice to 30 by the Speaker, the removal of the Speaker, etc. sidetracked other issues till the coming of the next election which was hardly three months away when the Rishang Keishing led ministry was sworn in.

Relationship among parties in Opposition from 1995-2000 in Manipur

Relationship among parties during the Congress led JLP ministry 1995-97

The 6th State Assembly Election of Manipur was held

on 16th and 19th February 1995. This time also, the opposition parties which were there during the time of the outgoing ministry contested the elections individually without entering into a formal pre-poll alliance. They were a heterogeneous, fragmented and divided lot. The party positions after the election results were announced were as follows:[37]

Party	Seats
BJP	1
CPI	2
Congress (I)	22
JD	7
SAP	2
Congress (S)	1
MPP	18
FPM	2
NPP	2
Independent	3
Total	60

This meant that no party won even a working majority. The Congress once again emerged as the single largest party after the elections followed by the MPP with 18 MLAs out of 60 seats in the assembly. As such, the struggle for power was again started between the Congress and the MPP, the two partners in the previous ministry.

There was struggle for power between the two groups one headed by Congress (I) and the other by MPP.[38] In the horse trading some JD MLAs split from their parent party and formed two new parties known as Progressive JD (PJD) (four MLAs) and JD (Sephu Group) (one MLA) and support the Congress (I). This meant that there were three Janata Party groups. Ultimately Congress (I) made a post-poll alliance with FPM, PJD, NPP, SAP, JD (Sephu Group), Congress (S) and some independents MLAs called Joint Legislature Party (JLP). The coalition ministry was sworn in on February 25th 1995 under the leadership of Congress (I) MLA, Shri Rishang Keishing. The opposition, on the other hand comprised the MPP (18 MLAs), CPI (2 MLAs) and Janata Dal (2 MLAs). Together they formed the United Legislature Front (ULF). The lone BJP MLA in the house, however, did not join the ULF.[39]

Meanwhile, within five months an internal crisis erupted within the ruling coalition. Ten MLAs [Progressive JD - 2, NPP - 2, SAP - 2, FPM - 2, JD (Sephu Group) - 1 and one Independent MLA] of it withdrew their support and formed another opposition front called the United Democratic Front (UDF). This meant that there were two camps in the opposition viz., the ULF and the UDF. With this the number of opposition members got increased to 33. However, the Speaker W. Nipamacha Singh who was clearly supporting the ruling side disqualified five opposition MLAs on the ground of defection. As a result, the strength of both the ruling and opposition remained tied at 27:27 in the house. Finally, when a motion of no-confidence was brought against the government on 30th July, 1995 the latter survived by a whisker defeating the motion by 27 to 26. This was because of the lone BJP candidate in the house deciding to abstain from voting.[40] This clearly shows that the opposition were not united and missed the opportunity to pull down the government. Of course, even if the motion got tied at 27:27, the government would have survived simply because then the Speaker shall have to cast his vote and he will be happy to save the ministry.

In the meantime the ruling side went on trying to attract some MLAs from the opposition parties. It managed to split the MPP into two groups with one of them forming a new MPP (K). This group later joined the coalition ministry. With this the strength of the ruling parties got increased to 37.[41] Obviously the ruling side could further consolidate its position whereas the credibility of the opposition got adversely affected all over again. This further proves that the opposition as a group was characterised not only by an absence of unity and cohesion among its members but was also vulnerable all the time to disintegration in the hands of the divisive designs of the ruling side. It could not able to keep its MLAs intact and this was a major factor for its inability to be an effective opposition.

The next few months saw the opposition parties making an effort to play a constructive and positive role. The opposition parties raised the issue of insurgency, ethnic clashes in the hills and the law and order situation of the State in the assembly.[42] They criticised the government for not spelling out a clear cut policy to deal with the problem of insurgency and insisted the government to solve it. They also demanded a human rights commission to be set up in the State.[43]

Relationship among parties in Opposition during MSCP led UF Ministry 1997-2000

As already mentioned elsewhere, coalition ministries often broke up not because of manoeuvrings of the opposition or public outcry against it but because of conflicts among coalition partners or within the individual partners of the coalition. About November and December, 1997, this perennial problem of intra-party factions within a party in coalition ministry crop up i.e. within Congress (I) of the JLP ministry. The crisis erupted when a group of Congress MLAs demanded a change in the CLP leadership.[44] The crisis become deeper and deeper and ultimately the Congress (I) was split.

The dissident group consisting of 23 Congress (I) MLAs formed a new party called the Manipur State Congress Party (MSCP) under the leadership of the Speaker W. Nipamacha Singh. As a result the coalition ministry headed by Rishang Keishing got reduced to minority and resigned.[45] With the fall of the government, a four party (MSCP - 25, MPP -11, FPM - 2, CPI - 1 and one Independent) coalition government led by Shri W. Nipamacha Singh under the name of United Front (UF) Government was installed on December 16, 1997 in the State.[46] This left the Congress (I) as the only opposition in the house with 15 MLAs.

The Congress, as the party in opposition tried to work in a constructive manner. It carefully observed each and every move of the government. When the government sought a motion of confidence in the house, it walked out of the house before the voting in protest against allegedly undemocratic conduct of the proceedings and failure to follow parliamentary norms. The opposition claimed that the Speaker did not convene the House Business Advisory Committee before taking up any business. The Opposition leader, Radhabinod Koijam protested strongly and criticised the failure to move a motion of thanks to the Governor's address to the house.[47]

As the 13th Lok Sabha elections, 1999 approached there were drastic changes in the political scenario of the State. By this time, the MPP without withdrawing from the MSCP led coalition tried to join hands with the Congress, the only opposition party in the State Assembly. The CPI, another coalition partner of the UF also did the same. In the meantime, the MPP and the CPI joined hands with the CPI (M), RJD and JD and formed one Secular Democratic Front (SDF) and asked the Congress (I) to join it. Actually, the SDF with the Congress wanted to put up a common candidate to defeat the MSCP. It convened a number meeting to sort out a consensus candidate for the election.[48] However, all the efforts to bring the Congress within the fold of the SDF went in vain as the Congress wanted to contest both the seats in Manipur.[49] Later, JD also withdrew from the SDF and ultimately, most of them decided to contest the elections on their own. Finally, the election was fought among the MSCP, SDF, Congress (I), NCP, RJD, and FPM for the two seats in Manipur. When the results were out, the Inner seat was won by MSCP, whereas the Outer went to the NCP.

Once defeated in the Lok Sabha elections, both the SDF and the Congress (I) seemed to have learnt a lesson. They realised that without cooperating with each other it will be difficult to overthrow the ruling parties. The main ruling party, MSCP is a partner of the NDA at the centre and the Manipuri voters normally look towards Delhi before they cast their vote. So the Congress and the SDF seriously thought of uniting before the State assembly elections which were to be held in the month of February or March, 2000. The SDF also formed a Joint Election Committee to fight the State election together. Some of the issues raised by the

SDF were protection of the territorial integrity of Manipur, eradication of corruption, promotion of communal harmony, and to defend human rights of the people.[50]

So far as the Congress (I) was concerned the Manipur Pradesh Congress Committee (I) (MPCC-I) was facing an internal crisis on the issue of its party Presidentship. The crisis was over with the induction O. Ibobi Singh as the President of the MPCC-I. After that the SDF and Congress-I started discussions to join hands and fight the State assembly election together. The outcome of the discussion was the admission of Congress-I into the SDF. Meanwhile the CPI (M) walked out of the Front. However, the remaining parties, MPP, CPI, JD (S) and Congress (I) decided to work together and agreed to put up common candidates in all the 60 seats if possible. They also decided that wherever it won't be possible to put up a common candidate, they will go for 'friendly contests' among them.[51] The SDF managed to put up common candidates in 24 ACs out of the 60 seats and have friendly contests in the remaining the remaining.[52]

Relationships among parties in Opposition from 2000-2002 in Manipur

Relation among the parties in opposition during the MSCP led UF ministry (2000-01)

The Seventh Manipur State Assembly Election was held on 12 and 22 February 2000. This election was different from the previous assembly election in many ways. For instance, in the election the people of Manipur witnessed pre-poll alliances for the first time. There were three alliances namely the SDF comprising Congress (I), MPP, CPI and JD (S), the Manipur Democratic Alliance (MDA) comprising BJP, SAP, JD (U) and KNA and the United Front (UF) of Manipur led by MSCP along with FPM.[53]

The pre-poll alliances however did not bring the desirable result in any of the groups by winning a majority of the seats in the assembly. The ruling UF secured highest number of seats with 29 with MSCP and FPM winning 23 and 6 respectively. Still it was two short of the majority. There were some uncertainties in other alliances because the UF may take away some MLAs and form a new government. Their apprehension was proven true when the UF managed to take away three elected MLAs (out of four) from the MPP and all the four elected MLAs from the NCP, and formed a new government. The defected MLAs formed new parties. The defected MLAs from the MPP formed a new party called as MPP (K) leaving only O. Joy Singh as the lone MLA of the MPP for the time being. About the four MLAs of the NCP, three of them formed a new party known as NCP (O) and the other remaining one formed the NCP (D).[54] This meant that there was no MLA of the NCP in the assembly though there were four immediately after the announcement of the results. Later, all the three groups joined the MSCP. They later on merged with the MSCP. It may also be noted here that the MSCP, a partner of NDA still not joined the BJP led ministry at the centre though it joined later.

Now the opposition parties in the State Assembly comprised BJP and the Congress having six and eleven MLAs respectively and MPP, SAP and JD (S) and JD (U) having one MLA each. Initially they expressed their intention to work together leaving their differences. The opposition parties also convened a joint meeting at the State Assembly Conference Hall on 8th May, 2000.[55] The meeting was attended by the MLAs from the Congress (I), the BJP, the MPP, the SAP and JD (S). They discussed the affairs of the State and demanded to place a White Paper in connection with the financial crisis faced by the State. They strongly emphasised the need for finding a long-term solution to the chronic problem of financial bankruptcy in the State. They also strongly condemned the government for the sudden imposition of the out-dated Prevention of Seditious Meetings Act in the valley district of Manipur. The opposition thought that the Act will curtail the democratic rights of the citizens of the State and the government may also misuse it. The meeting also agreed to fight jointly all the problems faced by the State inside and outside the assembly irrespective of party differences. They also resolved to work out a common strategy for their further line of action.[56]

They soon got busy trying to topple the UF ministry. They met again to discuss a joint strategy to topple the government. The meeting was held at the residence of former CM R. K. Dorendro, a BJP MLA and a leader of the MDA. The meeting was attended by 18 MLAs from different parties (Congress (I), BJP, MPP, SAP, JD (S) and NCP). All the members attending the meeting resolved to be united in their efforts to overthrow the government. The meeting unanimously agreed that removal of the MSCP led government will be imperative in the interest of the general public. R. K. Dorendro also assured his fellow MLAs that his party, i.e. the BJP was fully prepared to take all the necessary steps to topple the government.[57]

The unity of the opposition did not last long. Their resolve to be united was easier said than done as the BJP and SAP were allies of the NDA at the centre while they found themselves on different groups of the opposition. The BJP and its traditional rival Congress (I)'s attempts to sit united in the opposition was also doomed to fail because of the obvious reasons. All the parties in opposition as well their MLAs were not only interested in toppling the existing ministry but were also always ready to grasp a foothold in the existing government at the first opportunity. As such, only a few leaders came out openly to condemn and criticise the mistakes or weaknesses of the government while most of the others behaved like fence sitters inside and outside the Assembly, hardly raising any voice against the financial crisis, slipping law and order situation, charges of corruption on the MLAs and ministers, etc.

The people of the State were not happy about the role of the opposition. The opposition were not playing the role of constructive critics of the government. They were not able to project themselves as a viable alternative to the government.[58] The weakness of the opposition is a bonus for the government as this enable them to secure their position from possible onslaughts of the opposition.

It may also be noted here that among all the parties in opposition, it was mainly the BJP and the SAP of the MDA which took most of the initiatives to overthrow the government. This was obviously related with the fact that both were coalition partners at the centre. In a press release, the MDA stated that the alliance wanted to topple the ruling front which they described as a 'gang of thieves', not because they were running after power but in order to provide the public an alternative to a government which did not care for the welfare of the people. It further asserted that there were no differences of opinion among the opposition parties on the question of toppling the government. The MDA also warned the ruling party MSCP not to underestimate the ability of the MDA.[59] The leaders of the opposition parties also submitted an application to the Speaker seeking the disqualification of those nine MLAs who had defected to the ruling side and subsequently merged with the ruling party, MSCP. The opposition parties said that it was a violation of the Anti-defection law and the MLAs in question should be disqualified.[60]

The four parties, viz., the BJP, SAP, JD (U) and KNA forming the MDA group in the opposition, together tried every possible means to dethrone the government. It sent a fax message to the PM Atal Behari Vajpayee to send either CBI or any central agency to probe the various scams like lottery scam, the police uniform scam, the Public Distribution System (PDS) rice scam and the ex-gratia scam that the UF government of Manipur involved in.[61] All the parties in the two opposition groups also organized a meeting at the residence of the former CM, Rishang Keishing at Mantripukhri on 9th July, 2000. All the opposition MLAs except two attended the meeting. The meeting decided to move a censure motion against certain very corrupt ministers of the government. They also condemned the government as the most corrupt government of the State and resolved once again to unite all the opposition parties on the issue of toppling and replacing the corrupt UF government. The President of the meeting Shri Rishang Keishing said that the most urgent agenda before the opposition was to dismantle the anti-people UF government. The most significant thing of the meeting was that it gave an opportunity to iron out the differences and misunderstandings between the Congress (I) and BJP.[62]

The decision to unite and work together among the opposition parties did not last even a couple of months. In fact, two MLAs viz. N. Nimai Singh (Kakching AC) and Nursanglur (Tipaimukh AC) did not attend the aforementioned meeting which was very significant from the point of view of the tussle between the opposition and the ruling benches.[63] Besides, the differences between the BJP and the Congress (I) national bodies were all too great to achieve even a semblance of being allies between them at the State level. They may come together once in a while in connection with certain national and State issues but not in day-to-day politics. Indeed, one of the dominant congress leaders at that time openly proclaimed that "the two parties will never go together."[64]

Following these developments, the relation among the parties in opposition, particularly between the Congress and the BJP became all the more strained. They started criticising against each other. The State President of BJP, M. Bhorot Singh also openly claimed that the day the MSCP led coalition ministry fell, the Congress will also get split and many Congress MLAs will come over to the side of the BJP.[65] All these meant that the major parties in opposition were fighting against each other instead of fighting the ruling parties.

The weakness and division among the opposition parties were exposed all over again during the Kieshamthong assembly by-election.[66] Both the BJP and the Congress put up their own respective candidates. In the election the MPP one of the opposition parties supported the BJP. The decision of the (MPP) made the Congress (I) leaders very furious. The Congress leader and former CM Rishang Kieshing said that "the Manipur People Party, MPP, is a party without having any coherent ideology."[67] All these developments are further evidences of the failure of the opposition to work united against the ruling side. Differences abound them all the time.

The strained relation among the opposition parties continued till November 2000. However, a change came in December 2000. Three ruling MLAs - one from MSCP and two from FPM, defected and joined the opposition camp on December 3, 2000.[68] The two defected MLAs from FPM formed a new party called Progressive Federal Party of Manipur (PFPM).[69] At this moment the Congress (I) also split got reduce its MLA to one (Rishang Keishing, the former CM) in the State assembly on December 8, 2000. The breakaway group of the Congress (I) numbering 10 was headed by Radhabinod Koijam. They formed a new party called the Manipur Regional Congress Party (MRCP). This group subsequently entered into a new political alliance dubbed as the Manipur Democratic Front (MDF) comprising of six parties i.e. the MRCP, BJP, PFPM, MPP, SAP and JD (S). The strength of the ruling and opposition about this time was 35 and 24 respectively. While the ruling side comprised MSCP (30 MLAs), FPM (4 MLAs) and one Independent, the opposition comprised MRCP - 10 MLAs, BJP - 6 MLAs, PFPM- 2 MLAs, MPP - 1 MLA, SAP - 1 MLA, JD (S) - 1 MLA and Congress - 1 MLA.[70]

The new development suddenly changed the equation of opposition and ruling parties. About the parties in opposition, the relationship between the Congress (I) and the MDF became very bad. It was obviously because of the fact that the MRCP, dominant party within the latter was formed by 10 former MLAs of the Congress. The lone Congress MLA, Rishang Keishing also said that he did no longer support the opposition campers' strategy to topple the government.[71] But the MDF did not bother to listen to the lone MLA. Instead, it tried all the possible means to pull down the UF government, and forming a new government become its main agenda. It gave its best efforts to break the ruling parties specially the MSCP in order to overthrow the UF ministry. As a part of this venture, the MRCP and

PFPM merged with the SAP. This meant that the number of the SAP got increased to 13 from one. The central leader of SAP, Jaya Jaitley welcomed the new members of the party and expressed the hope that with the new strength, it would be able to serve the people of Manipur in a better way.[72] In fact, the SAP had started harbouring the ambition of forming a new ministry led by it. But, a new problem emerged among the parties in opposition. This was in relation to the question who will be the leader of the new Front. The MDF held a meeting on 16th January , 2001 and decided to keep the question of its leadership open for the time being. This was in addition to the fact that without support from some of the MLAs on ruling side they were not in a position to stake their claim to form a new ministry.[73] The MDF really needed some ruling MLAs to topple the government. The opposition parties were fighting for power not for the people of Manipur but for them.

Relation among the parties in opposition during the Samata Party led Peoples' Front Ministry (2001-01)

The struggle for power between the ruling UF and the MDF or the opposition sans the Congress (I) continued for the next three months. The constituent units of the UF for once could sustain their togetherness. Of course, it goes without saying that they succeeded in it not because of any other shared interest or ideology but that of looking for an opportunity to be a part of the government which they wanted to form by overthrowing the existing one. During this period neither the ruling side remembered to run the government nor the opposition remembered to be the vanguard of the public interests against possible onslaughts to it by the government.

Ultimately, the MDF succeeded luring eight MLAs from the ruling side and on 11th February, 2001 the strength of the UF ministry got reduced to 27 in the house of 60.[74] After two days, in a dramatic development, the leading party in the MDF joined hands with ruling parties to stake claim to form a new ministry. They formed a new alliance called as People's Front having 39 MLAs (MSCP - 22, FPM - 4, SAP - 12 and one Independent). Subsequently Radhabinod Koijam was sworn in as the new CM of Manipur on 15th February, 2001.[75]

The new political development in Manipur shows clearly that in politics there is no a permanent friend or foe. This is very much correct in Manipur. The SAP was very critical about the MSCP when they were in opposition but suddenly they become good friends and decided to work together. This proves the unprincipled nature of the parties in opposition. They had no hesitation in joining hands with those whom they criticised by saying all sort of things if such an alliance will allow them have their share of the power of the government.

It is also interesting to note here that the SAP was an important ally of NDA led by BJP at the centre. Yet, in Manipur the SAP ruled and the BJP sat in the opposition. During this time the politics of Manipur was really confusing. The political parties and leaders seemed to forget that they were running the affairs of the State. The political parties both in the opposition and the ruling front were only interested in gaining power. The composition and solidarity of the opposition continued to be as fluid as ever. Later, the lone Janata Dal (secular) legislator in Manipur Assembly, Dr Loken Singh, deserted the opposition camp and joined the United Democratic Alliance led by Radhabinod Koijam of the Samata Party raising UDA's strength to 40 in the 59-member assembly.[76]

About this time, the MSCP faction headed by ex-union minister Th. Chaoba (the other led by W. Nipamacha having already joined the Radhabinod Koijam led coalition ministry) formed a new party called the Progressive Manipur State Congress Party (PMSCP)[77] and merged with the BJP. With the merger of the PMSCP with BJP, BJP became the single largest party with the strength of 26 MLAs in the assembly though it had only six after the 2000 assembly elections.[78] With the new development the opposition side was left with the BJP having 26 MLAs and the lone Congress (I) MLA.

The lone opposition member, the former CM Rishang Kieshing called for dissolution of the 7th Manipur State Legislative Assembly, to pave way for a fresh mandate and renew mandate of the people. He further said that the MLAs of the State lost the faith of the people because of the unscrupulous and mercenary shifts in their loyalty.[79] He also observed that "lust for power was behind the frequent splitting of political parties in the State, and the consequent instability of the government."[80]

The fragile and instable nature of State politics continued unabated in the following months. The CM dropped six ministers from the council of ministers on the ground of charges of corruption and having nexus with underground elements. As a reaction to the action of the CM, seven ministers and two parties—FPM and NCP withdrew their support from the ruling People's Front government. They said that the reason for their withdrawal was the dropping of six ministers of the Front by the CM from the council of ministers without giving any reason. According to them the action of the CM weakens the Front partnership rather than strengthening it. They also demanded the resignation of the Radhabinod government claiming that it has been reduced to minority. As a consequence a no-confidence motion was brought in the assembly against the government on May 21, 2001. The motion was supported by 39 MLAs as against 17 MLAs voting against it. Following this, the Radhabinod ministry resigned. Those who voted for the motion were SAP - 12, MPP - 1, Independent - 1 and MSCP - 1. Those who voted against were BJP - 24, FPM - 2, NCP - 2, MSCP - 10, and JD (S) - 1. These 39 MLAs held a meeting on the same day and formed a new alliance called the Progressive Democratic Alliance (PDA).[81]

It may be noted here that the developments in the State had adverse effects inside the NDA at the centre. The relation between the SAP and BJP got considerably strained at the centre as the BJP had a major hand in the overthrow of the Samata Party led coalition in the State. However, the national leaders of the two parties exercised restraint and with their intervention the tension got somewhat eased with both deciding not to stake a claim to form a new government in Manipur.

At this crucial juncture the Speaker, Dr Dhananjoy staked his claim to form a new government, a move which was withdrawn in no time.[82] The political crisis was ended finally with the imposition of PR from June 2, 2001 in Manipur and the assembly was kept under animated suspension.[83] The PR continued till the ushering in of the SPF coalition ministry of the Congress (I), CPI, MSCP and NCP led by Shri O. Ibobi Singh of the Congress (I) after the Eight State Assembly Election held in February 2002.

During the Presidents' Rule many unwanted incidents happened in Manipur. In the second week of June, 2001 there were lots of protests, rallies and processions against the leaders and political establishment of Manipur in view of the extension of the ceasefire between the NSCN-IM and the Government of India without territorial limit. The extension of the ceasefire to Manipur was considered by the public as a direct affront to the territorial integrity of the State, and direct fallout of the fluid political situation gripping the State. The MLAs and the political leaders became the target of the people's criticism, anger and frustration. The people of Manipur thought that they were responsible for all the problems faced by the State as they remained continuously engaged in splits, mergers, breaking up of ministries, formation of new ministries, changing their political loyalties every now and then in their unscrupulous pursuit of power and in utter oblivion to the danger the Indo-NSCN (IM) have been posing to the unity and integrity of the State.

The situation became very tense and complex as the public's anger turned towards the MLAs and politicians. The anti-ceasefire agitators burned down the State Assembly Secretariat, chief minister officials' residence, office of the political parties including that of the MSCP, BJP, Congress (I), SAP and MPP on 18th June, 2001. 14 MLAs including the Speaker were also injured during the public lash out. The State forces tried their best to control the situation. They opened fire to the agitators to control the situation killing 14 protestors and injuring more than 50. Four more people succumbed to the injuries later. The government imposed curfew in the valley. The situation calmed down only after the central government dropped the clause 'without territorial limit' from the cease-fire agreement. The anti-ceasefire protests, agitations, etc. continued for months even after this.[84]

The agitations subsided by the end of 2001. By then it became clear to everyone that a mid-tem poll was inevitable. The parties also realized that the central government would not revoke the PR until a fresh mandate. So they started preparations for a mid-term election. The former CM W. Nipamacha Singh of the MSCP floated a new party called Manipur People's Conference (MPC) on 5th October 2001. At the same time the Democratic Revolutionary Peoples Party (DRPP) which was formed in 12th July, 1999 was renamed as the 'Democratic People's Party (DPP)' on 7th October, 2001. The DPP declared to fill up the political vacuum created after the ceasefire extension in the State and to bring about a political revolution in the State.[85] Meanwhile, the Election Commission of India also announced the 8th Manipur Legislative Assembly elections to be held on 14 and 21st February, 2002.

Before one proceeds further, it may be noted here that when the result of the previous State assembly election was out and a new ministry was formed, the parties in opposition were the Congress (I), BJP, MPP, JD (S), JD (U) and SAP. Later, after frequent floor crossings, splits and mergers, only one lone MLA of the Congress (I) remained in the opposition on the eve of the elections. This meant there was only one party in opposition when the new elections were announced. Having utterly failed to maintain even a semblance of unity or coordination among them during the tenure of the seventh assembly, it was not so surprising to find that none of these parties went together when the new elections were announced. All the parties inside the State for that matter contested the election separately. It means both the opposition and the ruling parties in the previous government decided to go alone to the electorate individually. This was quite in contrast to what one witnessed on the eve of the seventh Assembly Elections in connection with which one saw three pre-poll alliances viz. Secular Democratic Alliance (SDA) for the Congress (I), MPP, CPI and JD (S), Manipur Democratic Alliance (MDA) for the BJP, SAP, JD (U) and KNA and the United Front (UF) for the MSCP and FPM. This once again proves the failure of political parties, both as coalition partners as well as parties in opposition to forge a shared meaningful relationship so that they may evolve themselves as significant and meaningful structures of a democratic parliamentary system.

The elections to the eighth State Legislative Assembly were held on 14th and 21st February, 2002. Once again, no party could secure a majority in the house. The Congress (I) was the single largest party with 20 seats and followed by FPM with 13 seats. The verdict forced the political parties to join hands with likeminded parties in order to form a new government in Manipur. The Congress (I) entered into a post-poll alliance with the NCP (3 MLAs), CPI (5 MLAs) and MSCP (7 MLAs). The new alliance was called the Secular Progressive Front (SPF). Eventually, the Congress led SPF formed the new government under the leadership of Shri O. Ibobi Singh on 8th March, 2002.[86]

The opposition parties comprised six parties namely the FPM - 13 MLAs, BJP - 4 MLAs, SAP - 3 MLAs, MPP - 2 MLAs, DPP - 2 MLAs and MNC - 1 MLA. Of these, the BJP, SAP, MPP and FPM formed an alliance called Democratic People's Alliance (DPA).[87] The main objective of the alliance was to topple the new government. In fact, the DPA even released a 30 point Common Minimum Programme to be implemented if and when it comes to power. The agenda includes the territorial integrity and unity of Manipur, peace talk with the militants without any pre-condition, inter-ethnic council, sport policy, etc.[88] It also proclaimed, at least in words, its intention to play the role of a constructive critique of the government. The DPP also declared separately that it was ready to play the role of a constructive opposition and support any pro-people policy adopted by the government.[89] Later, it also joined the DPA. The FPM MLA Shri Chandramani also declared that the DPA will play the role of a constructive opposition by keeping close surveillance over the functioning of the Congress led SPF government minutely.[90] In a similar tone, the ex-CM Shri Radhabinod of the SAP also said that though SAP is in the opposition, it will not seek to dislodge the government. Instead, it will watch and study the performance of the government and will extend support if needed. He further clarified that if the DPA tries to go against the understanding worked out amongst the constituent partners and try to unnecessarily dislodge the government then SAP will distance itself from the DPA.[91] Thus, at least for once, the parties in opposition seemed to have together resolved to play the role of a constructive opposition in the years to come.

Conclusion and Summary

In a democratic setup one or more parties form the government and the remaining party or parties become the opposition of the government. It is universally accepted that parliamentary democracy can function on healthy lines only when there is a powerful and effective opposition to the party in power. The opposition consists of all those political party or parties which as a result of the last general election did not become part of the government. It is an inseparable part of the democratic political system. The absence of oppositional institution virtually meant an authoritarian or totalitarian form of government and not a democratic political system. There can be no democratic government without opposition and a responsible opposition is as important as the party in power in a parliamentarian democracy.

The role of the opposition in a democracy is very broad and comprehensive. The opposition functions as a watch dog of the government. The job of the opposition is to keep the government of the day on its toes by pin pointing its act of commission and omission. Another function of the opposition is to propose, expose, oppose and depose. They are also expected to propose measures which they think is very important but the government have neglected or have not bothered to touch, expose all the misdeeds and lapses on the part of the government to the public, and oppose all the policies and programmes which they consider as harmful, unjust and unreasonable for the people. The interests of democratic governance also demands that it should depose the government if the latter becomes anti-national and work against the interest of the people, and provide an alternative. It also should not only oppose and depose the government but should also co-operate and coordinate the government for the betterment of the people. They should play an effective and responsible role so that the government did not mislead the people.

The tradition of opposition emerged in Manipur before merging into India in 1949. The first democratic government was formed in 1947 under the leadership of Maharaj Kumar Priyobrata Singh. The first opposition party in Manipur was the Manipur State Congress. Coming to that of the nature of actions and interactions among the parties in opposition inside the State during the period from 1985 to 2002, it can be said that the opposition is expected to play an important role in the politics of Manipur like in any other democratic political system. Yet their role inside the State politics is far from satisfactory and constructive. Most of the time, the oppositions during this period were divided on party lines and they remained engaged more on the struggle for power. In a small State like Manipur it is desirable that all the parties in opposition are united so that they can check the working and movement of the government, and provide an alternative to the people. But most of the time the relation among parties in opposition was not cordial and they remained divided both inside and outside the assembly. They were kept either united or divided by their all consuming passion for gaining power.

They also remained a weak and heterogeneous group, characterised by lack of unity. It usually comprised many parties having different ideologies and beliefs. It makes it difficult for them to work together in pursuit of a common agenda for the people. As a result the relation between and among the opposition parties were often strained and their ability to be a responsible and effective opposition was always weakened. They come together occasionally. Yet the commonality of the opposition parties all the time remained that of the desire to topple the existing ministry so that they may get an opportunity to form the next ministry.

NOTES

1. Patagundi, S.S. The Opposition in the Indian Political System in D. Sundar Ram (ed), *Indian Parliamentary opposition*, Volume I, New Delhi, Kanishka Publishers & Distributors, 1996, p-221
2. As cited by D. Sundar Ram in Ram D. Sundar (ed), *Indian Parliamentary Opposition*, Volume I, New Delhi, Kanishka Publishers& distributors, 1996, p-1f.
3. Barkar, Rodney (ed), *Studies in opposition*, London, Macmillan St Martin's Press, 1971 p-4f.
4. Ogalo, Habil Slade O 'A Healthy Democratic Opposition' *South Asia Politics*, 3 (4), August 2004, p-21
5. Ram, D. Sundar *op. cit.*, p-3.
6. 'Government and Opposition-Roles, Rights and Responsibilities', http://www.thecommonwealth.org/shared_asp_files/uploadedfiles/67F8766B-F6A3-45B1-BC5A-C5B9E2903A49_ TRINIDAD LATEST-OVERVIEWPAPERJUNE2005.
7. Fartyal, H.S. *Role of opposition in the Indian Parliament*, Allahabad, Chaitanya Publishing House, 1971, pp-2f.
8. Dahl, Robert A. (ed), *Political Oppositions in Western Democracies*, New Haven and London, Yale University Press, 1978, pp-333ff
9. H.S. Fartyal, *op. cit.*, p-1
10. Ghita Ionescu and Isabel de Madariaga, *Opposition : Past and Present of a Political Institution*, Middlesex, England, Penguin, 1972, p-21
11. Duveger, Maurice *Political Parties: Their Organization and*

Activity in the Modern State, translated by Barbara and Robert North, London, Methuen & Co Ltd, 1964, p-413.

12. Schmitz, Gerald 'The Opposition in a Parliamentary System' www.parl.gc.ca/information/library/PRBpubs/bp47-e.html, Accessed on 22nd September, 2006.
13. Herr, Richard 'Opposition in a Small Westminster Parliament: The Case of Tasmania' htpp://www.parliament.wa.gov.au/web/webpages.nsf/Webfiles/ASPG+2006-Richard+Herr/$FILE/ASPG+2006-Richard+Herr.pdf , Accessed on 10th December, 2006
14. Ammal, K. Parvathy The Role of Opposition in Indian Legislature in Ram, D. Sundar (Ed) *op.cit.*, pp-154f.
15. Gehlot, N.S. *Opposition in Indian Political System: Problems of Role Perception'* Ram, D. Sundar *op. cit.*, p-179.
16. *Ibid.*
17. N. Joykumar Singh, Social Movement in Manipur (1917-1951), New Delhi, Mittal Publications, 1992, p-109
18. N. Joykumar Singh, Colonialism to Democracy, Guwahati, Spectrum Publication, 2002, p-164
19. Ibid, pp-40ff.
20. http://www.eci.gov.in/StatisticalReports/SE_1984/Statistical%20Report%201984%20Manipur.
21. Ammal, K. Parvathy, *op. cit*.
22. 'Self Style Opposition Front', *The Manipur Mail*, Imphal, January 8, 1985.
23. 'Janata Party Merges with Congress (I) in Manipur' *The Manipur Mail*, Imphal, February 5 1986.
24. Huiyen Lanpao, A Local Manipuri Daily, Imphal, October 23, 1989
25. 'Opposition Weakness Totally exposed', *The Manipur Mail*, Imphal, November 3, 1989.
26. 'Opposition Unity', *The Manipur Mail*, Imphal, January 24, 1990.
27. Sanatomba, N. 'Time will tell', *The Manipur Mail*, Imphal, February 4, 1991
28. 'MPCC (I) to Protest Against Governor', *The Manipur Mail*, Imphal, February 21, 1991.

29. 'CLP (I) to Boycott Governor's Address', *The Manipur Mail*, Imphal, February 23,1991.
30. 'MPP in deep crisis', *The Manipur Mail*, Imphal, February 17, 1991.
31. http://www.eci.gov.in/StatisticalReports/SE_1990/Statistical%20Report%20Manipur%201990.pdf
32. 'Rishang Elected CLP (I) Leader', *The Manipur Mail*, Imphal, December 14, 1994.
33. 'Rishang Group Commands Absolute Majority', *The Manipur Mail*, Imphal December 14, 1994.
34. 'Climax of Crisis: Too Late for Aversion?' *The Manipur Mail*, Imphal, December 24, 1994.
35. 'Climax of Crisis: Too Late for Aversion?' *The Manipur Mail*, December 24th 1994
36. 'Assembly being summoned on January 9', *The Manipur Mail*, Imphal, December 25, 1994.
37. http://www.eci.in/StatisticalReports/SE_1995/StatisticalReport-MR95.pdf
38. Singh, N. Joykumar *Federal Party of Manipur 1993-2000*, Akansha Publishing House, New Delhi, p-61.
39. Pakem, B. *Coalition Politics in North-East India*, Regency Publications, New Delhi,1999, p-94.
40. *Ibid.*
41. *Ibid.*, p. 95.
42. 'MHRC issue being studied', *The Imphal Free Press*, Imphal, March 12, 1997.
43. *Ibid.*
44. '15 CLP members demand change in leadership', *The Imphal Free Press*, November 24, 1997
45. Pakem, B. *op cit*, p-95.
46. 'Nipamacha in, Rishang out', *The Imphal Free Press*, Imphal, December 16, 1997.
47. 'UF Government wins confidence motion', *The Imphal Free Press*, Imphal, January 13, 1998.
48. "Opposition fails to unite", *The Imphal freee Press*, Imphal, August 8, 1999.
49. 'Opposition tries hard to rope in Congress', *The Imphal Free Press*, Imphal, August 21, 1999.

50. 'Opposition front may live to see Assembly poll', *The Imphal Free Press*, Imphal, September 9, 1999
51. 'Congress admitted into SDF, seat adjustments still to be finalised', *The Imphal Free Press*, Imphal, December 21, 1999.
52. 'SDF manages only 24 common candidates', *The Imphal Free Press*, Imphal, January 18, 2000.
53. Asish Gupta, 'Manipur Assembly Elections', *The Economic and Political Weekly*, New Delhi, March 11, 2000.
54. 'Defectors to form own groups', The Imphal Free Press, Imphal, March 9, 2000.
55. 'Opposition leaders to meet on May 8', *The Imphal Free Press*, Imphal, May 4, 2000
56. 'Opposition demands special session', *The Imphal Free Press*, Imphal, May 9, 2000.
57. 'Opposition prepare for assault on government', *The Imphal Free Press*, Imphal, May 18, 2000.
58. 'Opposition sloppiness strengthening ruling front', *The Imphal Free Press*, Imphal, June 14, 2000
59. 'MDA and company declare allegiance to Speaker', *The Imphal Free Press*, Imphal, June 19, 2000.
60. Opposition MLAs formally seek disqualification of 9 ruling MLAs', *The Imphal Free Press*, Imphal, June 21, 2000.
61. 'MDA urges PM to have scams probed', *The Imphal Free Press*, Imphal, June 22, 2000.
62. 'Opposition parties draw up government toppling pact over luncheon', *The Imphal Free Press*, Imphal, July 10, 2000.
63. Ibid
64. J Ngathingkhui and Suresh Sharma, 'At the personal level we can ally: Rishang' *The Imphal Free Press*, Imphal, August 10, 2000
65. 'Congress will split the day MSCP does: BJP chief', *The Imphal Free Press*, Imphal, August 20, 2000
66. A by-election was held on 29th September 2000 in the Kieshamthong constituency due to the untimely demise of the Keishamthong MLA, Dr L. Bhiegyachandra of the FPM.
67. 'MPP is a party without ideology: Rishang', *The Imphal Free Press*, Imphal, September 25, 2000.

68. 'Three MLAs ditch ruling camp', *The Imphal Free Press*, Imphal, December4, 2000
69. 'UF government's funeral closing in: O Joy', *The Imphal Free Press*, Imphal, December 5, 2000
70. 'Congress splits in opposition power gambit', *The Imphal Free Press*, Imphal, December 9, 2000.
71. 'Rishang to sever ties with opposition', *The Imphal Free Press*, Imphal, December 30, 2000.
72. 'Haokholet and Jayenta also jump onto Samata bandwagon', *The Imphal Free*, Imphal, January 6, 2001
73. 'Leadership issue in opposition MDF still unsettled', *The Imphal Free*, Imphal, January 17, 2001
74. 'Manipur ministry reduced to minority' www.tribuneindia.com/2001/20020212/nation.htm#1
75. 'Nipamacha Singh resign; new alliance in Manipur' www.rediff.com/news/2001/feb/13mani1.htm, also 'Koijam sworn in CM' www.tribuneindia.com/2001/20010216/nation.htm#5 Accessed on 12. 12. 08 also 'Nipamacha steps down, RB steps in',*The Imphal Free* , Imphal, February 14, 2001
76. 'Lone JD (S) legislator joins new alliance in Manipur', http://in.rediff.com/news/2001/feb/14mani.htm, Accessed on December 12, 2008
77. 'MSCP splits to form new group', *The Imphal Frees Press*, Imphal, May 9, 2001
78. 'Merger okayed, BJP seat to be largest party in assembly', *The Imphal Frees Press*, Imphal, May 14,01
79. 'Rishang for seeking fresh mandate', *The Imphal Frees Press*, Imphal, May 16, 2001
80. 'Rishang and Nipamacha chastise State politicians', *The Imphal Frees Press*, Imphal, May 21, 2001
81. *The Imphal Free Press*, 7th Anniversary Special Supplement, p. 54.
82. 'Speaker formally withdraws stake, PDA prepares to spring back after possible PR', The Imphal Frees Press, Imphal, May 31, 2001, also *Economic and Political Weekly* June 9, 2001
83. Manipur placed under President's Rule', *The Imphal Frees Press*, Imphal, June 4, 2001.
84. 'Sarjan Yumnam, 'The countdown to Manipur Assembly's Election', The Liberty Post: The Northeast Profile, October 15-31, 2001, p-7f

85. *Ibid.*
86. 'Congress led 30-strong alliance formed' http://www.e-pao.net/epRelatedNews.asp?heading=1&scr=270202 also see: 'O Ibobi elected chief unanimously' http://www.e-pao.net/epRelatedNews.asp?heading=1&scr=280202. Also see John Parrat and Saroj Arambam Parrat 'A new beginning? Manipur State Elections :2002' *South Asia Research*, 23 (1) May 2003 pp. 99ff.
87. 'DPP joins opposition alliance', *The Sangai Express*, Imphal, March 8, 2002.
88. 'DPA sets down agenda for governance', The Sangai Express, Imphal, November 9, 2002.
89. *Ibid.*
90. 'Optimism still reigns in DPA', *The Sangai Express*, Imphal, March 10, 2002
91. 'SPF will disintegrate on its own: RB', *The Sangai Express*, Imphal, March 14, 2002

5

Relationship between the Ruling and Opposition Parties

Introduction

A classical parliamentary democracy consists of elected representatives, a cabinet headed by a Prime Minister and an organized opposition within the parliament. It is assumed that the majority party or parties would form the government and the minority party or parties would function as the opposition. In democracy both the government and the opposition function with an aim to achieve a goal i.e. the welfare of the people.[1] It requires a good relation between them, and the co-operation, coordination and consultation between the government and the opposition on the national and states issues is a must. As such, the success of a democracy largely depends on the nature of relation between the ruling and the opposition.

The relationship between the ruling and opposition parties in Manipur is characterized by both elements of friendly cooperation as well as conflicting rivalry. There are certain issues which confronts the state and its people in connection with which they cooperate, co-ordinate, support and consult each other. At the same time, they have different opinions on many other issues of the state. They have had diametrically opposite views on several issues. Moreover, both the ruling and opposition parties often got involved in bitter struggles for power every now and then. Instances of the opposition parties trying to destabilize the ministry are all too frequent. Similarly, the ruling parties also often try to weaken the opposition parties by either breaking the opposition alliance or bringing party or parties from the opposition parties into their fold. These endeavors from both sides often lead to strained relationship between the two. The present chapter is an attempt to deal with the nature and dynamics of the relationship between the ruling and opposition parties in Manipur from 1985 to 2002 in all its comprehensiveness with the main focus being given on the conflicts or cooperation between them on basic issues, and their efforts to consolidate themselves or destabilize the other, etc.

Relationship between the Ruling and Opposition from 1985-90

Relationship between the Ruling and Opposition during the Congress-led Ministry 1985-88

The Fourth State Assembly Election was held in the last part of 1984. No party could win a clear majority in the election. However, Congress (I) won half of the seats, i.e. 30 out of 60 seats. Subsequently, the Congress (I) formed a government on January 4, 1985 under the leadership of Shri Rishang Keishing with the support of four Independent MLAs. The opposition parties comprised CPI - 1 MLA, Janata Party (JNP) - 4 MLAs, Kuki National Assembly (KNA) - 1 MLA and Manipur People's Party (MPP) - 3 MLAs.[2] The relation between the ruling and the opposition during the time was somewhat strained from the very beginning. This was mainly on account of their respective efforts to gain an upper hand in the struggle for power. The ruling party lost no time in trying to woo a number of MLAs from the opposition parties. The opposition parties, at the same time, also tried their best to destabilize the ministry.

What happened was that the Chief Minister was not so confident about the strength of his ministry in the legislature in spite of the support from 34 MLAs (30 congress + four Independents) in the House of 60 MLAs. Therefore the ruling party put their best efforts to encourage defection from the side of the opposition. Their efforts did not go in vain as they managed to convince the four Janata MLAs in the opposition. These MLAs joined the Congress (I). It may be remembered here that the Janata Party had four MLAs in the assembly at that time and their joining the Congress gave the impression that the Janata party got merged into the Congress. With this the strength of the Congress MLAs increased to 39. The ruling party also wanted the MLAs from the KNA and the MPP to merge with them.[3] The developments meant that the relationship between the ruling and the opposition in general and between the Congress and the State Unit of Janata Party in particular got strained.

The then President of the Manipur State Unit of the Janata Party Shri W. Kulabidhu Singh, clarified that the unit has not merged with the Congress (I) and the merger decision was the individual decision. He alleged that the defection by the four MLAs was untenable and against the spirit of the Anti-defection Law. He also criticized the state government for encouraging defection of MLAs and engaging in political horse-trading instead of trying to solve the deteriorating law and order situation and the hardships suffered by the general public because of unemployment, water scarcity, price hike, etc.[4] The President also filed a case before the Supreme Court challenging the admission of the four Janata Party MLAs into the Congress (I). He also had earlier submitted a case before the Gauhati High Court regarding the matter. However the case was rejected on the ground that courts were not supposed to inquire into proceedings of the legislature.[5]

Relationship between the ruling and opposition during the Congress led ministry 1988-90

As months went by, the relation between the ruling and the opposition got worsened. This was all the more evident during the time of Sagolband AC by-election in June and 1988. It may be noted here that the by-election was due to the resignation of Shri Salam Damodar Singh so that the CM Shri R. K. Jaichandra Singh can contest and become a member of the legislative assembly.[6] R. K Jaichandra was not a member of the Assembly when he became the CM of Manipur. He contested the election. The opposition parties also put up a common candidate Shri Moirangthem Kumar Singh of the MPP. The move from the side of the opposition to put up a common candidate with a view to defeat the Congress candidate was criticized by the then Joint Secretary, AICC, A. R Mallu, by describing it as an unholy alliance by parties bound only by their common interest of defeating the Congress. He taunted the opposition parties by saying how this will succeed in uniting "parties like the Janata, CPI (M), BJP, CPI and other regional parties which had different colors and problems?"[7]

The by-election was a straight fight by two candidates, one for the opposition and the other for the ruling. As the poll day got nearer, the ruling party kept on attacking the opposition as much as it could. The Congress MP, Shri N. Tombi Singh from the Inner Parliamentary Constituency said in his election speech that opposition unity was nonexistent and the opposition was too weak to be a force to reckon with. He further remarked that issues like inclusion of the Manipuri language in the Eighth Schedule should not be reduced to cheap election slogan as the opposition was doing. He also said that Congress party put up this issue above narrow party politics and cheap election stunts.[8] The by-election was won by the Congress (I) and the party observed that the victory has disproved the notion of a united opposition having the capacity to defeat the Congress party.[9]

A scandal also erupted in the state about this time over the issue of the budget concerning the purchase of fire extinguishers in July 1988. The opposition parties demanded to institute an enquiry commission to look into the scandals. The scandal seemed to bring an opportunity for the opposition to criticize and attack the government. The assembly was also in session at that time. As such, the opposition party had the advantage of raising the issue in the House. It demanded a high level independent enquiry committee to be instituted to look into the scandal. Heated discussions followed between the ruling and the opposition parties in the House. The ruling party refused to institute the committee. As a result, the opposition parties walked out of the House in protest against the refusal of the government to institute the enquiry commission.[10]

The strained relationship between the opposition and the ruling party continued unabated for the rest of the session. The ruling and the opposition parties also had major differences in the matter of the Budget, 1989-90. The opposition was not satisfied with the financial statement of the government. In the Budget session most of the time there were heated arguments between them. On 17th April, 1989 the Manipur Legislative Assembly passed the State Budget amounting to Rs 429,33,14,000 for the year 1989-90 after a heated debate between the ruling and the opposition parties. Just before the passing of the Manipur Appropriation (No.3) Bill, 1989, the members of the opposition parties, Shri O. Joy Singh, MPP and Dr M. Nara, CPI walked out of the House in protest against the ruling of the Speaker, who did not allow their proposal to discuss the allegation of financial mismanagement committed by the State Government.[11] The demand of the opposition parties were not allowed to be discussed in most of the cases. The ruling and opposition then got involved in serious arguments over the issue of a major flood which seriously affected the state that year. There were heated arguments between the two on the issue of admitting a call attention motion moved by Shri O. Joy Singh in the State Assembly.[12] The CM Shri Jaichandra boldly accepted the challenge thrown by the opposition member Shri O. Joy Singh of the MPP to have a debate on the issue. The entire episode was a clear evidence of the confrontationist stand both the ruling and opposition parties adopted towards one another.

The ruling and the opposition parties never lose a chance to criticize one another. The attack or criticism became worse as the day of the 9th Lok Sabha election approached. Both would usually try to win over the voters by highlighting the weakness of the other party or candidate. The ruling party Congress (I) charged the Independent candidates and the opposition parties for making the defeat of the Congress as their sole agenda thereby sidetracking other basic issues involved in the elections. It also criticized the opposition parties for defeating two very important bills for the people in the Rajya Sabha viz., the Panchayati Raj and the Nagarpalika Bills.[13] The party also attacked the parties in opposition individually one by one. It contended that the BJP had an insignificant number in the Lok Sabha, and that supporting them will be an exercise in futility. It also remarked that "under no circumstances Manipur voters can support such a party so remote from power and indulging in rank communalism."[14]

The party further remarked that CPI had very less number in the Lok Sabha and Manipur cannot afford to waste her voice by supporting them in this crucial situation. About the Janata Dal, the Congress (I) said that it does not exist in Manipur. They also attacked the MPP. They said that MPP is a local party and as such insignificant in the parliamentary politics. The Congress not only showed the weakness of the parties in opposition one after another but also highlighted the problems within the opposition. It said that the opposition parties like the BJP, CPI, JD, and MPP contesting the election on their own clearly shows the failure of the opposition unity.[15]

It may also be noted here that the inclusion of Manipuri language in the Eight Schedule of the Constitution was one demand which all the parties made during the election. All the parties which were there in Manipur during the time irrespective of their party differences took the same stand that they will put their best efforts to include the Manipuri language into the eighth schedule. However, they blamed each other on the issue. The CM Shri R.K Jaichandra warned the opposition parties not to try to gain political mileage out of language issue. Asking the opposition what they have done for the Manipuri language, he alleged that the opposition parties did nothing for the language except shouting slogans in some public meetings.[16]

The opposition, at the same time also blamed the ruling party for neglecting the issue. In the meantime, one Independent candidate, Shri Chingshubam Akaba, even promised that if the people choose and elect him then he'll speak the official language of Manipur i.e. the Manipuri, in the Parliament and pledged to fight unto the last if other communities try to stop him.[17] Ultimately, both the seats in Manipur were won by Congress (I). However Congress (I) could not form the government in Delhi. A coalition government was formed by the National Front (NF) under the leadership of Shri V.P Singh from the JD.

The installation of the NF Government in Delhi suddenly changed the political atmosphere of the country. Manipur was not an exception in this matter. The opposition parties in Manipur got a moral boost and felt energetic. They started attacking the ruling party very strongly. In the meantime, the general election for the state assembly was scheduled to be held in February, 1990. So, the opposition started flexing its muscle. Its members started criticizing each and every move of the government. The Government responded by saying that it would be far better if the opposition starts devising good policies and programs for the benefit of the people, and that indulging in mudslinging and character assassination will not them in winning elections. Describing the National Front ministry at the Center as an experiment in the field of united opposition, the Congress said that such coalitions may work in small countries such as Switzerland, Sweden, etc. but not in large countries like India.

Along with its criticism against all the opposition parties, the Congress also went on highlighting its achievements saying that it had created several job opportunities for youths through planning, that it has been instrumental in raising the literacy rate of the state to 41.35 which was higher than the national level. More education means eradication of illiteracy, ignorance and poverty. These are all because of the Congress party.[18]

Relationship between the Ruling and Opposition from 1990-95

Relationship between the Ruling and Opposition during the MPP-led ULP Ministry 1990-92

The Fifth Manipur State Legislative Assembly election was held on February 12, 1990. In the election no political party joined hands with another party to contest the election. It means that there was no pre-poll alliance in the election. In the election no party secured a working majority. The party wise break up of the election result was Congress (I) - 24, CPI - 3, Congress (S) - 4, JD - 11, KNA - 2, MPP - 9 and NPP - 1.[19] The mandate of the election gave a chance to the political parties for horse trading. All the parties put up their best efforts to forge a post-poll alliance with other parties so that they may form a new government. Finally, all the parties except the Congress (I) formed an alliance called the United Legislature Front (ULF). As the party which won maximum number of seats in the elections, the Congress expected the Governor to invite it to form the ministry. To their utter frustration or disappointment, the Governor invited the ULF to form the government. Thus, a new coalition government was installed in Manipur under the banner of ULF ministry led by Shri R. K. Ranbir Singh of the MPP.

The relation between the ruling parties and the opposition party looked to be very good in the beginning of the tenure of the ULF ministry. The opposition declared its readiness to cooperate with the ruling side. Yet, bickering started soon with the ex-chief minister, Shri R.K. Jaichandra Singh, alleging that the Governor of Manipur was pressurized by the centre to invite the ULF to form government in Manipur. He felt that the Congress (I) being the largest party in Manipur should have been invited to form the government. Still, the Congress, as the party in opposition said it won't indulge in the game of toppling the ministry so that the people may assess for themselves what the ULP ministry can do for them. It also said that it will play the role of a constructive opposition. The Ex-CM also expressed his doubt that the new government will be stable as it was formed by six parties. He said pulls and counter-pulls are bound to be there when they try to work together closely. The Congress (I) also reiterated that it will continue to fight for the inclusion of Manipuri language in the eighth Schedule of the Indian Constitution and that it will cooperate with the ruling parties if the government needs their help with regard to the inclusion of the Manipuri language in the eighth Schedule.[20]

However, the sequences of events which followed the coming of the ULF Ministry showed that the relation between the two was far from being cordial. The opposition lost no time in trying to pull down the coalition ministry. It openly declared that the ministry won't last long. It requested the Governor to proclaim President's Rule in the state on the ground that the government has failed to maintain law and order.[21] Yet all the efforts of the opposition failed to topple the ministry and the latter could sustain its position of power for some time. One of the ministers even taunted the opposition by saying that the opposition will go mad if the ULF ministry lasts the full term.[22]

As months passed, the relation between the ruling and the opposition deteriorated further. It was mainly due to a crisis within the ruling parties. By February 1991, the ULF ministry became faction ridden and it started showing cracks. In addition to this, the MPP which was leading the coalition ministry faced serious internal crisis. It was because of the differences of opinion among the MPP leaders. The problem of the MPP became very serious when the President of the MPP, Shri Houbam Bhuban Singh suspended the CM Shri R.K. Ranbir Singh from the party on 15th February 1991. To retaliate the suspension a requisition committee meeting attended by MLAs and ministers of the party removed Shri H. Bhubon from the Presidentship of the party and than suspended him along with Shri Kh. Chaoba Singh an ex-minister for six years from the party.[23]At this moment, the opposition tried to take maximum advantage of it. They were in no way about to miss the chance to pull down the government. So, they continued their criticism and attack towards the government with renewed vigor. The opposition parties demanded disqualification of Shri R. K. Ranbir Singh, the CM of Manipur from the membership of the house. It said that Shri R. K. Ranbir deserved to be disqualified from the House under the anti-defection law. Because his party President, Shri H. Bhubon expelled him from the party membership.[24]

The opposition also protested against the style of functioning of the Governor. The Congress party claimed that the head of the state was involved in trying to solve the crisis of a political party. It also reported that the Governor summoned both Shri R. K. Ranbir and Shri H. Bhubon at the Raj Bhavan and asked them to end the tussle. A spokesman of the Congress questioned whether the Governor was the guardian of the MPP or not? He further alleged that the Governor had misused the power vested on him by the constitution.[25] The Congress Legislature Party (CLP) (I) also boycotted the Governor's address on the first day of the state budget session 1991-92 to protest against what they called it as partisan attitude of the Governor. The CLP said that the Governor lowered the prestige of the high office by involving himself in the internal affairs of the MPP.[26]

The criticism and the attack on the government from the opposition party continued and the Congress (I) left no stone unturned in their efforts to form a new government. The opposition party demanded the dismissal of the ULF ministry. The Congress (I) questioned the Speaker, Dr. Borobabu Singh, why he did not declare Shri R. K. Ranbir, the CM as an unattached MLA.[27] Over and above, the opposition party also blamed the Governor of Manipur, Shri Chintamani Panigrahi. According to them, the Governor indulged in petty political affairs drawing him and the gubernatorial post to the political crisis of the state. Shri R. K. Dorendra, the Congress leader informed the press that their party is prepared to support any government formed without Shri R. K. Ranbir Singh, the CM.[28] At the same time, the ruling parties also blamed the Congress for trying to topple the government. The CM Shri R. K. Ranbir Singh criticized the Congress (I) for their ceaseless efforts to topple the government. He further said that it will never be successful.[29]

The crisis within the MPP, the leading party within the coalition ministry, shook the ULF ministry very badly but it managed to survive for some time. The ministry however came to an end when President's Rule was imposed in the state on 7th January, 1992 and the Governor kept the Assembly under animated suspension.

Relationship between the Ruling and Opposition during the Congress-MPP Ministry 1992-93

The Presidents' Rule in the state continued for three months. During the PR all the political parties and their leaders tried to work out an alliance so that they can stake their claim to form a new government. Political parties were negotiating and consulting among themselves to settle for an alliance to form a coalition ministry. In short, they were all busy negotiating and bargaining among themselves with a view to form a ministry.

Politics makes strange bedfellows. This cannot be truer than what happened in the politics of the state. The political parties negotiated for about three months. Then, finally, an understanding between the Congress (I) and the MPP, the two arch rivals till very recently, came to an understanding to work together. Together they demanded the President's rule in the state to be revoked and staked their claim to form a new ministry. Subsequently, a Congress-MPP coalition ministry under the leadership of Shri R. K. Dorendra Singh from the Congress was installed and a 13 member ministry was sworn in on 8th April, 1992.

The relation between the ruling and the opposition parties during the Congress-MPP ministry was overshadowed by the internal conflict within the ruling partners i.e. the Congress (I) and the MPP. The opposition parties became silent observers while the ruling parties were criticizing against each other. The coalition partners did not work like a team and they had internal problems from day one onwards. The bone of contention between the Congress and the MPP was that of the office of Speaker. The Congress (I) wanted to remove Dr. H. Borobabu from the post of the Speaker. However, the MPP was totally against it. Subsequently, the Congress (I) and the MPP started making charges and counter charges against each other openly in the public which obviously meant that the relation between the two coalition partners got serious strained.[30] In the simmering conflict and all holds bared fight between the two, whatever little maneuvers the opposition attempted went unnoticed by the general public.

In spite of all the differences and conflicts between the ruling and the opposition, there was one particular issue on which there was no division between them. The issue was that of the protection of the territorial integrity of the state. It is to be noted here that about this time, there was an increasing threat to the territorial integrity of Manipur. The people of Manipur were becoming more and more acutely aware of the implication the Naga insurgency with its demand for integration of Naga inhabited areas into a single political unit, independent or otherwise, will have on the territorial integrity of the state. Four districts of the state viz. Chandel, Senapati, Tamenglong and Ukhrul were being included in the demand for the unification. Besides, the Naga inhabited areas of Manipur in general and the Tangkhul inhabited areas of Ukhrul were becoming increasingly the mainstay of Naga insurgency since the formation of the NSCN (IM) in 1980.[31]

On this issue all the political parties both on the ruling and opposition side declared that any move to disturb the territorial integrity of Manipur will be opposed by all the political parties in Manipur. This was the reaction from the political parties to the decisive tendencies nurtured by certain insurgent outfits and their resorting to violence to terrorize their opponents. They also called upon all right thinking citizens to oppose all such disintegrating forces in the common interest of the state and protect the basic unity and oneness of the people living inside the state. The Congress (I) flayed the separatist movements demanding homelands and the like to be carved out of the state. The CM, Sri R. K. Dorendra Singh also stated that the divisive forces will be fought with determination and a political will by his government.[32]

Another issue in connection with which all the parties came together was that of the Kuki-Naga clashes in the hills of Manipur which started in the middle of 1992. The clashes which continued till the closing years of the decade were so severe that it claimed about 2000 lives and many more were injured. Many were also maimed for the rest of their lives. About 500 villages were attacked and about 7000 houses were burnt down to ashes. It also led to the displacement of about 15000 families and more than one lakh people.[33] When the clashes broke out, all the parties were unanimous in their condemnation of the clashes.

The young Legislators' Forum, Manipur which had member MLAs from both the ruling and opposition side also came out showing their solidarity with the victims of the clashes. They also took a 12-hour fast for restoration of peace and communal harmony in the hills of the state. A leaflet was also issued by the Forum and appealed to both the communities to eschew violence. It also observed that further continuation of the ethnic strife will hamper the development of the state particularly in the hill of the state.[34]

It may once again be noted that during the period from 1992 to 1993, the ruling-opposition differences or conflicts got sidelined by the persistent problem of intra-coalition conflicts. The Congress (I) and the MPP continued to pull one another's leg though they were in the same ministry. The MPP threatened to quit the ministry. However the Congress branded the threat to withdraw support from the coalition ministry as political gimmick to coerce the leadership to grant them extra benefits in the form of more ministerial berths. The Congress leaders openly started expressing their displeasure over the sharing of power with the MPP. They felt that the two parties had diametrical views on every matter.[35] The problem within the ruling parties was not over there. The Congress leader, former CM R. K. Jaichandra Singh met the Governor with some MLAs and told the Governor that the law and order situation in Manipur was at its worse as the government failed to check the then ongoing clashes. He said that the Congress-MPP ministry should be dismissed without any delay to check the deteriorating law and order situation in the state. He further demanded immediate intervention by the centre in the state affairs.[36] The situation continued for some time till the midnight of December 31, 1993, when President's Rule was declared for the state. Following this, the Governor took charge of the state administration and kept the assembly under animated suspension.

Relationship between the Ruling and Opposition during the Congress-led Coalition Ministry (1994-95)

The President's Rule was lifted on 12 December 1994 with the formation of a new ministry on this day. The ministry was once again a coalition ministry comprising the Congress (I) - 25, Congress (S) - 4, Janata Dal - 7 and KNA - 1 and was headed by the Shri Rishang Keishing of the Congress (I). This meant that the MPP which was a coalition partner with the Congress (I) in the previous ministry was now in the opposition. The constant conflicts between the two led to the downfall of the previous ministry. Now as the two were on the opposite sides of the house, the relationship got further worsened.

Once again conflict between the two centered round the office of the Speaker. The Speaker, Dr. H. Borobabu an MLA from the MPP and he was appointed as the Speaker when the MPP was a coalition partner in the previous ministry. Now the Congress (I) wanted to remove Dr. H. Borobabu Singh from the post of Speaker of the House. According to the Congress (I) party, the Speaker had lavishly utilized the power entitled to him under the 10th Schedule of the Indian Constitution.[37] At this crucial juncture, the Secretary of the Manipur Assembly Shri N. Hera with the Speaker's directive, sent show cause notice to 31 MLAs asking why they should not be disqualified.[38] The moved of the Speaker was supported by the main opposition party i.e., the MPP, the party he belongs to. The speaker ultimately, disqualified 23 MLAs from the House of 60.[39] The Manipur Assembly was scheduled to meet on December 23 to prove the strength of majority of the Congress led ministry in the House. On this day, many unprecedented things happened in the history of parliamentary democracy in the state. The session continued without the treasury bench. It also started without the Governor's address. The opposition declared that they have won the no-confidence motion.[40] The decision taken by the opposition parties on the controversial one-day session was not accepted by the Governor of Manipur. The Governor called a one day state assembly session on 9th January, 1995 so that the ministry could prove its strength in the House.[41] In the meantime the Gauhati High Court stayed the expulsion of the 23 MLAs from the assembly. This ultimately helped the Congress (I) led coalition ministry to win the no-confidence motion. It also replaced the Speaker Dr. H. Borobabu by W. Angou Singh. The ministry lasted till the next assembly election which was already scheduled to be held in February 1995. This enabled the Congress (I) to face the elections while being in power.

Before one proceeds further, certain things may be noted here. The relation between the ruling and the opposition was always a strained and conflicting one. More often than not, the office of the speaker was at the center of the conflict. The speaker failed to transcend his part affiliations and often exercised the power given to him by the 10th Schedule of the constitution in such a manner that will help his own party, i.e. the MPP. Another point that may be noted here is that Congress led coalition ministry at the center revoked the PR in Manipur when assembly elections were knocking at the door (around two months before the expiry of the assembly term). This meant that the Congress wanted to contest the state assembly elections as the party in power.

Relationship between the Ruling and Opposition from 1995-2000

Relationship between the Ruling and Opposition during the Congress led JLP Ministry 1995-97

The Sixth Manipur Legislative Assembly Elections were held in February, 1995. In the election, pre-poll alliances were not made among the political parties. All the political parties contested the election alone without any alliance or having any seat adjustment or seat sharing with other parties. The verdict of the election was a hung assembly. No party was able to secure majority in the House. Once again the environment was ripe for political horse trading among the parties. All the parties got busy in consulting and negotiating among themselves to forge post-poll alliances in their pursuit for the all important "power". Finally, the group headed by the MPP formed a post-poll alliance with the JD, CPI, SAP, NPP and ICS under the banner 'United Legislature Front (ULF)'. The strength of the six individual parties in the Front was MPP - 18, JD - 7, CPI - 2, SAP - 2, NPP - 2 and the Congress (S) - 1. Having amassed the required number, the Front staked their claim to form a ministry. Interestingly enough, about the same time the Congress also staked its claim to form the government claiming that it had the necessary number. Ultimately, the Congress won the battle for power and formed a new Congress led coalition government under the leadership of Shri Rishang Keishing on 25th February, 1995.

What actually happened was that some members of the ULF changed their side just before the installation of the government. This was possible through splits of party. The seven MLAs of the JD split into three. One group was called as Progressive JD having four MLAs, another group called as JD (Sephu Group) having one MLA and the original

JD was left with two MLAs. The ruling parties also formed an alliance known as 'Joint Legislature Party' (JLP) comprising the Congress (I) - 22, Progressive JD - 4, NPP - 2, SAP - 2, JD (Sephu Group) - 1, Congress (S) - 1, FPM - 2, and Independent - 3. It means the NPP, Congress (S) and the SAP changed its loyalty to the JLP and the newly formed parties i.e. the Progressive JD and JD (Sephu group) also supported it. The ULF was left with the MPP - 18, CPI - 2 and JD - 2. The lone BJP member did not support either side.[42]

The political atmosphere during the time was very fragile. The relation between the ruling and the opposition parties was very competitive as both tried to gain political power. The MLAs also kept on changing the sides of their support which meant that even after the formation of ministry by the JLP, the struggle for power was not over. The struggle for power created a conflicting situation between the ruling and the opposition parties. Both tried to lure away MLAs from the other side.

Soon after the formation of the JLP ministry, 10 MLAs from it again left the government. These included one Independent and nine MLAs from Progressive JD, NPP, SAP, FPM, JD (Sephu). They formed another opposition front called the United Democratic Front (UDF) as different from the other existing opposition group, i.e. the ULP. Accordingly, a no-confidence motion was brought against the Keishing coalition ministry on July 31, 1995. At this crucial moment, the Speaker, W. Nipamacha Singh disqualified five opposition MLAs to give more advantage to the Keishing ministry. With this, the JLP ministry managed just to survive with 27 voting for it, another 26 voting against it and the lone BJP MLA abstaining from voting. The abstinence of the BJP MLA saved the Speaker from having to cast his vote.[43]

The struggle for power was not over even after the no-confidence vote. The opposition parties have had a good chance to dislodge the ministry but they were outsmarted by the ruling side who acted in collaboration with the

Speaker. The defeat made the opposition parties very disappointed. On September 5, 1995, after the bitter experience, they decided to come together as one ULP and put up a combined opposition (with MPP - 18, CPI - 1, JD - 1, FPM - 2, SAP - 1) to the ruling side. By November 23, 1995, they initiated another no-confidence motion. However, the opposition's efforts to dislodge the ministry got another setback when the MPP got split into two. As a result, the motion was defeated by bigger margin of 37 against and only 16 for the motion.[44] It means that even after the two opposition groups joined hands together, they failed on both counts – in consolidating their own solidarity as well as in their efforts to defeat the government. This meant that there was a corresponding increase in the strength of the ruling side. Those opposition members who supported the government during the time of the no-confidence motion later merged with the Congress (I) and became the Congress MLAs.

All the above discussions meant that the relationship between the ruling and the opposition in Manipur so far has been not an ideal one. The relationship was characterized not by elements of mutual-cooperation but was one of conflict because of the never ceasing contest for power. Instead of trying to serve as a vanguard of the public interests and putting a check on the government from going against the interests of the people, the sole motive of the opposition remained to dislodge the ruling party or parties from their position of power and secure the same position for them. It was also always preoccupied with finding faults and highlighting loopholes drawbacks of the ruling side. The ruling side also always tried to encourage defections from the side of the opposition. Such efforts from both side greatly contributed to the strained relationship between the two. The line between the ruling and opposition also often got blurred because of the frequent shifting of loyalties by the parties and the individual MLAs.

The ruling and the opposition side were once again at loggerheads during the budget discussion for the financial years 1997-98. They criticized that the Governor's address lacked the political will to tackle the insurgency problem and maintain the law and order inside the state. It also criticized that the address did not mention anything about the important demands of the people around that time like that of the establishment of a state human rights commission. The CM, Rishang however dismissed the criticism by a master stroke. The CM said that the opposition members were not available for consultation at that time and expressed his regret that the opposition member only took up the matters not mentioned in the address leaving all the important matters mentioned there.[45]

There were, however, occasions when the two sides came together to cooperate, consult and coordinate with each other in connection with certain issues. For instance, the ruling and the opposition came together on the eve of the then Prime Minister I. K. Gujral's visit to Manipur in May, 1997. The CM convened an all-party meeting to discuss the matter to be discussed with the Prime Minister I. K. Gujral when he visits the state. All political parties came in the meeting except the BJP, and agreed to pressurize the Prime Minister to take up immediate action on some common issues like problems of insurgency, implementation of the Shukla Committee recommendation, shifting of the Assam Rifles from Kangla, extension of railway line up to Imphal, protection of territorial integrity, up gradation of Manipur University to a Central University etc.[46]

Overall, there were only a handful of issues on which both the sides agreed with each other. Otherwise, both tended to take a different stand on many issues which might be national or local. Moreover, the local parties had different ideas and interests as different from the national ones. These differences made it difficult for them to accept the standpoints of one another. There was also a tendency on the part of the opposition to support issues which the ruling side did not. A good example of this will be the demand for the creation of a Sadar Hills District. While the government was not ready for the creation of this district, the opposition went ahead with a *dharna* in support of the demand. It stated that the demand for the creation of the new district was supported by all the opposition parties, social organizations and the people and warned the government that further delay will create more complicacies.[47]

By the middle of December 1997, the Congress led JLP ministry fell apart. The fall of the ministry was mainly due to internal faction within the coalition ministry in general and within the Congress (I) which was leading the ministry in particular. About the last part of 1997, 15 Congress MLAs wanted to change the CLP leadership. They also threatened that otherwise more MLAs will be joining the dissident group and its members may increase up to 20.[48] The internal crisis of the Congress become deeper and deeper and it could not be solved even after the interference of the High Command in Delhi. Subsequently, the pro-change group of the Congress led by the Shri W. Nipamacha Singh, the Speaker, engineered a split from the Congress. The splitter group consisted of 23 MLAs and it formed a party called the Manipur Sate Congress Party (MSCP) under the leadership of Shri W. Nipamacha Singh. This was followed by Shri Nipamacha staking his claim to form the government and the Governor summoning a one-day special session on December 15, 1997 to test the strength of the Rishang ministry.[49]

Relationship between the Ruling and Opposition during the MSCP-led UF Ministry 1997-2000

The CM Shri Rishang Keishing tendered his resignation following his defeat during the vote of confidence in the state Assembly on 15th December, 1997. The motion for confidence was defeated by a margin of 22 votes. There were only 16 votes in favour of the motion while the entire opposition having 38 members voted against it. The Governor accepted his resignation.[50] With the fall of Rishang Keishing ministry, a four party (MSCP - 23, MPP - 14, FPM - 2 and CPI - 1) coalition government under the name United Front (UF) Ministry led by Shri Wahengbam Nipamacha Singh was sworn in on 16th December, 1997. This left the Congress (I) as the only party in opposition.

For obvious reasons, the relation between the ruling and opposition party was very strained from the word go. The Congress could not forget that the new ministry was the creation by its own previous MLAs who left the party because of conflicts over the leadership issue of the former JLP ministry which was eventually ousted. The strained relationship got it itself manifested in the form of the entire opposition staging a walk out on 12th January 1998, the day on which vote of confidence for the new ministry was scheduled to take place. The opposition party walked out of the House before voting of the confidence motion took place, protesting against the allegedly undemocratic nature of the proceedings and the failure to follow the parliamentary norms. The leader of the opposition, Shri Radhabinod Koijam protested strongly against the unparliamentarily nature of the proceedings of the House. He complained that the Speaker did not convene the House Business Advisory Committee before taking up any business. This was against the rules and beyond the Speaker's power, he added. The opposition also complained about the failure to move a motion of thanks to the governor's address to the House. The ruling parties however, moved the vote of confidence and passed the motion without the opposition. The Speaker, Shri Babudhon also clarified that the Business Advisory Committee (BAC) would meet only after it was reconstituted.[51]

The period of the UF ministry was known for bankruptcy of the state exchequer. The Government of Manipur was not able to pay even the monthly salary of its employees. The Banks in the capital, Imphal, refused to honor bills for payment of salaries of government employees passed by state treasury office.[52] It was an embarrassing and unfortunate situation for the state government. However, the ruling and the opposition party never sat down together and discussed the matter. Instead, both of them were blaming each other for the crisis. The Government said that the financial problem was due to the previous government. The opposition party, at the same time, also blamed the government for the financial mismanagement of the government.[53] The people of the state especially the common people were having a very difficult time because of the financial crisis. However, politicians did not work together to solve the problem. This was indeed a very unfortunate episode in the history of relationship between the ruling and the opposition in Manipur. Both failed to transcend their own differences and conflicting pursuits even at a time when the entire state and its people were under the grip of a serious financial crisis. Such a conflicting relationship between the two continued till the coming of the next assembly elections in February 2000.

Relationship between the Ruling and Opposition from 2000-02

Relationship between the Ruling and Opposition during the MSCP-led UF Ministry 2000-01

The Seventh Assembly Elections were held in February 2000. On the eve of elections there were altogether three pre-poll alliances among the political parties. They were 1. the Secular Democratic Front (SDF) comprising Congress (I), MPP, CPI and JD (S); 2. the Manipur democratic Alliance (MDA) comprising the BJP, SAP, JD (U), and KNA; and 3. the United Front of Manipur (UF) comprising the MSCP and FPM.[54]

A close examination of the composition of these three alliances revealed that many of the parties which were on the opposite side of the house joined hands together once the new elections were announced. For instance, the MPP and the JD (S) changed its side and tried to fight the elections together with the Congress. The Janata Dal which was there in the previous ministry with the MSCP also sided with the Congress to fight against its former ally. Such state of things once again proves the fact that shifting loyalties and alliances by the parties has been a lasting feature of the party system in Manipur and this significantly contributes to the thin line between the ruling and opposition sides.

The UF alliance secured the maximum number of seats with 29 out of 60 in the election. However it was short of two to get majority. The leaders of the UF started looking for some MLAs to get the required majority and form a new government. They somehow managed to win over the four NCP and three MPP MLAs. This meant that there were no members left in assembly to represent the two parties though they together won seven seats during the elections. One RJD and one independent MLA also decided to support the UF.

The MPP and NCP immediately started severely criticizing the MSCP. They charged the MSCP of "kidnapping" and hijacking their MLAs. The MPP alleged that the MSCP has kidnapped and confined their MLAs in the Chief Minister's official bungalow.[55] The NCP also sought the intervention of the Governor in connection with the 'abduction' of four of its newly elected MLAs by the MSCP.[56] At this moment, the MDA was also pondering as to whether to accept the offer of the UF or not regarding the formation of a new government.[57] Here it may be remembered that the MSCP was a partner of the NDA ministry at the center led by the BJP and the then the lone MSCP MP from Manipur was a Minister of State at the center. So, the MSCP had to go with the BJP and SAP in the state also. The State BJP and SAP bodies, however, decided not to go along with the MSCP in the formation of the ministry. Ultimately the UF managed to form the government with the support of the four MLAs from the NCP and three from the MPP, one RJD and one independent. The new government was sworn in on 2nd March, 2000.

The above developments meant that the relationship between the ruling and other parties was very much strained from the very beginning. The four MLAs of the NCP and the three MLAs of the MPP were expelled by their respective parties.[58] These seven MLAs on their part went ahead to form their own parties. The three MLAs from the MPP called themselves as MPP (K) while the four MLAs of the NCP decided to call themselves as NCP (D). This was followed immediately by these two parties merging with the MSCP.[59] The NCP and the MPP went on claiming that the merger was not valid and that their MLAs should be disqualified on the ground of defection. They also attacked the UF government for its abject failures on the law and order and economic front and demanded imposition of President's Rule inside the state with the assembly kept in animated suspension.[60]

It must be noted here that the NCP and the MPP were no longer represented in the state assembly as a result of all their MLAs joining the Congress (I). About the relationship between the ruling and the other opposition parties also, the relationship was a strained one from the word go. At the center of the conflict, once again, was the post of Speaker. The ruling parties wanted to remove Speaker from his post whereas the opposition parties were against it.[61] The opposition also wanted the Speaker to disqualify the nine MLAs who had defected to the ruling front and subsequently merged into the MSCP. The opposition submitted an application seeking the disqualification under the Tenth Schedule of the Indian Constitution.[62] The opposition efforts to get the nine MLAs (4 NCP, 3 MPP, 1 RJD and 1 Independent who have joined the MSCP) disqualified and destabilize the ruling coalition ministry, however, got a major jolt when the Speaker refused to admit a privilege motion moved by the opposition for the purpose. The entire opposition walked out of the House in protest against the action of the Speaker. As a result, the session continued without the opposition and it passed 47 demands for excess advance grants.[63]

Within no time the Speaker however, come to the side of the opposition. He openly announced (at a press conference) his firm resolution to bring down the government with the help of the opposition.[64] He also opened a camp in his official bungalow where 21 opposition MLAs were camping. He said that the UF government failed to control the law and order situation of the state and solve the financial crisis inside the state. He further alleged that the government was worries only for the payment of salary of government employees.[65] Obviously, the ruling parties wanted to change the Speaker as soon as possible while the opposition leader said that they would not allow the ruling parties to remove Dr. S. Dhananjoy Singh from the Speakership.[66]

The winter session of the House was also supposed to take place about this time and it was during this session that the relationship between the ruling and opposition became worst. The unfortunate incidence happened on 2nd December, 2000. On this fateful day the morning session went smoothly and the afternoon session followed. Things took an ugly turn after the procedural part was over and the discussions were to begin. First the intimation of the Governor's assent to bills was presented and then the CM tabled the report of the Business Advisory Committee. This was followed by the Chairman of the Committee moving the motion for extension of time for presentation of report. Then the Speaker took over and informed the House that four opposition MLAs made 10 different charges against the UF government and sought the permission of the House to move a no-confidence motion. He also announced that the President of the FPM, Prof. Gangmumei Kamei from the ruling side, sought permission for a counter motion expressing confidence in the UF government. The motion was admitted giving reason that the two was virtually the same. At this moment both the ruling and the opposition agreed to devote enough time to discuss the matter. Till now everything was alright. Then the Speaker stood up and announced that he would decide on how to conduct the motion and without further ado, announced the adjournment of the House sine die and walked out. At that moment, somebody switched off the lights in the House. Then, the pandemonium gave away to violence. The ruling members and the opposition members were exchanging blows against each other. They also shouted against each others. For instance, the IFCD minister Ksh. Biren shouted "You slave! How dare you raise your voice from the gallery? Arrest him." The opposition member O. Joy Singh shouted back to the minister "Mind your language, gentlemen." The violence continued till the house Marshal were put into action and drove everybody outside the House.[67] Two ruling and five opposition MLAs got injured in the unruly incident inside the Assembly Hall.[68]

The relation between the ruling and the opposition worsened day-by-day as the opposition continued its efforts to dethrone the ruling side with renewed vigour. They put up their best endeavors to get their objectives. Soon their efforts started yielding fruits. Three MLAs, one from the MSCP and two from the FPM left the ruling side and joined the opposition. It may be noted here that the one MLA who left the MSCP was one who got elected as an NCP MLA in the very first place. He had earlier left the NCP and had joined the MSCP and disqualification proceedings have already been started against him in the house with the Speaker having decided to reserve his decision on the issue for the time being. Now the same MLA returned to the NCP again saying that the UF ministry was not bothered with the welfare interests of the people as it was more concern with holding on to power.[69] The two MLAs from the FPM also criticized the UF ministry on the same lines. These two floated a new party called the Progressive Federal Party of Manipur (PFPM).[70]

The entire episode once again shows that the relationship between the ruling and the opposition was always in an extreme State of fluidity as the differences between the two were hardly in terms of ideology or principle or policies and programs. They were time and again brought together or divided mainly by the exigencies brought about by their pursuit of power.

Now the opposition parties started demanding intervention from the Center and also Proclamation of President's Rule inside the State. The NDA government however clarified in the Parliament that the Central government cannot intervene in the functioning of a state. This was mainly because of the fact that the NDA did not enjoy majority in the Upper House of the Parliament. The opposition leader in Lok Sabha, Mrs. Sonia Gandhi also expressed her opposition to any form of destabilization in the democratic institutions in the north-eastern region. The stand of both the NDA and the Congress threw cold waters to the aspirations of the opposition in Manipur. Emboldened by the developments, the UF ministry boasted that there is no failure of constitutional machinery in the State.[71]

Still, the opposition was not to give up so easily. The snub from the Centre rather made them more desperate in their efforts to topple the existing ministry. They wanted to topple the government somehow or other. They were unhappy and desperate with the attitudes of the Central leaders. At this moment, ten Congress MLAs out of 11 split the party and formed a new party called as Manipur Regional Congress Party (MRCP), headed by Shri Radhabinod Koijam. Subsequently, a new political alliance was forged by the MRCP with other six parties in opposition viz., BJP, NCP, PFPM, SAP, MPP, and JD (S).[72] Together they formed the Manipur Democratic Front (MDF). Its main objective was to remove the UF government. The leaders of the MDF went to Delhi and camped there to persuade the Central Government and their leaders to fulfil their demands.[73]

However many more twists and turns were yet to take place in the story. Soon the newly formed MRCP having 10 MLAs merged into the SAP. The PFPM (two MLAs) also merged into SAP. With this the strength of the SAP in the Assembly increased to 13.[74] The sudden increase in the strength of the SAP from 1 to 13 gave a new hope to the opposition camp to overthrow the government because the SAP was a strong partner of the NDA at the Center which was led by the BJP. However, the party leading the coalition ministry in Manipur, i.e. the MSCP was also a partner of the NDA at the Centre with its lone MLA sitting there as a Minister of State. However, in Indian politics, there is no guarantee that the parties in coalition at the center will also necessarily have a good relation in the state as well. Though the MSCP, BJP and SAP were close partners inside the NDA at the center, the latter two were in the opposition while the first one was leading the UF ministry inside the state. The BJP and the SAP were sitting not only in opposition but they were also trying to overthrow the MSCP led coalition ministry. The opposition parties further put pressures to the ruling parties by filing fresh application for disqualification proceedings against the four Minister Onjamang Haokip, Md Allauddin, Hankhanpao, and S. Chandra Singh under 10th Schedule of the Constitution. The first two, Onjamang Haokip and Md Allauddin, were elected on the NCP ticket. Hankhanpao was elected on the RJD and S. Chandra on the MPP ticket. However, they all defected to the MSCP. The four had already faced the disqualification proceedings but the Speaker Dr. S. Dhananjoy reserved his judgment in their cases.[75] This was when Nipamacha was leading the UF ministry and the Speaker was in good terms with him.

Soon the relationship between the ruling and the opposition became so bad that the MSCP considered pulling out of the NDA at the center. Actually the problem started within the MSCP. An internal crisis erupted inside the MSCP, the main ruling party during the time. The CM and party president Wahengbam Nipamacha and the MSCP working president, the then Union Minister of State for Food Processing, Th. Chaoba openly criticised each other and expelled each other. The CM declared that the MSCP's Central Executive Council (CEC) resolved to expel the MSCP working president, vice-president (administration) and general secretary (administration) from the party for six years for their anti-party activities on 10th February 2001. Moreover, they sent a fax message to the central leaders of the NDA informing them for the expulsion of the Union Minister of State for Food Processing, Th. Chaoba Singh.[76]

The working president of the MSCP, Th. Chaoba also retaliated to the CM on the same day. He announced the expulsion of the CM W. Nipamacha Singh and Deputy CM Dr. L. Chandramani along with six other ministers from the primary membership of the ruling MSCP for six years by the party Central Executive Council (CEC). He charged the CM and Deputy CM of failing to bring up the issue of the three month political crisis in the MSCP legislature party and failure of the government in maintaining the law and order. Shri Chaoba also charged the CM and his government of financial indiscipline. Both the groups claimed that they were the genuine MSCP and contended that their respective moves to expel the other were backed by the Central Executive Council of the MSCP. The crisis went unabated with Chaoba and his group joining hands with the opposition to topple the Nipamacha ministry. Chaoba also claimed that he enjoyed the support of 22 MSCP MLAs but 14 MLAs were still held as 'captive' at the Nipamacha side.[77]

Relationship between the ruling and opposition during the Samata-led Peoples' Front ministry (2001)

As the crisis reached its peak, Shri W. Nipamacha Singh stepped down as a CM of Manipur on February 12, 2001 in favor of SAP leader Shri Radhabinod Koijam. They formed a new alliance called as the United Democratic Alliance (UDA). The UDA comprised of 49 MLAS i.e. MSCP (Nipamacha group) - 22, SAP - 12, FPM - 4 and Independent- 1.[78] The new alliance was also known as Peoples' Front Alliance and claimed to have the support of 49 MLAs from six parties i.e. 6 - BJP, 12 - SAP, 23 - MSCP (excluding CM and seven other MLAs kept in unattached status), 1 - JD (S), 2 - NCP, 1 - MPP and 4 - FPM in the house of 60 with 59 effective strength.[79] Subsequently Shri Radhabinod Koijam was sworn in as the 24th Chief Minister of Manipur on February 15, 2001. Once the ministry was sworn in, the CM within no time claimed that he had the support of 57 MLAs in the House of 60.[80] This meant that there was only one MLA in the opposition for the first time in the history of Manipur, i.e., Shri Rishang Keishing of the Congress (I) as one seat (Kshetrigao Assembly Constituency) was lying vacant and the Speaker accounting for the other seat.

Throughout the period from 2000 to 2002, the relationship between the ruling and opposition was in a perpetual state of conflict. The two never succeeded in forging a relationship of mutual respect and cooperation even for a brief period. The reason is obvious. Shri Radhabinod Koijam won the election in the Congress ticket but later defected from the party and formed a new party, the MRCP which subsequently got merged into the SAP. The lone opposition member Shri Rishang criticized the ruling parties saying that they were responsible for the deteriorating law and order situation and financial crisis in the state. He demanded proclamation of President's Rule inside the state and also fresh State Assembly elections to seek a fresh mandate from the people.[81] He also observed that lust for power was behind the frequent splitting of political parties in the state and the resultant instability of the government was not in the interest of the public. He further said that the frequent changes in government in the state caused the people to lost trust in their representatives.[82]

The PF ministry also had the same fate as the earlier UF ministry. The Radhabinod ministry lasted only around three months i.e. from 15th February to 21stMay, 2001. It was due to internal crisis and not because of the opposition party. The lone opposition member was like a silent observer. Right after the installation of the ministry, internal problem erupted within the PF especially between the SAP to which the CM belonged, and the BJP. Both of them were partners of the NDA alliance at the centre. However, in Manipur the state unit of these parties had a strained relationship. Both the party wanted to lead the ministry. Initially, the BJP did not want to support the ministry as it wanted to lead the government. The BJP gave their support only after the intervention of the central leaders. As destiny would have it, before the PF could last any longer, soon the entire state was in the grip of, a deep crisis following the extension of the Indo-NSCN (IM) ceasefire leading to the burning of the assembly, party offices, etc. This was followed by the imposition of the President's Rule till a new government was formed after the 8th State Assembly elections were held in February 2002.

Conclusion and Summary

In a representative democracy, the party with a majority or a combination of parties would form the government and the minority party or parties would function as an opposition. The aims and objectives of the ruling and the opposition are more or less similar. Both their intention is to serve the people. They are expected to maintain a good relationship by lending co-operation and co-ordination between them on national and State issues. Indeed, the success of a parliamentary democracy depends on the nature of the relationships between the ruling and the opposition.

The relationship between the ruling and the opposition parties in Manipur during the period under study was not so much one of friendly co-operation but one of conflicting rivalry. A good relationship between the two used to be there once in a while. There were certain in connection with which there were co-operation and co-ordination between them. For instance, all the political parties in the state stood together on the issue of protection of the territorial integrity of Manipur. Inclusion of Manipuri in the Eight Schedule of the Constitution was another issue on which all the parties agreed. Both side also came out strongly condemning the ethnic clashes in the hills and appealed to all concerned for a quick and lasting solution to the problem. Otherwise, most of the time, they had diametrically opposite views on several problems arising inside the state. Moreover, both the parties got involved in the struggle for power all the time. There were too many instances of the opposition parties trying to destabilize the ministry. Similarly, the ruling parties also often tried to weaken the opposition parties either by breaking the opposition alliance or absorbing the smaller party or parties into their fold. All these efforts from both sides often led to strained relationship between the two. Finally, the relationship between the ruling and the opposition was always in an extreme state of fluidity as the differences between the two were hardly in terms of ideology or principle or policies and programs, and as the MLAs crossed the floor from one side to the other with alarming frequency. Time and again, they were kept together or divided mainly by the exigencies brought about by their all consuming pursuit of power.

NOTES

1. D. Sundar Ram (Ed), *Indian Parliamentary Opposition*, Kanishka Publisher, Distributors, New Delhi, 1996, p-2
2. http://www.eci.gov.in/StatisticalReports/SE_1984/Statistical%20Report%201984%20Manipur.
3. 'Janata Merges with Congress (I) in Manipur', *The Manipur Mail* (A local English daily), Imphal, February 5, 1986.
4. 'State Janata party President denies merger', *The Manipur Mail*, Imphal, February 16, 1986.
5. 'Admission of 4 Janata MLAs into Congress (I) challenged', *The Manipur Mail*, Imphal, August 1, 1986.
6. 'Damodar resigns from the state assembly', *The Manipur Mail, Imphal*, April 18, 1988
7. 'Congress party is ready to fight by-election in Sagolband Constituency', *The Manipur Mail*, Imphal, May 24, 1988.
8. 'Congress (I) heading for cat-walk victory in Sagolband: Nilamani', *The Manipur Mail*, Imphal, June 27, 1988.
9. 'Opposition unity crushed by People's solidarity with Congress', *The Manipur Mail*, Imphal, July 5, 1988.
10. 'Opposition walk out on fire extinguisher scandal issue', *The Manipur Mail*, Imphal, July 29, 1988
11. 'Assembly passed 1989-90 Budgets, Opposition walks out', *The Manipur Mail*, Imphal, April 18, 1989.
12. 'Jaichandra accepts Opposition challenge in Assembly', *The Manipur Mail*, Imphal, September 8, 1989.
13. 'Election Campaign', *The Manipur Mail*, Imphal, October 22, 1989.
14. 'For small States support to Opposition is counterproductive', *The Manipur Mail*, Imphal, November 2, 1989.
15. *Ibid.*
16. 'CM: Opposition Parties have done nothing for the Manipuri Language except shouting', *The Manipur Mail*, Imphal, November 6, 1989.

17. *Hueiyen Lanpao* (A local daily in Manipuri), November 17, 1989.
18. Dr. R.S.N., 'NF government will be a Failure Experiment', *The Manipur Mail*, Imphal, January 30, 1990.
19. http://www.eci.gov.in/StatisticalReports/SE_1990/Statistical%20Report%20Manipur%201990
20. 'Governor was pressurized by the Centre o invite the UF to form government says Jaichandra', *The Manipur Mail*, Imphal, March 2, 1990
21. 'Time will tell', *The Manipur Mail*, Imphal, February 4, 1991
22. *Ibid.*
23. 'MPP in deep crisis', *The Manipur Mail*, Imphal, February 17, 1991.
24. 'Disqualification of Ranbir from Assembly demanded', *The Manipur Mail*, Imphal, February 20, 1991.
25. 'MPCC (I) to protest against Governor', *The Manipur Mail*, Imphal, February 21, 1991.
26. 'CLP (I) boycott Governor's address', *The Manipur Mail*, Imphal, February 23, 1991.
27. 'Congress (I) demands dismissal of R.K. Ranbir', The Manipur Mail, February 18, 1991.
28. 'Ranbir and Yaima wanted to form government with Congress (I), says Dorendra', *The Manipur Mail*, Imphal, February 19, 1991.
29. 'Bhuban cannot expel me, says Ranbir', *The Manipur Mail*, Imphal, February 19, 1991.
30. N. Sanatomba, 'Congress (I) MPP relations badly strained', *The Manipur Mail*, Imphal, April 13, 1993.
31. S. Mangi Singh, Land, Ethnic – Relations and the 9th Assembly Elections in the Hills of Manipur in Ch. Priyoranjan Singh (Ed), *Tribalism and the Tragedy of the Commons, Land, Identity and Development: The Manipur Experience,* New Delhi, Akansha Publishing House, 2009, p.161.
32. 'Political Parties totally opposed to disintegration of Manipur', *The Manipur Mail*, Imphal, April 27, 1993.
33. S. Mangi Singh, *op cit,* p. 160.
34 'CM,Ministers, MLAs: Fast for peace', *The Manipur Mail*, Imphal, September 23, 1993.

35 'MPP making monkey tricks', *The Manipur Mail*, Imphal, September 23, 1993.

36. 'Jaichandra has met governor twice in 48 hrs accompany by 20 MLAs', *The Manipur Mail*, Imphal, September 23, 1993.

37. 'All eyes now to Speaker, Borobabu', *The Manipur Mail*, Imphal, December 17, 1994.

38. 'Behring says speaker acts arbitrarily', *The Manipur Mail*, Imphal, December 18, 1994.

39. 'Hangman in action 23 MLAs disqualified', *The Manipur Mail*, Imphal, December 23, 1994.

40. 'Climax of crisis: Too late for aversion', *The Manipur Mail*, Imphal, December 24, 1994.

41. 'Assembly being summoned on January 9', *The Manipur Mail*, Imphal, December 25, 1994.

42. B. Pakem, *Coalition politics in North-East India*, New Delhi, Regency Publications,1999, p. 94.

43. *Ibid.*

44. *Ibid.*

45. 'Deficit budget turns surplus overnight', *The Imphal Free Press*, Imphal, March 12, 1997.

46. 'All-party meet chalks out charter of demands to be given to PM', *The Imphal Free Press*, Imphal, May 21, 1997.

47. 'Opposition Parties ask Rishang Government to Step Down', *The Imphal Free Press*, Imphal, July 6, 1997.

48. 15 CLP members demand change in leadership', The Imphal Free Press, November 24, 1997.

49. Congress splits, rebels forms new party', *The Imphal Free Press*, Imphal, December 8, 1997.

50. 'Nipamacha in, Rishang out' and 'Rishang government tenders resignation', December 16, 1997.

51. 'UF government wins confidence motion', *The Imphal Free Press*, Imphal, January 13, 1998.

52. 'Banks refuse to honour government bills', *The Imphal Free Press*, Imphal, May 7, 1998.

53. 'Centre reimbursing Rs 100 cr to State', *The Imphal Free Press*, Imphal, July 3, 1998.

54. 'Manipur assemble election', *Economic and Political Weekly*, March 11, 2000, p. 883.

55. 'United Front claims support of 36', 'NCP alleges kidnap by MSCP', 'Ignore MSCP claim urge MPP chief', *The Imphal Free Press*, February 28, 2000.
56 'NCP seeks Governor's help', The Imphal Free Press, Imphal, February 29, 2000.
57. 'BJP and ally fail to arrive at decision to join government', *The Imphal Free Press*, Imphal, March 1, 2000.
58. 'Defectors expelled by own parties', *The Imphal Free Press*, Imphal, March 8, 2000.
59. 'MSCP in a haste to merge defectors to itself', *The Imphal Free Press*, April 10, 2000.
60. 'Merger not valid: NCP Chief', *The Imphal Free Press*, April 25, 2000.
61. 'MDA and company declare allegiance to Speaker', *The Imphal Free Press*, June 19, 2000.
62. 'Opposition MLAs formally seek disqualification of 9 ruling MLAs', *The Imphal Free Press*, June 21, 2000.
63. 'Opposition stages walk out against speaker's decision' *The Imphal Free Press*, July 26, 2000.
64. Speaker Dhananjoy draws first blood', 'UF declares resolve to remove Speaker', *The Imphal Free Press*, November 18, 2000.
65. *Ibid.*
66. *Ibid.*
67. 'House session day one ends in Pandemonium', *The Imphal Free Press*, Imphal, December 2, 2000
68. 'House session day one ends in Pandemonium', *The Imphal Free Press*, Imphal, December 2, 2000
69. 'Three MLAs ditch ruling camp', *The Imphal Free Press*, December 4, 2000.
70. 'UF government's funeral closing in: O Joy', *The Imphal Free Press*, December 5, 2000.
71. 'PR move unfair: FPM', *The Imphal Free Press*, Imphal, December 24, 2000
72. 'Congress split in opposition power gambit', *The Imphal Free Press*, December 28, 2000
73. '18 opposition MLAs camping in New Delhi', *The Imphal Free Press*, December 30, 2000

74. 'Haokholet and Jayenta also jump onto Samata bandwagon', *The Imphal Free Press*, Imphal January 6, 2001.

75. 'Opposition files more disqualification pleas', *The Imphal Free Press*, Imphal and 'Fresh move to axe 4 MLAs' *The Sangai Express*, Imphal, January 11, 2001

76. 'Nipamacha, Chaoba expel each other from MSCP', *The Imphal Free Press*, Imphal, February 12, 2001

77. Ibid, also 'Seven of eight who left CM's camp tender resignation', *The Imphal Free Press*, Imphal, February 13, 2001.

78. 'Nipamacha steps down, RB steps in', *The Imphal free Press*, Imphal February 14, 2001.

79. 'Political somersaults galore as parties jump on RB bandwagon' *The Imphal Free Press*, Imphal, February 15, 2001

80. 'RB sworn in as 24th Chief Minister of Manipur' *The Imphal Free Press,* Imphal February 16, 2001.

81. 'Rishang for seeking fresh mandate', *The Imphal Free Press*, Imphal, May 17, 2001.

82. 'Rishang and Nipamacha chastise state politicians', *The Imphal Free Press*, Imphal May 22, 2001.

6

Summary and Conclusion

Democracy is the best form of government and the successful working of parliamentary democracy depends on the existence of a healthy and meaningful set of political parties and party system. Political party is one of the most essential requirements of democracy. Political parties can be studied in two ways. First of all, they can be studied in terms of their organizational structures, goals, functions, characteristics, etc. by taking them as distinct entities. Secondly, they can also be studied in terms of the various patterns of inter-party relationship they have inside a political system or as Maurice Duverger puts, "the forms and modes of their co-existences."[1] Douglas W. Rae defines it as the network of competitive relationships between political parties.[2] G. Sartori further wrote that party system is the system of interactions resulting from inter-party competition.[3]

Party system is commonly classified according to the numbers of parties competing for power. There are three types of party system viz. one party system, two party system and multi-party system. One party system is one where only one political party is there inside the political system. In one party system, normally other political parties are not allowed to exist, e.g. China. A two-party system is the party system where only two political parties have a realistic chance of winning an election, and all or nearly all the elected offices are held only by the candidates of the two party. It means political power really alternates between two parties – one becomes the ruling party and the other the opposition. According to M. Duverger, in two party system, for practical purposes only two parties share the parliamentary seats; one assumes the entire responsibility for government, the other limits itself to the free expression of criticism in opposition.[4] The examples of two-party system are the U.K and the U.S.A. M. Duverger observed that "the simple majority single-ballot system favours the two-party system."[5] This is known as Duverger's law. This law did not apply in countries like India and Canada. These countries follow the 'simple majority single-ballot systems' but have the multi-party system.[6]

Multi-party system is a system in which more than two parties are competing for political power in a political system. It is based on the democratic ideals which allow every opinion freely to organize, unite and separate with the change of political situations. It offers many choices and options to the voters, and the voters can choose among many parties and candidates, according to their wishes. Multi-party system is usually associated with coalition politics. This is because parties normally fail to secure majority in the elections. India is a good example of multi-party system. Even, in the just concluded election of the Lok Sabha, 2009 no party secured majority. Subsequently, a coalition ministry headed by the Congress (I) under the banner of United Progressive Alliance (UPA) was sworn in on May 22nd 2009, headed by Dr. Manmohan Singh, of the Congress (I).

Multi-party system can be divided into three broad categories. In the first category, many small parties exist in a political system and they are very competitive. Here, none of the parties is large enough to command majority of the vote or a majority in the legislature. The second category of multiparty system exists where one party garners a sizeable proportion of the voters and the remainder of the electorate is divided among several small parties. The third category of multiparty system prevails where parties inter into alliances after or before the elections, enabling one coalition to rule.[7] In fact, the type party system in Manipur during the period of study falls in the third category. However, the second category of multi-party system is witnessed since the 8th State Legislative Assembly, 2002 till date. At present, the Congress (I) has emerged as the dominant party in Manipur as evidenced by its being in power since 2002 and also by the fact that it has won 31 of the 60 seats of the present assembly.

Party system is dynamic; it varies from time to time according to the changing political scenario of the state. Different party systems may evolve after the results of an election.[8] This is true in the Indian context. The party system in India varied from time to time. In the beginning, it was one-party dominant system till 1969. This was the phase when the Congress was voted time and again with an overwhelming majority in the Parliament. This was followed by a brief spell of multi-party system from 1969 to 1971, after Congress split into two - Indira faction and Syndicate faction. Once again, Congress (I) dominated the electoral politics of India from 1971-77 and brought the one-party dominant system during this phase. The fourth phase from 1977 to 1979 was a phase of two party system. The Janata Dal and the Congress accounted for over 80 per cent of both the votes and seats. The fifth phase from 1980-89 saw a reversal to the one-party dominant system where the Congress controlled the political scenario of the country. The sixth phase is the phase of multi-party system which followed after the 1989 Lok Sabha elections. From 1989 till date none of the parties have won a majority in the Lok Sabha. As a result, national politics has become coalitional in nature. There are pre and post election alliances to get a workable majority in the House. There are specially two alliances at the national level – one headed by the BJP known as the National Democratic Alliance (NDA) which came into being in 1999 and the other by the Congress which was formed after the 14th Lok Sabha elections in 2004 and called the United Progressive Alliance (UPA). These two alliances compete with each other for political power and triumph in the electoral politics of the nation at present. Therefore, the Indian party system is known as the bipolar party system from 1999 onward till date.[9]

Coming to the state of Manipur, party politics emerged during the British period. The ancient Manipuri politics was the politics of the palace. Political consciousness on democratic lines developed during the 1930s. It was mainly the result of the introduction of modern education but the two World Wars and the Indian freedom struggle too had an impact upon the people which also contributed to the growth of political consciousness among them. Subsequently, many political parties like the Nikhil Manipuri Mahasabha (1938), Manipur Praja Sanmeloni (1940), Manipur Praja Sangha (1946), Manipur State Congress (1946), etc. came into existence. Most of the parties emerged during the time were somehow or the other related with Hijam Irabot Singh, the charismatic leader who championed wide spread socio-economic and political reforms during the 1930 and 1940s. The Manipur Praja Sammeloni (1940), Manipur Praja Sangha (1946), Manipur State Congress (1946), etc. were also formed with the initiative of Hijam Irabot Singh.

The party politics of the 1930s and 1940s of Manipur were mainly concentrated on demanding democratic political reforms inside the state. The ever increasing demand for political reforms during the closing years of the colonial rule continued unabated immediately after the departure of the British as well. These demands bore fruit in the form of the Manipur State Constitution Act, 1947. The first ever elections in Manipur were held under the provisions of the Constitution in June and July 1948. Some of the parties contesting the elections were the Manipur State Congress, Manipur Krishak Sabha, Socialist Party, Praja Shanti, etc. However, none of the parties won majority in the legislature. As a result, a coalition ministry headed by the Praja Shanti and supported by the Krishak Sabha and Hill members was formed. The ministry, however, did not last long as a result of the merger of Manipur into the Dominion of India with effect from 15 October 1949.

Inter-party relationship within the party system as emerged during the British period was not very competitive. The action and interaction among them were not so conflicting as it were friendly because their aims and objectives were more or less same. This trend continued to some extent during the post-British era and after the merger into the Indian Dominion. The people really wanted to establish a responsible government in Manipur. Political parties took up the issue and fought for it. Though, there were differences among parties, they coordinated and cooperated among themselves to fight for a common cause. They joined together and formed the "All Manipur Statehood Demand Committee (AMSDC)" in 1968 and "the All Parties Statehood Demand Coordinating Committee (APSDCC)" in 1972 to actively pursue together their common goal. This trend continued till the grant of statehood to Manipur in 1972. After that they parted ways in search for political power and gain control over the state government.

However, from the mid 1960s onwards, inter-party relationship became competitive and conflicting in nature. Defection followed at an alarming rate and in the process political stability of the state got seriously affected. Political defections were so frequent that no government could last its normal tenure of five years. In fact, after the installation of the first elected Territorial Assembly in 1967 till 1972 (the year Manipur granted statehood), there were three ministries and President's Rule on two occasions. The trend continued even after Manipur became a state of the Indian Union. From 1972 to 1985, the state witnessed eight ministries and President's Rule on four occasions. Not only defection, change of party loyalty by the party members, merger and split, etc. were the norm inside the state politics with the people always giving a fractured mandate. No single party could assert so dominant a position so as to form a ministry on its own after elections. This meant that most of the governments formed in the state were coalition ministries. As a result, the politics of Manipur became coalitional in nature and it became an inevitable and indispensable part of it. In fact, there were eight coalition ministries during the period from 1985 to 2002, excluding the one formed in 2002.

The concept of coalition emerged out of a multi-party government where a number of minority parties join hands with a view to run a government, which is otherwise not possible in a democracy. Coalition ministry is formed under two circumstances. First of all, a coalition government is formed due to national emergency like in Britain during the First and Second World War. Secondly, it came into being when no party commands even a working majority in the legislature. It is this type of system which prevailed in Manipur.

Many political parties also emerged during the period from 1985 to 2002. These parties were short-lived entities with fluid personnel. For instance, the Federal Party of Manipur (1993), Manipur State Congress Party (1997), MPP (K) (1997), JD Progressive, (1995), JD (Sephu) (1995), Progressive Federal Party of Manipur (2000), Manipur Regional Congress Party (2001), etc. Among these parties except the Federal Party of Manipur (FPM) and the Manipur State Congress Party (MSCP), all failed to last even two-three months. The FPM and the MSCP are also no longer there at present. The MSCP merged with the BJP in 2006 and the FPM also merged with MPP on the eve of the 9th State Assembly elections, 2007.

Most of the leaders of the parties which emerged during the period from 1985 to 2002 were also former leaders of Congress (I). For example, Shri Radhabinod Koijam of Samata Party who led the People's Front ministry was a Congress leader till he floated a new party, the Manipur Regional Congress Party in 2001 which got subsequently merged with the Samata Party. Now, he is the President of NCP. In the same way, Shri Wahengbam Nipamacha Singh, the former Chief Minister of state, started his carrier inside the Congress (I) till he launched the MSCP in 1997. He again floated another party, the Manipur National Conference on the eve of the 8th State assembly elections, 2002, and then joined the RJD again. At present he is a member of the BJP. Others like MPP (K) (1997), JD Progressive, (1995), JD (Sephu) (1995), Progressive Federal Party of Manipur

(2000), Manipur Regional Congress Party (2001), etc. went into oblivion within a few months time.

Overall, the party system which was there during the period from 1985 to 2002 was one of a multi-party system without a dominant party. There were many parties but no party was able to dominate the political scenario of Manipur. This feature was there in the party system of the state right from 1972. In fact, no party ever won a majority in the state assembly elections so far. It was only in the present Assembly that a party won a majority after election. This was also possible only after by-elections in two assembly constituencies. Otherwise, the Congress (I) won only 30 out of 60 assembly constituencies in the 9th State Assembly elections, 2009.

Regarding the relationship among the coalition partners, Coalition ministries were formed by entering into alliances with the sole purpose of having a share of the governmental power rather than on the basis of shared ideologies, principles or policies and programs. Several pre-poll alliance partners changed their side after elections when a ministry was about to be formed. In other words, political parties entered into post-poll alliances to form a coalition ministry by abandoning their pre-poll alliances, promises, election manifestoes, policies, programs, etc.

Usually, even after forming the coalition ministry, the coalition partners failed to establish a meaningful coalitional relationship among them. Their main motive remained gaining as many ministerial berths as possible. As a result, jumbo size ministries were formed in the state. Yet, jumbo size ministries did not bring stable government, though political leaders believe in it. Moreover, coalition partners failed to continue as a team when new elections were announced. They contested the elections of their own in many occasions. It further vindicates the fact that while entering into alliances, the most important concern of the parties was that of sharing power and nothing else.

By and large, the inter-party relationship within a coalition ministry was that of a conflicting one and not a cordial one. The coalition partners failed to maintain stable and good relationships among them. In other words, the relationship they shared was often characterised by lack of coordination and cooperation and most of the time the relationship they shared was not one of mutual trust and cooperation but one of conflict and distrust. The stability or otherwise of the coalition ministries also depended on the intra-party relationship of the leading party of the ministry. Very often, ministries fell due to the intra-party conflicts among the coalition partners. These show not only the failure of the parties to achieve unity and solidarity among them as a group of parties but also as individual parties.

Small parties also often tended to change their political affiliations. Within the coalition they will support different leaders from time to time with a view to garner their own position of power. They won't even hesitate at all to cross over to the opposition side thereby leaving the ministry in a lurch and seriously endangering the stability of the ministry. This further proves the feeble and fragile nature of the relationship which the coalition partners shared among them. All these also meant that the coalition partners failed to transcend their own ambition to grab power anyhow by any means. Prospects of sustaining their own position of power or gaining a position power were the main concerns which kept the coalition partners together. They will also part ways for the same reasons. As a result, all the time they failed to achieve unity and solidarity among themselves. This in turn led to the failure of the emergence of a healthy coalitional relationship among political parties forming a coalition ministry.

The opposition is expected to play an important role in the politics of Manipur like in any other democratic political system. Yet their role inside the state politics is far from satisfactory and constructive. Most of the time opposition parties during the period from 1985 to 2002 were divided on party lines. In a small state like Manipur it is desirable that all the parties in opposition are united so that they can check the working and movement of the government with a view to promote the interests of the people and provide an alternative to them. But most of the time the relation the parties in Opposition share is not very cordial and not united inside and outside the assembly.

Most of the time, the opposition remained a weak, heterogeneous group, characterised by lack of unity. It usually comprised many parties having different ideologies and beliefs. It makes it difficult for them to work together in pursuit of a common agenda for the people. As a result the relation between and among the opposition parties were strained most of the time and their ability to be a responsible and effective opposition was always weakened. They come together occasionally. Yet the commonality of the opposition parties all the time remained that of the desire to topple the existing ministry so that they may get an opportunity to form the next ministry.

Their lack of proper co-ordination and understanding on various issues led to their failure to evolve themselves as a meaningful group and project themselves as a viable alternative to the government. The Opposition as a group was also characterised not only by an absence of unity and cohesion among its members but was also vulnerable all the time to disintegration due to divisive designs of the Ruling side. This was all the more so because there were inter-party as well as intra-party conflicts within the Opposition. As a result, Ruling parties often succeeded in absorbing parties in Opposition. This further meant that the latter often failed to keep its MLAs intact and this was a major factor for its inability to be an effective opposition.

About the relationship between the Ruling and Opposition parties in Manipur, it was characterized by elements of friendly cooperation once in a while. Otherwise, it remained one of conflicting rivalry. There were certain issues during the period from 1985 to 2002 in connection with which there were co-operation and co-ordination between them. For instance, all the political parties inside the state agreed on the issue of protection of the territorial integrity of Manipur, shifting of the Assam Rifles from Kangla, finding a peaceful solution to the problem of insurgency inside the state though political dialogues, etc.

Apart from these few exceptions, they had diametrically opposite views on several problems confronting the state. Moreover, both often got involved in the struggle for power every now and then. The Opposition was always on the lookout for opportunities to destabilize the government. Similarly, the ruling parties also often tried to weaken the Opposition parties either by breaking their alliances or absorbing the smaller party or parties in the Opposition. All these efforts from both side often led to strained relationship between the two. Moreover, the relationship between the Ruling and the Opposition was always in an extreme state of fluidity as the differences between the two were hardly in terms of ideology or principle or policies and programs. They were time and again brought together or divided mainly by the exigencies brought about by their pursuit of power.

Instead of trying to serve as a vanguard of the public interests and putting a check on the government from going against the interests of the people, the sole motive of the Opposition remained to dislodge the ruling party or parties from their position of power and secure the same position for them. It was also always preoccupied with finding faults and highlighting loopholes drawbacks of the ruling side. The ruling side also always tried to encourage defections from the side of the opposition with a view to further strengthen its own position of power. Such efforts from both side greatly contributed to the strained relationship between the two.

Overall, the single most important motive behind the parties while conducting their relationship with other parties has always been that of securing power. This has always been the only shared attitude among the parties which brought them together or drove them apart. Ideologies, principles, common policies or programs hardly mattered to the parties. All these have contributed to the failure of the emergence of a healthy and meaningful party system inside the state during the period from 1985 to 2002.

Obviously, the stability of the government was seriously disturbed during the period of study from 1985 to 2002. This has been proved by the fact that during this period four State Assembly elections were held including the 8th State Assembly elections, February 2002 and there were ten ministries including the SPF ministry installed in March 2002. It means that the average life span of a ministry was only about one year and seven months. This clearly shows the type of political instability the state faced during the period.

Finally, it may be noted that eighth State Assembly Elections, 2002 ushered in a new phase in the history of party system in Manipur. The stringent provisions of the 91st Amendment Act left hardly any room for defections. This meant not only stability of the government with the SPF ministry lasting the entire normal tenure of the eighth State Assembly but also an end to the fluid nature of the composition of the Ruling and Opposition sides. The line dividing the two which was always blurred earlier has also become clear and sharp. Obviously, the situation has strengthened the position of the Congress inside the state as the party in power since then. The party consolidated its dominance by winning 30 seats out of the 60 in the ninth Assembly elections which got further increased to 31 after two by-elections. As a result, it has a clear majority in the House. The Congress further enhanced its eminent position in state politics winning both the IMPC and OMPC during the 15th Lok Sabha elections, 2009. All these proves the emergence of Congress as the dominant party inside the state leaving the MPP far behind with only five seats in the state assembly, thereby ushering in a new era of multi party system with a dominant party in Manipur which is akin to what Jean Blondel said. With the present stringent anti-defection laws; its being in power at the Center and also winning both the Lok Sabha seats of the state; and enjoying a clear majority in the State Legislature; a change in the present trend is not foreseeable in the near future.

NOTES

1. Duverger, Maurice, *Political Parties; Their organization and Activity in the Modern State*, London, Methuen & Co Ltd, 1967, p. 203.
2. Dougl as W. Rae, *The Political Consequences of Electoral Laws*, (revised edition), New Haven, Yale University Press, 1967, p. 45.
3. Sartori, Giovanni, *Parties and Party System: A Framework for Analysis*, London, Cambridge University press, 1976, p. 64.
4. Duverger, Maurice *op cit,* p. 207.
5. *Ibid.,* p. 217.
6. Brain D. Humes, 'Multi-Party Competition with Exit: A Comment on Duverger's Law', in Public Choice, Vol. 64. No 3 (1990) p-229, www. Jstor.org/stable/30025231, Accessed on 17/02/2009, Joseph M. Colomer, 'It's Parties that choose electoral Systems (or, Duverger's Laws Upside Down)', in *Political Studies*, Vol. 53, 2005, p-1ff, also Rekha Diwakar, 'Duverger's Law and the size of the Indian Party system' in *Party Politics*, vol. 13 No. 5, p-539ff, www.ppq.sagepub.com, Accessed on 19/5/08
7. *Lexicon Universal Encyclopedia*, Vol. 15 (p), New York, Lexicon Publications Inc, 1983, pp. 402f.
8. Laver, Michael and Kenneth Benoit, 'The Evolution of Party System between Elections', *American Journal of Political Science*, Vol. 47, No. 2 (April 2003), Published by Midwest Political Science Association, pp-215ff, www.jstor.org/stable/3186134, Accessed on 17/02/2009
9. Sridharan, E. 'The Fragmentation of the Indian Party System, 1952-1989: Seven Computing Explanations', in Zoya Hasan (ed), *Parties and Party Politics in India*, New Delhi, Oxford University Press, 2004, p. 492.

Bibliography

A: Books: Authored and Edited

Anderson, Janathan, Berry H. Durston and Millicent Poole, (1991), *Thesis and Assignment Writing*, Wiley Eastern Limited, New Delhi

Ashraf, Ali and L. N. Sharma, (1999), *Political Sociology: A New Grammar of Politics*, Universities Press (India) Ltd., Hyderabad.

Awasthi, Dr S. K, (1999), *The Constitution of India*, Dwivedi Law Agency, Allahabad

Barker, Rodney, (ed) (1971), *Studies in Opposition*, Macmillan, St Martin's Press, London.

Basu, Durga Das, (1994), *Introduction to the Constitution of India*, Prentice- Hall of India Private Limited, New Delhi.

Belloc, Hilaire and Cecil Chesterton, (2007), *The Party System,*Norfolk, VA, U.S.A.

Bernard, Jean- Pierre, Silas Cerqueira, Pierre Gilhodes, Helene, Graillot, Leslie F. Manigat, and Hugo Neira, (1973), *Guide to the Political Parties of South America*, Translated by Michael Perl, Penguin Books, Great Britain.

Bhandari, Ashish, (1997), *Politics and Development: Theory and Strategy*, Kanishka Publishers, Distributors, New Delhi.

Bhuyan, B.C., (1989), *Political Development of the North-East*, Volume -1, Omsons Publications, New Delhi.

Bhuyan, Dasarath, (2007), *Role of Regional Political Parties in India*, Mittal Publication, New Delhi.

Blondel, Jean, (1969), *An Introduction to Comparative Government*, Weidenfeld and Nicolson, 5 Winsley Street, London W_1.

Bogdanor, Vernon, (1983), *Multi-Party Politics and the Constitution*, Cambridge University Press, London.

Bogdanor,Vernon and David Butler (ed), (1969), *Democracy and Electoral Systems and their Political Consequences*, Cambridge University Press, London and New York.

Bone, Robert C, (1972), *Action and organization: An Introduction to Contemporary Political Science*, Harper and Row Publishers, New York, Evanston San Francisco, London

Brass, Paul R, (2nd edition), (2004), *The Politics of India since Independence*, Cambridge University Press, U.K.

Brennan, T., (1972), *Politics and Government in Britain*, Cambridge University Press, New York.

Chander, N. Jose, (2004), *Coalition Politics: The Indian Experience*, Concept Publishing Company, New Delhi.

Chandra, Bipin, Mridula Mukherjee and Aditya Mukherjee, (2000), *Indian After Independence*, Penguin Books, New Delhi.

Chatterjee, Partha, (ed), (1997), *State and Politics in India*, Oxford University Press, New Delhi.

Chaturvedi, Sadhna, (1999), *India 50 Years of Independence: 1947-97, Status, Growth and Development of Political Parties*, B.R. Publishing Corporation, Delhi.

Chaube, SK, (1999), *Hill Politics in Northeast India*, Orient Longman, Patna.

Conn, Paul H, (1971), *Conflict and Decision Making: An Introduction to Political Science*, Harper and Row Publishers, New York.

Dalh, Robert A. (ed), (1978), *Political Opposition in Western Democracies*, Yale University Press, New Haven and London.

Das, Hari Hara, and B.C Choudhury, (1999), *Political Theory: Traditional and Modern Theory*, National Publishing House, New Delhi.

De Souza, Peter Ronald and E. Sridharan,(ed) (2006), *India's Political Parties*, Sage Publications, New Delhi, Thousand Oaks, London.

Dev, Bimal J, and Dilip K. Lahiri, (1987), *Manipur: Culture and Politics*, Mittal Publications, Delhi.

Dodd, Lawrence C, (1976), *Coalitions in Parliamentary Government*, Princeton University Press, Princeton, New Jersey.

Dun, E. W, (Rp.) (1992), *Gazetteer of Manipur*, Manas, Delhi.

Duverger, Maurice, (1969), *Political Parties: Their Organisation and Activity in the Modern State*, Translated by Barbara and Robert North, Methuen 7 Co Ltd., London.

Fartyal, H.S, (1971), *Role of the Opposition in the Indian Parliament*, Chaitanya Publishing House, Allahabad.

Gassah, L.S., (1992), *Regional Political Parties in North- East India*, Omsons Publications, New Delhi.

Gelb, Joyce and Marian Lief Palley, (1971), *The Politics of Social Change: A Reader for the Seventies*, Holt, Rinehart and Winston Inc., New York

Gopalaswami, R. A, (1970), *Indian Polity: A Plea for Reform*, Nachiketa Publications Ltd., Bombay.

Groennings, Sven, E.W. Kelley and Michael Lieserson (ed) (1970, *The study of Coalition Behaviour: Theoretical Perspectives and Cases from four Continents*, Holt, Rinehart and Winston, Inc., New York.

Gunther, Richard, Jose Ramon Montero and Juan J. Linz, (ed) (2003), *Political Parties: Old concepts and New Challenges*, Oxford University Press, New York.

Hartmann, Horst, (1971), *Political Parties in India*, Meenakshi Prakashan, Meerut.

Hofstadter, Richard, (1970), *The Idea of a Party System*, University of California Press, Berkeley, Los Angeles and London.

Ionescu, Ghitaand Isabel de Madariaga, (1972), *Opposition: Past and Present of a Political Institution*, Penguin Books, England, Australia and U.S.A.

James, Judson L, (1969), *American Political Parties: Potential and Performance*, University of London Press Ltd., London.

Jennings, W. Ivor, (1972), *The British Constitution*, Cambridge University Press, London.

Jeyaseelan, L, (1996), *Impact of the Missionary Movement in Manipur*, Scholar Publishing House (P) Ltd., New Delhi.

Karam Monimohan Singh, (1989), *Hijam Irabot Singh and Political Movements in Manipur*, B.R. Publishing Corporation, Delhi.

Kashyap, Subhash. C, (ed) (1997), *Coalition Government and Politics in India*, Uppal Publishing House, New Delhi.

Kashyap, Subhash. C, (ed), (1971), *Elections and Electoral Reforms in India*, Sterling Publishers Private Ltd., Delhi.

Key, V. O, Jr., (1964), *Politics, Parties, and Pressure Groups*, (Fifth Edition), Thomas Y. Crowell Company, New York.

Kothari, C.R. (2003), *Research Methodology: Methods and Techniques*, (Second Edition), Vishwa Prakashan, New Delhi.

Koul, Lokesh, (1984), *Methodology of Educational Research*, Second Revised Edition, Vikas Publishing House Pvt. Ltd., New Delhi.

Ksh. Shyamkanhai, (1974), *Manipurgee Leingaklon Amasung Leingak Pathapki Itihas (1762-1949)*, Author, Imphal

Ksh. Shyamkanhai, (1974), *Manipurgee Leingaklon Amasung Leingak Pathapki Itihas (1950-1972)*, Author, Imphal

Kumar, Dr. Sunil, (2004), *Parties and Coalition Politics: A Comparative Study*, Uppal Publishing House, New Delhi.

LaPolambara, Joseph, (1974), *Politics within Nations*, Prentice Hall Inc., New Jersey.

LaPolambora, Joseph and Myron Weiner, (ed), *Political Parties and Political Development*, (2nd Print), Princeton University Press, Princeton.

Laski, Harold J, (1945), *Parliamentary Government in England*, George Allen and Unwin Ltd., London.

Le Duc, Lawrence, Richard G.Nieme and Pippa Norris, (1996), *Comparing Democracies: Elections and Voting in Global Perspective*, Sage Publications, New Delhi.

Lees, John D., and Richard Kimber, (ed), (1972), *Political Parties in Modern Britain: An Organisational and Functional Guide*, Routledges and Kegan Paul Ltd., London.

Lt. Col. H. Bhuban Singh, (1988), *The Merger of Manipur*, Author, Imphal.

MacLver, R.M, (1966), *The Modern State*, Oxford University Press, London.

Maisel, Louis and Joseph Cooper, (ed), (1978), *Political Parties: Development and Decay*, Sage Publications, Beverely Hills/ London.

Mayer, Lawrence C., (1989), *Redefining Comparative Politics: Promise versus Performance*, Sage Publications, London.

Mc Donald, Neil A, (1963), *The Study of Political Parties*, Random House, New York.

Mehre, Ajay K., D.D Khanna and Gert W. Kueck, (ed), (2003), *Political Parties and Party Systems*, Sage Publications, New Delhi, Thousand Oaks, London.

Merki, Peter H., (1970), *Modern Comparatives Politics*, Holt, Rinehart and Winston Inc., New York.

Mukherjee, Subrata, and Sushila Ramaswamy, (ed), (1998),

Political Science Annual, 1997: Special Volume on India at 50, Deep and Deep Publication, New Delhi.

N. Joykumar Singh, (1992), *Social Movement in Manipur*, Mittal Publications, New Delhi.

N. Lokendra Singh, (1998), *Unquiet Valley*, Mittal Publications, New Delhi.

Naik, J.A, (1983), *The Opposition in India and the Future of Democracy*, S. Chand and Company Ltd., New Delhi.

Nalwa, Vanit, (1992), *The ABC of Research for Behavioural and Social Sciences*, Wiley Eastern Limited, New Delhi.

Naorem Joykumar Singh, (2002), *Colonialism to Democracy: A History of Manipur*, 2819-1972, Spectrum Publication, New Delhi.

Naorem Sanajaoba, (ed), (1988), *Manipur: Past and Present; The Heritage and Ordeals of a Civilization*, Volume 1 (History, Polity and Law), Mittal Publications, Delhi.

Narang, AS, (1994), *Indian Government and Politics*, Gitanjali Publishing House, New Delhi.

Neumann, Sigmund, (ed), (1950), *Modern Political Parties: A Process to Comparative Politics,* Chicago Press, U.S.A.

Ng. Kumarjit Singh, (1986), *Emergence of Regional Political Parties*, Volume 1, North Eastern Region, Imphal.

Ostrogorski, M. (1902), *Democracy and the Organization of Political Parties*, Translated by Frederick Clarke, Mc Millan and Co Ltd, London and New York.

P. Bhorot Singh, (1997), *Elections in Manipur*, Imphal

Pakem, B, (1999), *Coalition Politics in North-East India*, Regency Publications, New Delhi.

Parrat, John (2005), *Wounded Land: Politics and Identity in Modern Manipur*, Mittal Publications, New Delhi.

Pennings, Paul, Hans Keman, and Jans Kleinnijenhuis, (1999), *Doing Research in Political Science: An Introduction to Comparative Methods and Statistics*, Sage Publications, New Delhi.

Priyoranjan, Ch., (2009), *Tribalism and the Tragedy of the Commons, Land, Idendity and Development: The Manipur Experience*, Akansha Publishing House, New Delhi.

Rae, Douglas W., (1967), *The Political Consequence of Electoral Laws*, (Revised edition), Yale University Press, New Haven.

Rajkumar Maipaksana, (1996), *Manipurda Ihan Hanba Satyagraha Aandalon*, Imphal.

Ram, D. Sundar (ed) (1996), *Reading in the Indian Parliamentary Opposition*, Volume 1 and 2, Kanishka Publishers, New Delhi.

Ranney, Austin, (1975), *The Governing of Men*, Fourth Edition, The Dryden Press Hinsdale, Illinois.

Richard S. Katza and Peter Nair (ed), (1994), *How Parties Organize*, Sage Publication, New Delhi.

Sartori, Giovanni, (1976), *Parties and Party Systems: A Framework for Analysis*, Cambridge University Press, New York.

Schattschneidre, E. E, (1942), *Party Government,* Rinehart, New York.

Sharma, Ranbir, (1977), *Party Politics in a Himalayan State*, National Publishing House, New Delhi.

Singh, Ravindra Pratap, (1981), *Electoral Politics in Manipur*, Concept Publishing Company, New Delhi.

Singh, V.B and Shankar Bose, (1987), *State Elections in India 1952-85*, Data Handbook on Vidhan Sabha Elections, 1952-85, Volume 3, The East and North-East.

Sirsikar, V.M and L. Fernandes, (1984), *Indian Political Parties*, Meenakshi Prakashan, Meerut and New Delhi.

Soyam Chandradhari Singh, (1972), *Manipurgee Itihasta Irabot*, Soyam Publication, Imphal.

Sundar Ram, D, (2000), (ed), *Coalition Politics in India: Search for Political Stability*, National Publishing House, New Delhi.

Swan, Abram De, (1973), *Coalition Theories and Cabinet Formations*, Elsevier Scientific Publishing Company, New York.

Thumm, Garold W, and Edward G. Janosik, (1967), *Parties and the Governmental System: A Book of Readings*, Prentice-Hall, Inc., Englewood Cliffs, New Jersey.

Varshney, Ashutosh, (ed) (1989), *The Indian Paradox- Essay in Indian Politics*, Sage Publications, New Delhi.

Wallace, Paul and Ramashray Roy, (ed) (2003), *India's 1999 Elections and 20th Century Politics*, Sage Publications, New Delhi/Thousand Oaks/London.

Wilson, James Q, (1973), *Political Organizations*, Basic Books Inc., Publishers, New York.

B: Dictionaries and Encyclopedias

Lexicon Universal Encyclopedia, (1983), Volume 15 (P), Lexicon Publications, Inc., New York.

McLean, Iain and Alister McMillan, (ed), (2005), *Oxford Concise Dictionary of Politics*, Indian edition, Oxford University Press, New Delhi.

Plano, Jack C and Greenberg, Milton, (1972), *The American Political Dictionary*, Third Edition, The Dryden Press Inc., US.

Sills, David L (ed), *International Encyclopedia of Social Science,* Volume 10, Macmillan, New York and London.

The New Encyclopaedia Britannica, (1998), Volume 25, Micropadia, Encyclopedia Britannica Inc, USA

C: Government Publications/Documents

Statistical Abstract of Manipur (2004), Directorate of Economics and Statistics, Government of Manipur.

The Gazette of India, Extra Ordinary, The Schedule Castes and Schedule Tribes Order (Amendment) Act, 2002.

D: Research Articles and Journals

American Journal of Political Science, Volume 47, No. 2 (April 2003)

Frontline

Volume 17- issue 05, March 04 – 17, 2000,
Volume 17 – issue 07, April 1-14, 2000
Volume 19 – issue 06, March 16-29, 2002,
Volume 18 – issue 12, June 09-22, 2001
Volume 18 – issue 13, June 23-July 06, 2001
Volume 18 - issue 14, July 07- 20, 2001
Volume 18- issue 15, July 21 – August 03, 2001
Volume 18- issue 17, August 18 – 31, 2001
Volume 19 – issue 05, March 02 – 15, 2002

Liberty Post: The Northeast Profile, Vol. 1, No. 5, October 15-31, 2001

March 11 2000, June 9 2001, July 6 2002, December 13 1997, February 9 2002, December 16 2000.

Party Politics, Volume 13, No-5

Political Studies, Volume 53, 2005
Public Choice, Volume 64, No. 3, 1990
South Asia Politics, Volume 3, Issue 4, August 2004
South Asia Research, Volume 23 No.1 May 2003
The Economic and Political Weekly
The Oriental Anthropologist, 2005 (1)

E: Newspapers

Huiyeng Lanpao (local Manipuri daily)
Manipur Mail (local English daily)
Poknapham (local Manipuri daily)
Praja Tantra (local Manipuri daily)
The Imphal Free Press (local English daily)

The Resistance (weekly) April 26, 1977, February, 1, 1977
The Sangai Express (local English and Manipuri daily)

F: Unpublished Thesis

Devi, K. Shusila *Origin and Growth of Legislature in Manipur up to 1972*, unpublished Ph. D dissertation, Imphal, Department of History, Manipur University.

Singh, Ksh. Kenedy *Parties and Politics in Manipur (1985-2000)*, unpublished M. Phill dissertation, New Delhi, Centre for Political Studies, 2000.

Singh, S. Mangi *A Study of Some Selected Socio-Political Problems in Manipur,* Ph. D dissertation, Imphal, Department of Political Science, Manipur University, 1996.

Singh, Th. Arke *Party System in Manipur (1972-85)*, Ph. D dissertation, Imphal, Department of Political Science, Manipur University, 2008.

G: Personnel interview

Hoakip, Holkhamang, Dated July 20, 2006.
Horam, Prof. M. Dated April 17, 2006.
Kamei, Prof. Gangumei Dated May 2, 2006.
Luwang, Nimaichand, Dated May 4, 2006.
Singh, A K Sanaton, Dated June 5, 2006.
Singh, Moirangthem Ibohal, Dated July 7, 2006.
Singh, R.K. Dorendro Dated August 22, 2006.
Singh, Th. Chaoba, Dated August 28, 2006.
Singh, Yumnam Yaima, Dated June 10, 2006.

Index

***